Shakespeare's Beehive

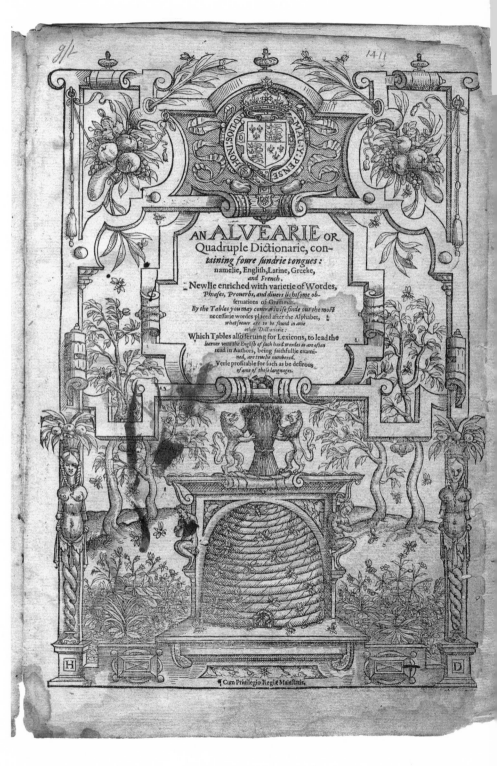

AN **ALVEARIE** OR
Quadruple Dictionarie, containing foure sundrie tongues:
namelie, English, Latine, Greeke,
and French.

Newlie enriched with varietie of Wordes,
Phrases, Prouerbs, and diuers lightsome ob-
seruations of Grammar.

By the Tables you may contrariwise finde out the most
necessarie wordes placed after the Alphabet,
what soeuer are to be found in anie
other Dictionarie:

Which Tables also seruing for Lexicons, to lead the
learner vnto the English of such hard wordes as are often
read in Authors, being faithfullie exami-
ned, are truelie numbered.

Verie profitable for such as be desirous
of anie of those languages.

¶ Cum Priuilegio Regiæ Maiestatis.

Shakespeare's Beehive

AN ANNOTATED ELIZABETHAN DICTIONARY COMES TO LIGHT

George Koppelman

&

Daniel Wechsler

AXLETREE BOOKS

NEW YORK

2014

Standard edition

ISBN 978-0-9915730-0-4

Signed numbered edition

ISBN 978-0-9915730-1-1

Signed lettered edition

ISBN 978-0-9915730-2-8

For Becky,

my devoted wife of forty years, who has been
hearing about this particular Elizabethan dictionary
for the last six of them, and for our son, Sam, who
has helped usher it into the digital age.

— GEORGE KOPPELMAN

For Tatiana,

who endured a great many restless days and nights,
and for our two wonderful sons, Jan and Marcus.
And to the memory of my father, Adam Wechsler,
an avid collector of books, who lived long enough
to hear the first whispers, but nothing more.

— DANIEL WECHSLER

Contents

A Note to the Reader . . . . *page* ix
Editorial Conventions xii

PART ONE
The Romance:
Or, How to Start a Case for Shakespeare's Dictionary

Prologue 3
A Few Thoughts on Old Books 5
Early Modern Dictionaries 11
Shakespeare Goes to London 17
A Heavily Annotated Copy 24
Personal Markers 29
Paleography 40
Shakespeare on Handwriting 55
Shakespeare as Reader 63
Becoming a Believer 69

PART TWO
The Evidence:
The Annotations as They Relate to the Works

Hamlet 79
The Narrative Poems 101
The Sonnets 121

The Early Comedies 147
The Early Histories 170
Falstaff 200
The Trailing Blank 219
Baret as Shakespeare's Beehive 254
What's in a Name? 275
"My Darling" 283

Afterword 298
Acknowledgments 305
Sources 306
Notes 320
A Note on the Authors 339

A Note to the Reader

W E A R E, each of us that make up Axletree Press L L C, professional rare booksellers, and we view the effort printed here as a single-item catalogue. Its companion piece is our website for the dictionary in question: shakespearesbeehive.com. The dictionary can be viewed there in its entirety. The object itself has for some time been housed in a private unit at a secure facility.

We look forward, in due course, to being able to provide it a more appropriate home.

"Baret was in effect the standard English diction- ary of Shakespeare's schooldays, and must have had powerful influence in shaping the English definitions of Shakespeare's generation. But it is not likely that Shakespeare would have preserved the patterns so ac- curately if he had not himself turned many a time and oft to Baret for his varied synonyms."

    – T. W. Baldwin on John Baret's *Alvearie*

POLONIUS: *What do you read, my lord?*
HAMLET: *Words, words, words.*

    – *Hamlet*, act 2, scene 2

"You have to read something other than the diction- ary. I mean, if you're not Shakespeare, why bother reading the dictionary?"

    – An Upper East Side mother overheard admonishing
    her daughter at Bel Ami Café, off Madison Avenue,
    in New York City, December 2013

Editorial Conventions

THROUGHOUT the following study we embody citations from our copy of Baret's *Alvearie*, or *Quadruple Dictionarie* in a regularized format designed to convey both the characters used in the printed dictionary text and the annotations that we find in the margins and within the text columns. Both the printed Baret texts and the annotations are represented in their original spellings, which include features peculiar to the early modern period in which they were made. Although certain elements may at first be difficult to relate to the modern alphabet and familiar spellings and punctuation, such as the lack of the letter "J," the combined usages of "U" and "V," the common spelling shift of words ending in "y" to "ie," and doubled consonants such as "dogge" for "dog," we feel it is essential for the strength of our linguistic arguments that they be conducted within the parameters of the Elizabethan and early Stuart English language.

There are no page numbers in Baret's *Alvearie*. To allow readers to quickly locate an entry, we use the same numbering system for individual definitions that Baret uses. For example, at the Baret number 98 under letter "B," we find the following definition: *to Bang, or beate with a cudgell.* If we were to refer to this definition, we would cite B98. To help distinguish and highlight the annotator's work in the context of our own analysis, anything that the annotator adds to the page – either by supplying words, or by marking the text without using words – we have represented in red. If you see red, you know that the annotator has added these words or marks to the page.

We have also chosen to cite printed excerpts from Shakespeare's works using the original printed texts. For the poems and sonnets, we cite from the original quarto printings. For the plays that were first printed in the First Folio of 1623, we cite that original text. In addition, to allow our readers to more easily access the plays, for each citation we provide a reference to the modernized passage, by act, scene, and line numbering, as it appears in *The Oxford Shakespeare: The Complete Works* (2nd ed.), under the general editorship of Stanley Wells and Gary Taylor (Oxford: Clarendon Press, 2005).

Part One

The Romance: Or, How to Start a Case for Shakespeare's Dictionary

Prologue
A Few Thoughts on Old Books
Early Modern Dictionaries
Shakespeare Goes to London
A Heavily Annotated Copy
Personal Markers
Paleography
Shakespeare on Handwriting
Shakespeare as Reader
Becoming a Believer

Prologue

ON THE EVENING of April 29, 2008, through joint
venture, a bid of $4,300 was placed on eBay for a book
printed in London in the year 1580.[1] The book was John
Baret's *Alvearie*, or *Quadruple Dictionarie*, and that Elizabethan
dictionary, and, more notably, the particular copy offered to the
public on that date, is what the following pages are all about.

The precise bid was arrived at following a series of brief day-
time exchanges, across email and telephone. In not untypical
antiquarian bookseller fashion, the debated figure continued to
rise the more we each contemplated the lingering disappointment on the chance that we might lose out, in this instance, on a
sixteenth-century Elizabethan dictionary with handwritten annotations. Not everyone will relate to such nervousness, but in
our profession there are items that excite and those that don't,
and this was one that, for us, carried from the beginning a sense
of romance and intrigue. This, in spite of the fact that we had
not yet come across Mr. T. W. Baldwin and his pronouncement,
a conclusion that we imagine will represent a certain portion of
the debate going forward.

The auction closed at $4,050. Only $250 separated us from
never having had this experience, and a long experience it has
already been.

One week after the auction ended, our copy of Baret's *Alvearie*
arrived in New York City from Canada. As rare booksellers, we
then began to do what we have done repeatedly. We started to
describe an item new to our inventory with the goal of reaching
the utmost limits in terms of appeal. This is not meant to sound

magnanimous. Add too much luster and gloss to your descriptions, and it will seem as though you are trying too hard. Some books warrant very little description. But there are those occasions when you feel there is work to be done, and through the process of investigation an angle is found that previously went undetected. The homework, the investigation, is what makes the job fun.

Many of the books and manuscripts that are acquired in our business have at least some description available at the time of acquisition. One has the choice to either build upon the pre-existing write-up, or start from scratch. Our copy of Baret was offered on eBay with a few rudimentary, though not amateurish, paragraphs. Annotations were mentioned and several of them pictured, although nothing more was said, this not being unusual. The physical book and its general contents were accurately described, with one not insignificant exception: the book lacked two leaves of preliminary matter; as such, it was incomplete. We have from time to time amused ourselves by wondering how many members of the antiquarian book trade would have returned the book on account of its incompleteness (a common and accepted practice), and either saved themselves a mountain of time and trouble, or, potentially, for a refund of $4,050, returned to the previous owner William Shakespeare's own personal dictionary.

Presumably, if it had been returned, the book would have been reoffered and sold to someone else. Or the seller could have sought out the under-bidder to make the sale. In any event, it is impossible to know if a comprehensive study such as the one that we are in the process of conducting would ever have been attempted.

A Few Thoughts
on Old Books

THERE IS, to start with, a fundamental truth concerning old books that many people may not know: simply, that extraordinarily large numbers of them printed centuries ago survive to the present day. This is a commonly understood fact among those who have spent significant time with antiquarian books: through research, devotion as hobbyist, by retail trade or librarianship, and certainly by those who through marriage or similar partnership are forced to live with them. But, outside of these circles, we consistently encounter people who will ask, with utter but understandable astonishment: *That* book is from 1580, or *that* book is from 1550? No doubt there is something inspiring about any book that old or older, and even ones from more immediate centuries, but the fact is that old books as a rule do not vis-à-vis their age qualify as rare, nor does age guarantee them otherwise extraordinary distinction. This does not mean you can expect to turn up books from the sixteenth century at your local public library sale, but it does suggest that a book can live a life of its own for a very long time, and lay low, as it were, without receiving special attention to a potential mystery, even from those people most intrigued by them.

Our newly acquired book looked and felt modest in all respects, both at first impression and even now, although we have long since abandoned routine handling, and for several years running have worked from our self-photographed digital facsimile. Shortly after acquisition, we elected to re-attach the loose boards to allow for studying the book more carefully, and also just to make it more appealing. The binding, not original, was a product of work done during the mid to late eighteenth century. The packaging was simple, nothing lavish or unusual, and the marbled boards over time had received their battle scars in the usual forms of various scuffs and stains. Many other extant copies surely presented better to both trained and untrained eyes. This was, in all honesty, a book that could easily have gone unnoticed, and that, at least, was something that encouraged us as we became more and more entrenched in our own conversation, and wondered time and again how no one had ever noticed the yield from the annotations inside.

In spite of the reality that copies of Baret's *Alvearie* itself are not especially rare according to the standards of the trade, a survival, and the survival of any old book, does have requirements, the two principal ones being luck and care. For a book to survive from an initial publication in 1580 to the present day requires a combination of both, and our book, in spite of its unassuming appearance, had been accordingly blessed.

A thorough examination of the contents revealed the main text block to be in excellent condition. That the bulk of the pages held up so well is partly a result of the quality of the paper. Although there is scattered marginal staining from long ago, you can feel the durability of the paper as the leaves are turned, particularly in the middle sections; listen carefully, and you gain an appreciation for the crisp sound as one page passes onto another. The relative thinness to the paper, early on and at the end, is an effect of exposure to the air different from what was received by the protected bulk, but aside from the inevitable aging to the first gathering of leaves and the last, the main text block of the dictionary remained, through the centuries and up until the present day, in a considerably fresh state of preservation. This is noteworthy information. It suggests that our book was loved and cared for by its first owner – or, if it passed swiftly through different sets of hands, its first real owner, the one responsible for annotating the book, and establishing it, in the way that annotators do, as permanently his copy.

Most likely, the book was not lent out to others. Once it became the annotator's book, it was his book, and a cherished one. In the time since the annotations were made, we are guessing that relatively few resting places have been in play, but that is just an educated guess. What we do know is that those homes it did have, private owner or institutional, invariably offered advantageous conditions, neither too dry nor too wet, and rough handling was not a factor in the aging process.

As wonderful as it would be to retrace the actual "landing shelves" of this book, the reality is that much will never be known. There are some clues, but even then huge gaps must be acknowledged. From a small ink stamp on the binder's front free endpaper it has been determined that later owners were the nineteenth-century English novelist and book lover Georgiana Fullerton[2] and her husband Alexander Fullerton. Eventually, it landed in the hand of the antiquarian book trade, and found its way to Canada. How long our book has lived an active life within the trade is unclear, but it felt safe to assume when we started, and it certainly does now, that this book's annotations had never before been carefully studied, and that no prior dealer, or private owner for that matter, had attempted to make hay of identifying the annotator as part of earlier descriptions or private studies.

There may be voices of objection at these old book ramblings, but there is something exceedingly important to establish in these early chapters, before we get into the examination of the annotations alongside the works, and that is the demystification of what an old book is, and how examples handled by famous and ordinary individuals alike have made their way through time.

In our personal collections, as well as our inventories past and present, we have handled numerous remarkable association copies, including books with Shakespearean connections. Books that currently we could slide across a table into welcome arms include volumes from the libraries of Ben Jonson and Edmond Malone, born many years apart, but each known for his book collecting as well as his importance relative to Shakespeare. We could present a copy of Grinnell's *Psychology of Shakespeare* from the library of Charles Dickens, with his Gadshill bookplate. The book contains several annotations in Dickens's hand, including an insightful addition to the margin during a discussion of *Macbeth*.

Our association copy treasures are not limited to books from one period, or relating to one particular author. We can hand over Jack Kerouac's own copy of an *Anthology of English Literature* signed "John Kerouac." The book, fittingly, is in deplorable condition. Tucked away are Olivia Shakespear's own copy of *The Shadowy Waters* that W. B. Yeats had presented to her, Thomas Carlyle's copy of *Candide*, and Samuel Taylor Coleridge's own copy of a book entitled *The American Mariners*. One of us recently sold, somewhat regrettably, James Boswell's copy of Pine's *Virgil*.

The goal in naming these books is not commercial. We have, each of us, invested ourselves to the point where, as far as books are concerned, there is really only one that matters. The world of books is filled with treasures, and private and institutional collections are blessed to boast similar survivals such as the ones that we have just named. We have never in this process lost sight of the fact that the establishing of this one association copy as the most glorious one of all, towering in importance above all the others, was an entirely different matter.

Long before we acquired our copy, we were well aware that there are no formally accepted examples of particular volumes that can be traced to Shakespeare's ownership or use. That there are no surviving books from his library with ownership markings that have ever gained a substantial majority acceptance was understood from the beginning to be a huge problem for us. To consider altering that stance based upon our book would require an enormous leap of faith on the part of scholars regardless of what evidence might be found inside.

We are not Shakespeare scholars, although we do know substantially more about the man and his work, and the time and place (where and when he lived), than we did at the outset. In consideration of T. W. Baldwin's assessment,[3] of which we did not have the slightest inkling when we made our bid, we cannot help but wonder after studying the book for as long as we have, had more people investigated the accuracy of his claim, then, no doubt, the whole notion of a copy of Baret would be different today, akin to a copy of Shakespeare's Holinshed, his Plutarch, his Ovid, or his Florio. But essentially there never was a critical uproar generated, and so the *Alvearie* never made its way into the pantheon of exalted sourcebooks on which the plays were partly built.[4]

Our speculation, the driving force behind our book, is that Baret's *Alvearie* is indeed part of the canon of source material, and is predicated on Baldwin being correct: that in the course of his intellectual development, Shakespeare did turn to Baret, and turn to him "many a time and oft," not just casually once or twice, or a modest number of indifferent times.

The idea that Shakespeare may have often turned to *any* copy of Baret – there was magic for us in the simple thought of that alone, and, to a large extent, we went about our business of exploring the nooks and crannies of the text of Baret's *Alvearie* as a means of testing Baldwin's general assessment of it in regard to Shakespeare. We encourage greater examination of Baldwin's claim, and, should a scholar prefer not to get involved in the messy business of authorship in regard to the annotations in our copy, there is certainly a bounty remaining in these annotations for exploration relative to the language of the period that is almost without limits, from whatever point of departure one wishes to choose.

Early Modern Dictionaries

PART OF our preparation included familiarizing ourselves with as many details regarding sixteenth- and seventeenth-century English and continental dictionaries as we could uncover, and looking at as many examples as we could locate.

Early modern dictionaries were used for bilingual translation, for examples of word usages, and as troves of synonyms. Ian Lancashire identifies the 1573 (trilingual) and 1580 (quadruple) editions of Baret as one of the string of "original" or seminal works of early English lexicography.[5] Baret's triple dictionary was the third to appear in English, the first having been published by John Veron in 1552 (Latin–English–French), and the second being John Higgins's revision of Huloet's dictionary (English–Latin–French) in 1572.

John Baret, who taught Latin in Cambridge, named his dictionary the *Alvearie* (Latin for "beehive"), because he would send his students out to the college collections to find varied usages of his "hard words," referring to them as "diligent bees" who brought their finds back to nourish the "hive." (See our Baret's title page depicted on our frontispiece.) The term "hard words" (words too learned or obscure for ordinary readers) originated with Baret, who discusses the meaning in his preface, stressing that he thought it best to concentrate on these hard words rather than familiar ones. By providing separate Latin and French indexes and word numbering for quick cross-reference in the main dictionary, Baret makes it easy for the reader to access the equivalent of any Latin or French word.

Baret included a modest number of Greek equivalents in the

first edition; when he died in 1578 he was still revising his dictionary to include much material from new sources and greatly supplementing the Greek. Abraham Fleming (c. 1552–1607), author, translator, literary editor, compiler, and Church of England clergyman, was a contributor and the primary editor as the new edition moved toward completion and eventual publication two years after Baret's death.

The *Alvearie* owes much to Thomas Cooper's *Thesaurus*, on which it was largely based, as well as to Robert Stephanus's *Dictionarium Latino-Gallicum*. The Cooper, in which Latin entries come first, was published initially in 1565. It went through several editions, and, like Baret, is cited by Baldwin as having been instrumental in Shakespeare's development, and as being a source with which he must have been intimately familiar.[6]

However lofty the praise Baldwin offers to Baret (and to Cooper), let us keep in mind that the attention is rather buried in his vast two-volume study, which is primarily noted for its pioneering findings regarding the rigorous Latin-based curriculum of the King's New School that Shakespeare would have attended in Stratford.[7] While Baldwin provides some detail and elaboration, the sweeping statement on Baret's significance is more or less left behind, almost as a tease. Historically, mentions of the importance of Baret to Shakespeare are relatively slight, although a number of eighteenth- and nineteenth-century editions of the collected works offer frequent references to Baret in the critical notes. Edmond Malone's library contained a copy (sold in the auction conducted after his death for 1£),[8] so it is not surprising that we see many references to Baret in his important edition of Shakespeare's collected works. Much more recently, Patricia Parker, in *Shakespeare from the Margins* (1996), implies that when one wants to begin a serious study of Elizabethan language, it makes good sense to start with the dictionaries of the time, and she lists Baret as the first of her examples.[9]

Among the antiquarian book trade, and at auction, copies continue to surface with a fair degree of regularity, although we could trace only one copy that referenced Shakespeare in its catalogue description. The renowned firm of Bernard Quaritch excerpted the passage from Baldwin just as we have done, when (relatively recently) offering a copy of the 1580 *Alvearie*, going so far as to catalogue the book under the heading: *Shakespeare's Thesaurus.*[10] Their Baret was unmarked by annotations, and this allowed them to quote Baldwin playfully and without controversy, although with a clear interest in attracting possible buyers.

The main point on the subject of Baret from a standpoint of reputation is that over time very little fanfare has been generated that would have led to exhaustive investigations. The largest online database of early printed English books, EEBO (Early English Books Online), helps to confirm Baret's relative obscurity. The website contains two viewable photocopies of Baret, but unlike the case for, for example, Cooper's *Thesaurus* of the same vintage, the search tools will not bring up Baret's text. An extraordinarily large number of texts are word searchable on EEBO; the fact that Baret is not one of them helps to underscore that very few scholars have any real familiarity with Baret, let alone in relation to Shakespeare. The scholarly community will have an opportunity once our study is released to fully study Baret's *Alvearie* in this capacity for the first time.[11]

If Baldwin was right – and we pause to examine the problem purely as a numbers game – the odds are long, but hardly unfathomable. The number of copies printed is uncertain, as for most books from this period, but it's a safe guess that in the range of 750 copies of the 1580 edition were printed. Mathematically, the chances of a copy being Shakespeare's, assuming the same likelihood of survival for each copy, is one in whatever number was printed. Between the copies in special collections around the world, the frequency of copies appearing at auction, and the unknown number of copies in private hands, we can roughly guess that fifteen percent have survived. Let's imagine that one hundred copies have survived. Since we have no prior knowledge of whether Shakespeare's copy was one of those survivors, the odds are still one in whatever the number of copies that were printed. In some ways, the survival of Shakespeare's copy was becoming, especially in consideration of what we had uncovered in the annotated texts of this Baret, one piece at a time, a relative long shot, but not an impossibly far-fetched notion.

In the time since acquiring our annotated copy, we have purchased three additional copies of the 1580 edition. Each of these is in an early binding, and yet none contain evidence of readership with annotations of any real sort that would allow you to speculate. Unlike ours, each of the other Baret copies contains at least one ownership signature, and included among the three is a copy presented to the lexicographer Robert Nares, who would go on to publish one of the first works on the obscure vocabulary and proverbial language of Shakespeare and his contemporaries. His copy is entirely free of annotations.

Using less ambitious means, we have obtained four copies of the Cooper, a much more common title, with only one of the four containing notable annotations. These annotations are mainly in Greek, and of a sober scholarly nature, but the annotator quits not long after aggressively marking the first quire both marginally and interlinearly. This is a pattern one often sees in annotated books: the annotator does not make it all the way, or even very far at all. One imagines fatigue or the new attraction of a more recent acquisition being the principal factors in most cases.

An extreme example of an exception to this pattern with which we are familiar is a copy of Huloet's dictionary in the collection of the Folger Shakespeare Library in Washington, D.C. There is an old note penciled inside (not the Folger's) claiming that the copious annotations throughout belong to the hand of the man credited with revising the book, John Higgins, himself also a writer. Whether or not the annotations in the Folger's copy belong to Higgins, a close examination proved them to be dramatically afield from our annotations in terms of content, spirit, and paleographic qualities. Locating a more vociferously annotated book than the Folger's aberrational Huloet would not be easy. The annotations are so overpowering, so excessively robust and demanding, that to the naked eye the printed text itself almost functions as the washed-out palimpsest, with the manuscript additions dominating the page and the attention on the eye. As far as a method on the part of the annotator is concerned, there is no interrelation between annotation types such as we find in our Baret, and will introduce shortly. It almost looks as if another dictionary has been entered in the surrounding spaces and, quite often, over the top of the printed one. The personality of the annotator is lacking in nuance, and it is unlikely that one could find in the swirling mass of annotations any personal effects; it is simply a brute force task that, however awesome, obliterates information with the excess of information it provides. We might add that the Folger's Huloet is in a beautiful contemporary crimson leather binding, not the sort of book that could have escaped attention from eager book connoisseurs and prominent librarians (although we were the first visitors, apparently, to examine it in quite a long while).

Our main conclusions on early modern dictionaries will likely need to be tested over more comprehensive surveys, but we are confident in asserting that finding copies annotated with any degree of thoroughness is uncommon, and, even if they are vigorously marked, you will not see results in any manner remotely approaching the successes that we have found in our Baret, when the annotations are studied alongside Shakespeare. Realistically, we might ask, will *any* sort of a similarly engaging and complex Shakespeare picture emerge when you examine a single other annotated copy of any book anywhere?

Or, if one were to seek the same comparisons of the annotations to all of the other writers of the Elizabethan period that have left behind a significant set of texts, could a similar close correlation of our *Alvearie* annotations with any of their canons, and personas – both known and speculated – be found?

Our search for other dictionaries was not limited to those printed in England. Among sixteenth-century continental dictionaries examined, one has stood out to us over all the others. A certain Jean Scapula had cut his teeth working as a proofreader for the legendary sixteenth-century French scholar and printer Henri Estienne, and in 1580, the same year as our edition of Baret's *Alvearie*, Scapula put to the market a Greek and Latin dictionary of his own, published in Basel. A copy of this large folio book that we acquired (bound in a 1584 dated binding of full vellum) turned out to be copiously annotated throughout in a tiny, equally eager and sincere, contemporary hand. But the annotator, unlike with our Baret, is no mystery. His marginalia efforts complete, he has offered at the rear, for posterity, his name: Henricus Hirschdörfer. It's a marvelous thing, this book, but quite another thing to find people that actually *care*. There is no news story to be developed from Hirschdörfer's annotated copy of the first edition of Scapula's *Lexicon Graecolatinum Novum*, that much we can be sure of, as marvelous as it may be.

Shakespeare Goes to London

L ET US interject into the discussion some of the historical facts concerning Shakespeare that encourage us to take copies of Baret's *Alvearie* seriously, irrespective of Baldwin's strong textual assertion, but most definitely in combination with it.

The entire 1580s record of Shakespeare is, understandably, slight. We can say understandably because that is what one would expect prior to his establishing himself in the theater world in London. The keeping of an individual's historical record was generally limited to birth, marriage, family baptisms, and burial; and for many notable writers of the time, even these have vanished. In addition, in that litigious society, records were kept of its many lawsuits, and many of these survive. Guilds kept careful dated lists of their apprentices, and specifically the records of the Stationers' Company, which licensed and regulated printers, have survived. What we do have is the recording of his marriage to Anne Hathaway in 1582, the birth of his daughter Susanna in 1583, and the birth of his twins Hamnet and Judith in 1585. Sometime after the birth of the twins, Shakespeare makes his way to London, and the next references we have to him are as an "upstart" London poet and playwright in 1592.[12] What Shakespeare was doing in the period prior to establishing himself in the theater or when he actually began writing or "doctoring" plays for his acting company has been a matter of ongoing conjecture with no clear resolution.[13]

But one thing is virtually certain: During this period, the so-called "lost years,"[14] Shakespeare must have immersed himself in books. His body of work is so rich in allusion to works composed earlier or contemporary to him that this time was surely the most robust when it came to his own reading. Not only do the plots of most of the plays bear the marks of literary and historical plots that came before, but the language itself, while transformed in unparalleled fashion, nonetheless owes an enormous debt to sourcebooks that he must have, at minimum, gained brief access to, and, much more likely in at least some cases, made his own in a more permanent sense.

The question of where Shakespeare would have gotten access to books in the first place may seem as elusive as the "lost years" problem. But enough pieces of the puzzle exist to hazard a good guess.

Richard Field, also of Stratford, and roughly two years older than Shakespeare, had established himself in London prior to Shakespeare's arrival there. Field was the son of a tanner, Shakespeare the son of a glover. Shakespeare's father had dealings with Field's father, and the two sons would have been acquainted, almost certainly when they both attended the Stratford grammar school, before meeting again in London.

Field apprenticed for the French Huguenot printer Thomas Vautrollier, who had emigrated to England, and following Vautrollier's death not only took over the business but married his widow, Jacqueline. It has often been speculated that this could help to explain Shakespeare's knowledge of French and his later relations with London's French Huguenot community at the turn of the sixteenth century.[15] Certainly his close ties to Field initially, not long after his arrival in London, would have improved his chances of gaining easy access to the books that he would rely heavily on for source material.

The relationship between the two men and books was clearly ongoing, as Field's career and Shakespeare's both evolved. One of the more celebrated Shakespeare sourcebooks was North's

Plutarch, which Field printed in 1595. Equally important were the foreign language books published under Field's imprint that helped cement Field's reputation and that likely proved useful to a young and energetic Shakespeare. Field also published books on handwriting.

But as significant as the back-home Stratford connection and the role in providing books may have been, these are not the primary reasons why historians are so confident in asserting the relevance of Field to Shakespeare during Shakespeare's early London years. Field printed Shakespeare's two long poems – first, *Venus and Adonis* in 1593, then *Rape of Lucrece*, in 1594. For *Venus and Adonis* he served not only as the printer, but also as the publisher. Whereas the assumption over time has generally been that Shakespeare took little interest in the careful treatment of his plays in print,[16] the quality of the printing and textual accuracy of the narrative poems suggests that Shakespeare either took a far greater role in overseeing the production, or that Field himself was simply a better caretaker of these carefully executed works.

The overall picture we get of the two men can be reduced to this: With their backgrounds, their interests, and their collaboration, Shakespeare must have worked intimately with Field. To some degree, at least, Shakespeare found himself mingling, whether through socializing, employment, studying the references to be found, or any combination of these matters, in the relatively insular world of Field's associates: the licensed and regulated printers of London, the people who surrounded themselves with the books that we know, from Shakespeare's own work, provided great influence upon him.

Among those who have speculated on Shakespeare's relationship with Richard Field is Katherine Duncan-Jones. Duncan-Jones goes so far as to assert that Shakespeare may have lodged with Field when he arrived in London.[17] It has even been suggested that "the two men teamed up occasionally for the journey back to Warwickshire."[18] All "biographical fantasy" aside, writes Jonathan Bate, "the point is a serious one. Thanks to his undoubted friendship with Richard Field and his very probably acquaintance with John Florio, Shakespeare had easy access to [these] books."[19]

This "undoubted friendship" with Field also may help explain Shakespeare's French abilities. French was not taught in English schools at the time, and many have wondered where Shakespeare would have learned it. The profusion of French annotations in our *Alvearie* initially caused some concern, but learning of the relationship with Field was part of what helped to lessen it.

On the subject of Shakespeare and the French language, René Weis imagines that "the only plausible explanation is his friendship with Richard Field's French family."[20] While Shakespeare makes use of French in a number of plays, the most significant inclusion is in *Henry V*, where an entire scene and a good portion of a second scene are written entirely in French. The use of French demonstrated in these scenes may seem superficially naïve, but the verbal dexterity in fact befits only a person who understood the language intimately.

Beginning at the turn of the century Shakespeare lodged with a French Huguenot family, and one can reasonably speculate that Field and his French Huguenot wife may have played a role here as well.[21]

Shakespeare's "artfully halting French"[22] is not limited to *Henry V*. There are scenes in *The Merry Wives of Windsor* where "he affectionately parodies French accents and mistakes in English," demonstrating an intimate knowledge of French culture and giving further weight to his connections with Field as a means of explanation.

Of course, the sourcebooks themselves may also have played a role and, here, the *Alvearie* is no exception. Immediately after citing the importance of Baret generally, Baldwin writes: "It might also be added that Shakespeare could have acquired a considerable French vocabulary from Baret – and that his generation must have had its English vocabulary considerably tinged with the French because of the mere fact that both Huloet-Higgins and Baret based their English-Latin dictionaries upon the French-Latin dictionary of Stephanus."[23]

This generation that "must have had its English vocabulary considerably tinged with the French" has been an area of discussion for other Shakespeareans. In the words of Stanley Wells, "The English language [of the Elizabethan period] was struggling to achieve a vocabulary and expressive power comparable to that offered by Latin. This process involved much coining of new words, often on the basis of, especially, Latin and French, and encouraged the use of old words in new forms, senses, and combinations. Shakespeare was an indefatigable innovator."[24]

In a tantalizing late find for us, Andrew Murphy recently noted that "through Field, Shakespeare was able to find employment in the print trade, most likely at the press of Henry Denham, who, at the time, was just embarking on the considerable task of printing Holinshed's *Chronicles*. Shakespeare worked as a proofreader at Denham's, in the process making the acquaintance of Denham's apprentice, William Jaggard, whose own firm would, much later, be responsible for printing the first collected edition of Shakespeare's plays."[25]

This seemed too good to be true: Shakespeare working for the man who printed not only the most celebrated of all Shakespeare sourcebooks (Holinshed), but also the book (Baret) for which we were attempting to make a case based upon the evidence within the particular copy that we had already studied and been increasingly in awe of over a period of several years.

Alas, Murphy quickly covers himself and points out that this is not his own claim; he is simply channeling one of those "lost years" stories that would be fun to believe in, but that can never be proven. He credits the "story" to William Jaggard, who, in 1933, delivered an address at Stationers' Hall in London, *Shakespeare Once a Printer and Bookman*.[26] Jaggard, a distant relation of the William Jaggard who printed the First Folio, is apparently indebted to an 1872 work by William Blades, *Shakespeare and Typography*,[27] which explores the notion that Shakespeare likely worked with books at some point during the "lost years" and gained access to the world of London's printers via his relationship with Richard Field.

Much more recently, the website of the Shakespeare Birthplace Trust, an independent charity that promotes Shakespeare's life, works, and times, has added speculation in this regard, while discussing a certain copy of the first edition of North's Plutarch from 1579, printed by Thomas Vautrollier around the time he hired Richard Field as an apprentice. The provenance of the book can be traced from ownership inscriptions on the title page dating back to the year of publication: "The book was given to Henry Stanley, 4th Earl of Derby by William Chaderton, who became Bishop of Chester in 1579; the book passed to the 5th Earl, Ferdinando, Lord Strange, whose company of players presented some of Shakespeare's first plays, including Titus Andronicus." Ferdinando's widow, Alice, has added an inscription, "later deleted and obscured, but which can be read by ultra-violet light," wherein she presents the book to a "William." No claim is made, obviously, as to whether this "William" was Shakespeare. But Field's "life-long" friendship to Shakespeare is mentioned, as well as Field's future involvement in printing the narrative poems, and it is suggested that "it is possible that the young Field shared proof-reading the work with the future playwright, and this introduction led to his extensive use of the book in later years."[28]

Splendid as it would be for us to see the proofreading theory concluded as fact, such a goal is not possible, much as it is impossible to settle on any of the "lost years" theories absolutely.

E. K. Chambers declares that "in a sense, these conflicting theories refute each other,"[29] and yet, if one breaks down all of the speculative stories from this period – and there are an astonishing number – a most amusing truth is revealed: *at least* one of them is almost certainly correct.

It is our feeling, based upon the evidence in our copy of Baret's *Alvearie*, that Jaggard may have gotten it right when he imagined in his address at Stationers' Hall in London, back in 1933, Shakespeare working in the print house of Henry Denham. If we entertain ourselves with the possibility that this is a fact, and not one person's speculation, that Shakespeare worked as proofreader for Henry Denham, and that our copy of Baret was acquired by him at that time, this revisionist history could also go a long way in explaining how thoroughly Shakespeare understood his Holinshed, the most famous of all sourcebooks. In our Baret, also printed by Denham, we do see frequent and distinct hallmarks of proofreading at various points throughout by the annotator. However, it becomes equally clear, once the book is studied carefully for some time, that these moments are merely a backdrop to an exploration of words on the part of a robust lover of language, a language lover who has peppered the extensive exploration of words with occasional personal flags and personal memories.

At some point after first marking it, this book becomes the proofreader's, whoever this person was. What emerges is a web of annotations demonstrating an interest in words that has nothing at all to do with proofreading.

A Heavily Annotated Copy

THAT THIS particular book should have annotations at all would not have come as a surprise to an antiquarian bookseller or scholar accustomed to dealing with old books. Although there has been a trend over time in paying closer attention to annotated books, without knowledge of a particular owner, many collectors have historically preferred clean copies to books with writing in the margins, whether casual or obsessive.

Not long after we acquired our copy of Baret, we began an informal study of the annotations, and gradually noticed a pattern of Shakespeare-related annotations, often in a surprisingly strong way. This is not to say that we found connections to the texts everywhere we looked; yet there were often enough for us to take note and begin to have fun with the idea, the grandest of all possibilities.

Our dictionary was heavily annotated, so there was a lot of evidence, which was a good thing, but it was not annotated to such a degree that the annotator had abandoned selectivity. A dictionary heavily annotated with no regard for organization and substance might be considerably less desirable, because the brute and generic force of the method and the accompanying examples could be deemed at odds with identifying a specific individual. We were faced with what felt like an ideal balance. Examples ran from the first page to the last, but despite the huge number of markings in consideration, the effort that produced the abundance was restrained and thoughtful – at times, even modest.

Of significant importance, after a number of readings, one could see that the markings – whether added words or symbols – were part of a characteristic method and were continually interrelated, and the whole was suggestive of a single annotator at work over an indeterminate but clearly substantial amount of time.

We eventually went about recording the entire body of annotations (this document can be seen in its entirety on our website), and decided it useful to think of them as composing two distinct categories. These terms are ours, and we use them throughout this study. The first category, which we refer to as the "mute" annotations, consists of three primary types of indicative markers found at various printed individual words or phrases located throughout the Baret dictionary text.

The first type of mute annotation is the underlining of a single word or a group of words found in a prefatory or editorial paragraph or a word definition. Here, at M531, the annotator has underlined *snoute*, *Shrew*, and *blindmouse.*

> 531 | ✳ A field mouſe ſoith a long ſnoute, called a Shꝛew, oꝛ a blindmouſe, ſohich if he go ouer a beaſts backe, the beaſt ſhalbe lame in the chine, and if he bite, it ſwelleth to the hart, ᵹ the beaſt dieth. Mus araneus. Plin. μυγάλη.

The very first annotation in our book is on the title page itself, where *lightsome* is underlined.

The second type of mute annotation is the slash [/] mark placed in the margin adjoining headword definitions.

> ¶ Jeſſes, hanging at haukes legges. Lemniſci, corum, maſc. gen. Plin. Pedicæ accipitrum. λημνίσκοι. Lanieres, ou longes, à tenir les oiſeaux ſur le poing. | I 8

For all headword definitions in Baret, the ¶ character precedes the word being defined, as in the above example at location I/J28, / ¶ **Jesses, hanging at the haukes legges**. The annotator's added slash indicator in the left margin is clearly marked.

The third type of mute annotation is the small circle mark [o] placed in the margin at a subsidiary definition or usage example. Many of these circles also bear an additional dot alongside the circle. These circle marks are the most plentiful of all, totaling roughly 4,000, and function for the annotator as do the slash marks, except they do not appear at the head definitions but only at subsidiary definitions, as here at M313 – *Mercilesse, rigorous.*

The second primary category, which we refer to as "spoken" annotations, consists of approximately 1,000 single words or phrases found added in manuscript, in the annotator's hand.

These occur throughout the book, interlineally within the text columns, in the pages' narrow vertical margins, and in the more ample top and bottom margins. The annotations really need to be seen to gain a full appreciation for how extraordinarily small they are. Here, at the S710 definition, ¶ **to Spell, or put letters together,** the annotator has added, interlineally, the three-word phrase charmes and spells.

In cases where the annotator struggles for room in adding a spoken annotation, a device we term a "mouse-foot" is entered to indicate where an annotation that is written in either the top or bottom margin actually belongs within the column of definitions on that page.

2.5"

The mouse-foot can be seen at the left of this scan in the central vertical column separating the two columns of text on the page. It is carefully positioned in the center column between the definitions for *a Lap* and *the Laps* between L90 and L91. In this instance the annotator directs the annotation into the bottom margin, where he has added **to** L, a rare case where he has not completed his thought.[30]

Among our observations, once we had completed our compilation, was that the mute annotations were more or less entirely uniform in appearance and manner of usage from beginning to end. Among the mass of spoken annotations, a great percentage had been formed by extracting text from, specifically, the underlined mute markings, and then transferring that extracted text to a new alphabetical location. Most importantly, we began to grasp how the annotator was working through the dictionary. The highly engaging method of annotating the book was consistent throughout and most unusual.[31] As our examination continued, we were staggered by the number of mute markings at Baret usage examples where we find a straightforward phrase converted into a Shakespearean phrase, often by a simple "lift," but more commonly by a reversal of the word order found in the Baret text, the addition of a related but unexpected wording from a neighboring example, etc. There was also a strong correlation of spoken annotations with citations in the *OED* as first or very early usages by Shakespeare, generally in the figurative sense. And the annotations as a whole appeared to demonstrate a deliberate and discernable pattern of usage on the part of a primary annotator beginning to work not long after the book was published.

So far, it was all lining up nicely. And yet, we were hardly at the point of becoming true believers, convinced that we could make a case for Shakespeare as annotator. After all, the contrarians to our thesis were sure to point out, these were just words, and Shakespeare used a *lot* of words.[32]

For someone obsessed with innovation in regard to words, the *Alvearie* must have represented a dream tool, with its emphasis on variable options and its pooling network of sources, proverbial phrases, and multilingual comparisons. The obsessive annotator of our copy may indeed embody the sort of language-obsessed person one would expect to find in the margins, but the critical question before us is this: in the absence of a name added to the page, how can one possibly begin to feel comfortable suggesting a specific annotator?

There is no getting around the fact that many will not be comfortable with the proposition at all. But a fairly substantial body of evidence that is stamped with personal markers must be introduced. The annotator may not have left his name to the page in a direct sense, but personal information does pass through his fingertips and onto the page more discretely, allowing us to better understand the man behind the network of annotations, both spoken and mute.

Personal Markers

IT TOOK some considerable time to discover, but our annotator has imitated the font of a lead capital letter as they are printed in Baret with two letters, and with two letters only. Five times with the "W" and three times with the "S," the annotator mimics the elaborate upper-case examples as printed in the *Alvearie* type font at the start of a word.

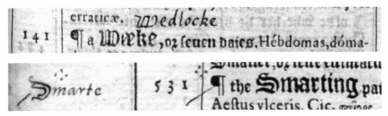

A page-by-page scan of the entire book reveals that these odd "artistic" tries occur within and under these two letters only. Could these playful attempts have been purely the result of a moment's fascination with those initial letters alone, and be devoid of personal meaning? As calligraphic formations, the "W" and the "S" as printed in Baret are hardly more curious, more artistically appealing, than the other letters. In the case of *any* other annotator, one would be *encouraged* to suggest that they may have held, for the person holding the feather, distinct personal meaning. But as evidence in support of our hypothesis, caution would, no doubt, be expressed and be expressed strongly.

Whatever conclusions are arrived at in regard to authorship, this much cannot be argued: The "W" and the "S" are clear choices on the part of the annotator. He does not take them too seriously, as they are just several in number, but these (we imagine spur-of-the-moment) copies appear to have been drawn purely on a sub-conscious level, and they fall entirely outside of the soon-to-be introduced handwriting argument of Italic vs. Secretary, because neither handwriting script comes close to containing either example. Our annotator, whoever he was, highlights the "W" and the "S."

He also occasionally highlights in the margins extracts from the Bible. Twelve of the spoken annotations are biblical quotations, a healthy enough number to bear significant weight, and most of these are followed by short indications of chapter and verse. In comparing the English Bible translations of the period, we observe that, without exception, whenever a translation differs, our annotator's biblical citations are closer to the Great Bible translation (1540) and the Bishops' Bible translation (1568). That neither the Geneva nor the yet-to-be printed King James Bible were in the annotator's head is significant for multiple reasons, including providing critical information on how to improve our sense of narrowing the period from which the annotations date.

After the composition of *Henry V*, Shakespeare's biblical allusions turn sharply to the Geneva Bible,[33] but before 1600 the echoes are notably not from the Geneva translation. According to Jonathan Bate, an allusion to the officially sanctioned Bishops' Bible over the Geneva "would have come from the memory of listening in church."[34]

Many of the biblical quotations in our margins are not exact transcriptions, but usually differ slightly in some of the wording, which tells us that they were written from memory, not taken directly from a published Bible immediately at hand. Most of the biblical quotations appear to contain a single word that is pivotal for the annotator. When the annotator inserts the quotation according to where that pivotal word would fit alphabetically, he has essentially entered a memory from church into the margin.

Here is one example. In the lower margin, under the word *faine*, our annotator cites Psalm 71.

My lips will be faine when I sing unto thee Ps. 71.21

☞ Psalm 71, line 21:

Coverdale Bible (1535) My lippes wolde fayne synge prayses vnto the.
Great Bible (1540)   My lyppes wylbe fayne, whan I synge vnto the:
Bishops' Bible (1568) My lyppes wyll be ioyfull when I syng vnto thee.
Geneva Bible (1587)   My lippes will reioyce when I sing vnto thee.
King James Bible (1611) My lips shall greatly rejoice when I sing unto thee;

With the five early English Bible translations of Psalm 71, line 21, shown above, we can see how this example coincides with Peter Milward's findings, in *Shakespeare's Religious Background*, that "when he uses the phraseology of the *Psalms*, it has been noted that Shakespeare follows the Great Bible, as used for the *Psalms* in the *Book of Common Prayer*."[35]

Clearly, the presence of the Baret sentence *To faine in singing* triggered our annotator's remembrance of the words from Psalm 71 of the Great Bible and caused him to write them into the bottom margin of the page. We do not find any use of this line in the works, but this annotation is surely a case of a personal memory of an incident from his life coming to the surface through a word association and being thus recorded.

Two additional spoken annotations that the annotator adds for *faine* are extracted from prefatory Baret texts: We are faine to use comes from a Baret phrase in the preface to letter "A." I was faine to seeke is taken from an even earlier preliminary text, *To The Reader*. On both occasions the annotator marks the prefatory texts with underlining before later adding the spoken annotations. All three of the words, *faine*, *use*, and *seek*, together with the third-person pronoun, are found together in one speech, which may or may not be a coincidence:

☞ *Much Ado About Nothing.* Claudio (5.1.123–25; Q1600, H2b)
We haue beene vp and downe to **seeke** thee; for **we**
are high proofe melancholie, and would **faine** have it beaten
away, wilt thou **vse** thy wit?

Another biblical word that the annotator recalls from the Great Bible and enters into the narrow left margin, between A530 and A531, is one that already in Shakespeare's day was becoming archaic. The three lines in the narrow margin –

areed vatici
(nor) marc
14

– should simply be read as areed vatici (nor) marc 14. This single-word quotation (we perceived that *vatici (nor)* was likely the Latin equivalent, and that turned out to be correct) proved the most elusive, and we were not able to verify it until we followed Peter Milward's advice and added the Great Bible translation into our search base. At once, we came upon *Areade* in place of *prophecy* used in each of the other translations, including the earlier Coverdale Bible. What made this particular quotation especially difficult is that all of the translations actually do have the two-word phrase *a reed*, used in a different context as part of Mark 15 (not 14), but the annotator's inserting it under the "A"s would have differed from his consistent method in the other eleven annotations where he inserted the biblical phrase under the principal "action word" of the phrase rather than the first word. Coming upon *Areade* in the Great Bible further confirmed Milward's general findings and was a very satisfying reassurance of our growing confidence that Shakespeare was the annotator of our *Alvearie*, despite the fact that it does not appear in the canon. (Milward would not, of course, have been able to incorporate the Great Bible's singular use of *Areade* as part of his determination.)

🖙 Coverdale Bible (1535) Mark 14.

Then beganne there some to spyt vpō him, and to couer his face, and to smyte him with fistes, and to saye vnto him **Prophecie** vnto vs. And the seruauntes smote him on the face.

🖝 Great Bible (1540) Mark 14.

And some begāne to spit at him, & to couer his face, & to beate hī with fistes, ād to saye vnto him, **Areade**: And the seruauntes boffeted him on the face.

🖝 Bishops' Bible (1568) Mark 14.

And some began to spyt at hym, and to couer his face, and to beate hym with fistes, and to say vnto hym, **prophecie**. And the seruauntes dyd beate hym with roddes.

🖝 Geneva Bible (1583) Mark 14.

And some began to spit at him, and to couer his face, and to beate him with fists, and to say vnto him, **Prophesie**. And the sergeants smote him with their roddes.

🖝 King James Bible (1611) Mark 14.

And some beganne to spit on him, and to couer his face, and to buffet him, and to say vnto him, **Prophecie**: And the seruants did stricke him with the palmes of their hands.

Areade is one of the period spellings along with *Areed*, and it can be defined as a synonym of *prophecy*, although its principal meaning is given in the *OED* as "to determine by counsel, to decree" or, hence, "to declare by supernatural counsel, oracularly; to divine, augur, soothsay, prophesy." The Latin word included as part of the annotation, but split in half because of the narrow margin, *vatici (nor)*, is one of the three Latin words listed in Baret's Latin index — *vates*, *vaticinium*, and *vaticinor* — that all refer the reader back to P779, a ***Prophesie***, where we see the annotator's little circle mute annotation. Shakespeare heavily uses *prophesy* and its variants (27 times), *prophecy* and its variants (24), and *prophet* and its variants (31).

One of our twelve biblical annotations is from the 46th Psalm, and it would be disingenuous not to mention it, as it is sure to draw the most attention as a result of the whimsical but widespread speculation surrounding a particular set of coincidences that are found in the translation of that psalm as printed in the King James Bible published in 1611. These involve the number "46" as well as this particular passage that our annotator has added in the left margin at K87.

he knappeth the speare in sunder

Knapped appears twice in the Shakespeare canon, *asunder* (along with *sunder* and its variants) 27 times, and *spear* 10 times. *Sunder* is always used opposite the peace-making sense of the psalm. Once again, the wording is critical, as it eliminates both the Geneva and the King James Bible being in the ear at the time of annotation, because both of these later translations use *cutteth* in place of *knappeth*. The annotation is closest to the three earlier translations:

Coverdale Bible (1535) **He** breaketh the bow and **knappeth the spear in sunder**

Great Bible (1540) **He** breaketh the bowe & **knappeth the speare in sonder,**

Bishops' Bible (1568) **He** breaketh the bowe, & **knappeth the speare in sunder,**

Geneva Bible (1587) He breaketh the bowe and cutteth the speare,

King James Bible (1611) He breaketh the bow and cutteth the spear asunder

But what will raise eyebrows, should we gain traction, is the link to a possibility that has been suggested for many years – namely, that in 1610, as the King James Bible translation was nearing completion, many of the celebrated poets of the period may have been consulted informally by the committee of translators for help with the more poetic passages of the Hebrew Bible such as the Psalms and the Song of Solomon.

Because of the set of coincidences in the 46th Psalm, attention especially falls on Shakespeare. If he had been among the poets chosen, *and* given the 46th Psalm, could he have taken the opportunity to adjust the exact placement of *shake* (as the 46th word from the beginning) and *spear* (as the 46th word from the end) as a hidden "signature," made even more intriguing because he would have been 46 years old at the time? This theme of poets used as KJB translators was even taken up by Rudyard Kipling in his last published story, "Proofs of Holy Writ,"[36] which portrays Ben Jonson and William Shakespeare happily imbibing in Shakespeare's garden in Stratford one afternoon and becoming more and more inebriated as they work together to improve the translation of Isaiah 60 that had just been brought down to them by a messenger on horseback from Oxford.

We are most definitely not leaning on the 46th Psalm heavily as a reason for our final hypothesis, but as observers and recorders of the evidence, we would be coy to shy away from certain annotations, or pretend that these will not be noticed once the magnifying glass is handed over from us to everyone else. There are twelve biblical annotations, and one of them is taken from the 46th Psalm and includes the word *spear* – there is no sidestepping this fact. If our annotator did participate in the KJB translation of the 46th Psalm, he obviously then was already familiar with the Bishops' Bible version and would seem to have chosen to retain the word *cutteth* from the Geneva Bible in place of the Bishops' Bible's *knappeth*.

As evidence that the 46th Psalm is still a debatable topic, the *TLS* recently printed a lively exchange on the matter across three issues from December 2011, to January 2012. Their reviewer, who initiated the discussion, concluded, after an exchange of letters, by saying, "No one, certainly not I, would seriously argue for anything except coincidence in all this. Nevertheless, as a matter of logic, it surely has to be either 'improbable chance' or 'improbable design.'"[37] We are in accord and certainly feel, given the recent illuminating scholarship regarding the known translators of the KJB,[38] that, at most, with the discovery of our annotated

Baret, we may have moved the matter to a chance of slightly less improbable design.

Another personal marker is also sure to arouse strong feelings among those that have argued strongly on the issue from one side or the other. Three IHS monograms are penned beside variant spellings of the *yew* tree. Each monogram is penned slightly differently, perhaps to match the variation noted in the spelling by Baret.

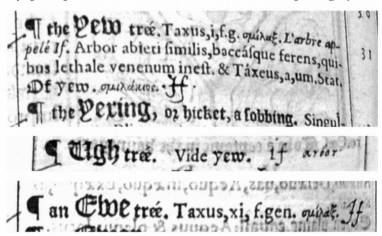

The extra care given to these monograms further supports the possibility that they were intended as religious markers with personal meaning, but also, by their placement, were meant to be private markers that would attract very little attention. In fact, the cross above the letters usually found in Jesuit usage of the IHS monogram is absent but perhaps can be represented by the *yew tree* itself.

Shakespeare uses *yew* six times in the works, including the famous brew of the weird sisters at the start of *Macbeth*. A yew tree was said to have grown in his yard in Stratford. No doubt he was familiar with both its medicinal properties and the association with Christ and the wood used for the cross. In a detailed book that explores botanical usages in the works, *The Plant Lore and Garden-Craft of Shakespeare* (1896), the author relates an alternative word for yew, *hebana* or *henbane*, with the depiction of poisoning from the plant that Hamlet hears from his father's ghost: "It may well be asked, how could Shakespeare have known of all these effects, which (as far as our present search has discovered) are not named by any one writer of his time, and some of which have only been made public from the results of Yew-poisoning since his day? I think the question can be answered in a very simple way. The effects are described with such marked minuteness that it seems to me not only very probable, but almost certain, that Shakespeare must have been an eye-witness of a case of Yew-poisoning, and that what he saw had been so photographed on his mind that he took the first opportunity that presented itself to reproduce the picture. With his usual grand contempt for perfect accuracy he did not hesitate to sweep aside at once the strict historical records of the old king's death, and in its place to paint for us a cold-blooded murder carried out by means which he knew from his personal experience to be possible, and which he felt himself able to describe with a minuteness which his knowledge of his audiences assured him would not be out of place even in that great tragedy."[39]

Shakespeare's personal connection to the yew plant aside, the most serious potential interest here, as far as his life is concerned, falls into the Catholicity debate, sometimes characterized as Lancastrian Shakespeare.[40] To make matters more complicated still, beyond simply the drawing of the three IHS monograms alongside the three variant spellings of *yew*, the annotator draws a slash line above the printed word *Shake* to allow for the entering of the spoken annotation shaft, for the intriguing composition *Shakeshaft*. The speculation behind the theory of Shakespeare as schoolmaster in Lancashire under the name "Shakeshafte" is part of the scholarship related to Catholicity, and Shakespeare's possible recusant sympathies.

These intriguing annotations are undoubtedly present in our book and surely deserve mention, but we do not feel we need to further stress the Catholicity of our annotator, only to relate in these introductory remarks what will provide additional complication for those unwilling to cede any chance that Shakespeare or his works can be explicitly tied to this book. Commentators have suggested that if indeed William Shakeshafte was William Shakespeare, the use of the name Shakeshafte was itself a sign of his wariness and the distance he preferred to keep from the Cottam and Campion circles, and we find no other annotation evidence in our Baret that would hint at any further connections.

The evidence we have identified as the most personal in this heavily annotated book culminates with the trailing binder's blank, a blank leaf whereupon an extraordinarily odd assortment of words are written, the majority translated from English into French. The words on this page are not reactive to pre-existing printed text on that page. As such, it is different from every other page in the book that warrants consideration. The entire sample emerges from a mind, the same mind that has engaged with the printed text throughout, but is here given no guidance, no suggestions. The word salad is a Baret word salad, words that the annotator has almost without exception previously negotiated and marked in varying capacity, but the selection is unique, and, when put to the test, dynamic Shakespearean patterns are formed. A selection that looks like nothing yet reveals everything must ultimately be reconciled in any counterargument.

One imagines these annotations to be not only the final ones to appear in the book, but certainly among the last ones added to it. There is also the opportunity to see a sizeable number of words on a single page in the *same dramatically mixed hand* as one sees throughout the book. This helps to squash the argument that the variability throughout is a sign that multiple primary annotators are at work. This mixed hand, the heart of the paleography question, is the subject of the next introductory chapter.

Whether by implausible coincidence or something more, the

words themselves on this trailing blank produce extraordinary connections within the tight framework of Falstaff plays, and even a bizarre connection to the opening scene in *Merry Wives of Windsor*, which has historically been speculated to reference Sir Thomas Lucy of deer theft fame. Yet, there is no structure to the word arrangement on the page to possibly indicate the annotator is a Shakespeare reader making a commentary on the works (or life) of Shakespeare.

Pointless it would be from any angle to be blind to the personality of the annotator. The letters "W" & "S," the IHS monograms, the select group of biblical citations from memory, and the word salad of French and English words that looks haphazardly arranged on the trailing blank are each distinct from the printed text, and are revealing as to who this person may have been, or at least help us to understand more about him and his background.

As we dig further, we uncover a preponderance of natural history annotations, interest in the language of clothing and costume of the period critical to stagecraft, and annotations that connect with our understanding of Shakespeare's father. Curiously, none of these aspects stand out at first glance, but they are there, and they add to the personality we can properly grant the annotator irrespective of whether they can help build a case for a specific annotator.

If one considers the occasional marks befitting a proofreader, the annotations may realistically have started out as part of a vocational exercise. The overwhelming methodology itself, however, is clearly personal, and there are enough highly personal moments throughout, beyond the method, to obliterate the notion that this book was primarily a source for professional revision and not a single man's dictionary that held a secure position through the years on his most cherished bookshelf.

Paleography

ANY ARGUMENT in favor of the annotations belonging to Shakespeare must begin with, at the very least, a plausible defense of the paleography. One can say "plausible" because books belonging to Shakespeare with annotations attributable to him are thought not to have survived – if indeed he ever made annotations in his books. So knowing precisely, or even remotely, what such an annotated book would look like is, to a large degree, a matter of conjecture.

When we talk about paleography in relation to the annotations in our copy of Baret, the discussion begins with three primary concerns: the variability demonstrated in the formation of the letters throughout, the determination of whether it is reasonable to assume that the full body (or very close to the full body) of the marginalia is the work of a single person, and the question of how to establish as close an approximation as possible on the dating of the handwriting.

Paleographers can usually ascertain a decent range in assigning estimates to the dates of handwritten annotations. But even then, with Elizabethan books, one is talking about a window over some not inconsiderable number of years that will bring no satisfaction to those wanting hard proof, as paleography is by no means a hard science, especially as the ink from the period can only be tested generally, with a margin of error often greater than the paleographer's estimate. When we argue strongly that the annotations on the trailing blank are most likely no more than a year away from 1598, we will have come to that conclusion by means other than scientific testing. Given that it is scientifically impossible to guarantee anything close to a precise date for the ink on this page and on other pages, we have no choice but to gain some semblance of plausibility from paleographers before perceptions of authorial authentication can be gauged.

Establishing a reasonably tight time frame – a plausible time frame – wherein the annotator is most likely to have annotated is aided by other factors in addition to the nature of the handwriting script, which we will get to momentarily. Spellings, shorthand usages, and the biblical citations would be among these other factors. Paleographers may well assign a plausible range as wide as beginning in 1580 (date of publication) and ending as late as 1650. But the later portion of this range is, in our opinion, something of a stretch. Assigning a date following the death of Shakespeare would require imagining an annotator somehow recalling (as opposed to copying) much earlier biblical translations – and also imagining an annotator using already archaic words and spellings, and making small, frequent textual changes to a dictionary no longer in fashion, all while making consistent use of a number of notably Elizabethan abbreviations (i.e., mouse-foot; tilde) that would decrease in vogue as the seventeenth century advanced. It is our conclusion that a late-sixteenth-century to turn-of-the-seventeenth-century speculation seems far more likely, and this is not at all unsupported by the paleography; it simply can never be proven scientifically one way or the other through the testing of the ink, or the naked examination of the marks, and we must be willing to accept that.

On the question of single annotator vs. multiple annotators, we have already noted that the profusely employed mute annotations – annotations that number well into the thousands – are executed and utilized consistently throughout the book from beginning to end. That these non-word markings – especially the more one studies the annotator's tendencies – are so convincingly and even irrefutably tied to the handwritten additions of words (the spoken annotations) should, by itself, give credibility to the determination that there is a single primary annotator. The case is only strengthened the more deeply we examine it.

The Elizabethan period contains a diversity of handwriting styles, each of which contains its own variable range of letter formation.[41] We are concerned with the two primary scripts of the period: the more newly introduced Italic hand and the native Secretary hand. Each of these styles is represented in our book, but with the Italic contributing, overwhelmingly, the lion's share.

Other writers of the period, such as the poet Edmund Spenser, are known to have used two, or even three, distinct hands, with book marginalia among the variety of writing that frequently would have been executed using the increasingly popular Italic script. But most of these "other writers," Spenser included, were separate from Shakespeare in terms of background and acknowledged university attendance, and this represents a distinction to paleographers that have emphasized the difference in backgrounds as having contributed to handwriting preference and capacity. The question is, should the trepidation of imagining Shakespeare learning to use an Italic hand be warranted, especially as it is acknowledged that we have no accepted examples of Shakespeare's marginal hand?

In terms of letter formation and penmanship style, variation alone, even in a modern annotated book, does not eliminate the possibility that a single person is doing the annotating. But this is especially true when examining books from the Elizabethan period. The preference for variation is nowhere more dramatically represented in our book than on the all-important trailing blank, where the display of variety in letter formation strikes one as almost whimsical. Among the many aspects that stand out in studying this page – relative to all other pages that we are faced with – is the open space in which our annotator is given an opportunity to operate. This offers a chance that exists nowhere else in the book: to see a large writing sample in one place. There is, oddly, a profound sense of harmony in spite of the variant letter formations within both the Italic and Secretary formations. In keeping with the pattern throughout the book, in the French and Latin annotations that are made alongside the English annotations, we typically see more variable elements, whether they be of English Secretary hand, or a wider variety of Italic forms – differences, perhaps, that the annotator has used to help distinguish between them at a glance. Most significantly, the tremendous variation that we see present in the formation of letters throughout the book matches, in great detail, the wide variation found in the letter formations on the trailing blank. The Elizabethan attraction to variation is here in full bloom, and the variation is evident sometimes even in a single annotation.

Leon Kellner is not a major name in the historical landscape of paleography. Yet it is Kellner who, in 1925, provides a most lucid summation on this principle of variation: "What strikes us moderns as inconsistency, perhaps as incongruousness, was not considered as such by the Elizabethans. Uniformity was shunned, variety commended as a grace of style. In spelling, in declension and conjugation, in the structure of sentences, in word-formation we notice a deliberate preference for variation. If, then, variation was considered a grace of style in grammar, it may be assumed to have been no mere carelessness to use letters of different script in the same letter or composition. Shakespeare's signatures are direct proof of his having had no objection to the Mixed Hand."[42]

What exactly does a mixed hand imply? This leads our discussion into the problem of the meager bits and pieces of handwriting that *have* been determined to be in Shakespeare's own hand. Regrettably, none of the handwriting examples available to us are in confirmed marginal additions to books, including books that we know that Shakespeare must have used. This presents a problem, in that the distinctions that make up annotations in books (sometimes referred to as a book hand) might not necessarily be compliant with how the same person's handwriting would look if the composition were a poem, or a scene in a play, or a letter to a friend (all examples of a writing hand), and certainly may not be at all compatible with how a person would sign his name.[43] And even within these various styles, we encounter variability based on time and circumstance. Comparisons with the handwriting in our Baret, therefore, are difficult, and may never be conclusive.

There are six known surviving signatures of Shakespeare on legal documents; for starters, none of them are even spelled the same. Whereas some will point to this as a sign of alarm, it merely reinforces how haphazard notions of spelling were at the time. The six signatures, along with one two-word addition, "By me," found on his will just in front of a signature, have generally been viewed as the only universally accepted examples of Shakespeare's hand. It needs to be conceded that a majority of today's experts seem now to be in favor of Hand D[44] in the *Sir Thomas More* manuscript, a collaborative effort on the part of multiple playwrights, wherein three of the pages made as part of a later revision are thought to be Shakespeare's. These three pages – still cautiously referred to as Hand D – are argued to be Shakespeare's through linguistic dissemination as much as on paleographic evidence.[45] With no other alleged Shakespeare manuscript with which to compare it, one must acknowledge that the author of Hand D is still a matter of some conjecture.

What is not a matter of conjecture when it comes to Hand D is the style of the handwriting. The style of Hand D is a fluid, cursive, English Secretary hand. The consensus among paleographers of yesterday and today repeatedly emphasizes and maintains that this is the script that Shakespeare would have used; it was, after all, the one he would have learned in grammar school.

That the overwhelming majority of the letters formed in this copy of Baret (especially those written in English) fall under the broad categorization of an Italic hand as opposed to Secretary hand is a hurdle for many paleographers, and we understood that it would be a major source of contention were we ever to feel comfortable in the strengths of our argument to bring it forth publicly. The presumption that Shakespeare used a Secretary hand is backed up not only by the signatures and Hand D (if indeed the three pages are in his hand) but also by errors in the early printings – errors that appear to derive from the misreading of words and letters written in Secretary.[46]

That said, the handwriting of our annotator includes many words and letters written in Secretary, mostly occurring in the French and Latin additions, wherein we also see a tendency toward using cursive, although separation is frequently maintained for the sake of legibility. The Italic formations, by contrast, are almost always in disconnected letters – seldom, if ever, in cursive. Here is an example where the English word skulle is added in disconnected Italic letters, and the French tete l'homme morte (head of dead man) is written in a mixed hand, with elements of Italic and Secretary, and an increased use of cursive:

Even while acknowledging that the contributions from the annotator in English are almost entirely Italic, it is important to note that, from one page to the next, it is a variable Italic marginal hand and not an elegant Italic writing hand, such as the example of a letter from poet George Peele in 1595, or in a Ben Jonson manuscript from 1609, both held in the British Museum.

Our emphasis on this distinction is straightforward, but no

less relevant. So constrained are the spaces that the annotator is almost by necessity, as well as design, required to abandon a writing hand, and be deliberate for the sake of legibility. The great majority of the annotations are written in detached letters, this necessitated by the narrow confines of the spaces. The confines are often so genuinely small that to write a sequence of words in a secretarial hand would require obliteration of the neighboring printed text. If the annotator wished to annotate the book both marginally and interlineally and still see what he had written, he needed to be careful.

This brings us to the one Shakespeare signature to which we do see similarity in terms of the letter formations in our book. Often referred to as signature "C," it is one of two signatures produced on back-to-back days on the Blackfriars Gatehouse sale and mortgage documents.

SIGNATURE B   SIGNATURE C

Sir Edward Maunde Thompson, a former director and principal librarian of the British Museum, discusses these signatures as "the two constrained signatures"[47] because of the minimal allotted space on which they were penned. He notes that signature "C" is "somewhat laboriously written down in disconnected letters thereby losing the natural run of the hand."[48] This is in complete harmony with the person annotating our book – the annotator who has squeezed in bits and pieces, observations, cross-references, and, in some instances, memories, with no other choice but to lose the "natural run of the hand."[49] For the sake of legibility, given the space restrictions and the likely challenging arm angles, etc., it is only logical that the majority of entries would benefit by being made in disconnected letters. Because the letters in signature "C" are disconnected, Thompson stresses that they have also been made "with deliberation."[50] This is a vital point, but the conversation should be from there extended.

We have observed, but have not seen it noted elsewhere, that Shakespeare seems most concerned with restricting himself to the label when signing his name. One of the other two signatures even races over the labels' edge, but not Shakespeare's. Why is this significant? Shakespeare took a certain approach when he signed the label, and that approach seems to mirror the value our annotator places on respecting the limits imposed by the printed lines, as he repeatedly makes a point of not going over the edge – not always successful, but enough so on a regular basis that it bears highlighting on the subject of our book's paleographic evidence. Often he will rely on a tilde to reduce the number of required letters. Consider this example, where a concerted effort has been made to respect the limits of the space by incorporating not just one tilde but two, simply to avoid going over the line (almost successful):

The continual respect for space as the annotator relies on small, disconnected letters likely accounts for the similarity between elements in certain annotations and signature "C." We discovered, for example, that the "h + a" combination of the signature is in spirit – and, to a strong degree, in appearance – in line with the same pair of letters we find in combinations over a large number of spoken annotations that contain them together (e.g., shaft). The second "s," the "p," and the "e" at the end of the label also all bear likenesses to numerous annotations throughout the book. The known dimensions of the seal itself allow us to apply measurements of these letters and compare them even more closely with what we find spatially in our Baret.

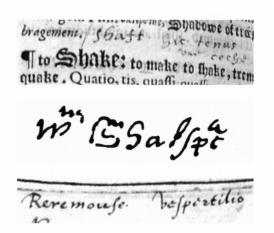

The basis for our comparisons is somewhat skewed, as we imagine a period of roughly fifteen years between most of the very last annotations made in our book and the March 1613 date on the Blackfriars mortgage seal. Nevertheless, in what contains the most disconnected letter formations found anywhere in the signatures – even if the style has been forced upon him by the size of the seal – we must acknowledge some stylistic likeness when comparisons are applied. These are understood not to be exact replicas – they need not be, nor should they be expected to be, but they are close enough in look and feel to justify notice.

In spite of the clear-cut differences between signature "C" and the other Shakespeare signatures – differences that Thompson attributes to the constraints of the label – signature "C" is nonetheless regularly acknowledged to likewise be written in Secretary. None of the disconnected letters are interpreted as Italic, per se, and yet even a modern reader is able to distinguish between what looks like a recognizable Italic "p" in Shakespeare's signature "c," whereas the "p" from a day earlier is not remotely of Italic quality.

In isolating this example alone in our book, consider one of the annotator's "p" formations (from a French annotation, non per) and compare it with the two from minuscule "p" formations in signatures "B" and "C."

If a variation on a familiar childhood game "one of these three is not like the others," is played, the "p" in signature "B" is swiftly eliminated. Our goal in providing the preceding illustrations is not to insist upon a eureka moment, but to highlight the enormous difficulty in eliminating an annotator based upon paleographic difference, whether that difference be the formation of a single letter, a combination of letters, or even in – the broadest terms – a variety of script.

Factor in the additional elements of time elapsed and difference in purpose to what we find in these select letter formations alongside signature "C," and it must be conceded that we are in the game – especially in light of all the other evidence that overpowers the desire to fall back on prefigured estimations of Shakespeare's marginal hand that are, in themselves, highly unscientific. And while it would be a misrepresentation to say that every instance yields the results that we have reproduced here in our extracted examples, allow us to return to the point of emphasis in regard to variability, and to use, once again, the variation seen and commented upon in the two mortgage signatures produced but a single day apart. One need not be an expert in Renaissance paleography to be struck by the difference. "When we turn to the mortgage deed ["C"] we naturally expect to find a signature uniform with that of the purchase deed executed a day earlier. It is therefore surprising to find a difference."[51] These words of Thompson's punctuate, emphatically, the critical need to emphasize the Elizabethan preference for variation when studying the annotations in our Baret going forward. It should especially come as no surprise to see variation in the hand throughout our book, where the large mass of annotations were likely made over some number of years, and certainly over an exceedingly large number of annotating stints.

One final thought on signature "C" before moving on. Let us for a moment imagine that this signature was not found on a legal document, but rather in a sourcebook. It would be easy under such an imagined circumstance to see how the signature would rather swiftly be denigrated as a forgery. It is plainly obvious that it would be impossible, based upon the other signatures, to authenticate it. The fact that signature "C" exists at all tells us something important regarding what is seen as authentic and what has come to be viewed as a misrepresentation: one has to be open to other evidence. In the case of signature "C," the "other evidence" holds authority because it is executed on a legal document that cements its validity. In the case of the annotations in our book, the "other evidence" does not bear the irrefutable imprint of a legal document, but, although murky, is incalculably vaster in scope. The sum of what we find from a linguistic standpoint should not be dismissed or written off as trivial, especially if there proves to be a complete absence of other books where similarly powerful results can be demonstrated with comparative marginalia.

If there is one objective that is more relevant than any other in Part One of our defense of the grandest of possibilities, it is that our copy of Baret's *Alvearie* and the marginalia it contains is nothing if not genuine. Our own eyes and experience told us this from the outset, and it was only more substantially reinforced the further we worked our way into the analysis. This will almost universally not be in dispute when others who are familiar with looking at annotated books are allowed a detailed and sustained inspection. There is no conspiracy to be found among the annotations in our copy of Baret. Only the most bitter, misguided, and misinformed responses – now that we are going public, we must prepare for anything – would suggest otherwise. The linguistic elements that make up the annotations, as well as the paleographic elements, are wholly the product of someone's organic and very diligent approach toward the book and stand no chance of being understood as the product of a calculated attempt to deceive.

This honest, legitimate effort on the part of the annotator is why, while we are on the subject of paleography, we must again remind our readers of an unusual piece of evidence: how on occasion the annotator imitates the font of a lead capital letter as printed in Baret. This previously asserted observation is intimately connected to the question of paleography and cannot be ignored as being outside the argument. As much of the handwriting in our book is destined to be viewed as "generic" with nothing to distinguish it from other period hands, it is even more reason to take seriously this attention restricted to two letters only out of twenty-two (there is no capital example of X or Z; IJ and UV are one).[52]

Following the release of the film *Anonymous*, Stanley Wells was interviewed on the subject of the need to offer resistance to anti-Stratfordian misrepresentation, as opposed to the more regular strategy of simply ignoring those who believe that Shakespeare could not have written Shakespeare.[53] At one point, Wells was asked why there are no books from Shakespeare's library. He answered that there might be one or two around somewhere, and that maybe one or two that bear an unconfirmed signature could in fact be genuine. This led to an inquiry on our part into one sourcebook in particular, held by the British Museum: Florio's *Montaigne*, published in 1603, and signed "William Shakespeare" at the front.

The *Montaigne* apparently "belonged to Rev. Edward Patterson, a clergyman in the county adjoining Warwickshire, who is known to have shown the volume to his friends before the year 1780."[54] Eventually his son took it to the British Museum. "Neither he nor his son ever attempted to put their possession to profitable use. The fine art of Shakespearian forgery was then unknown."[55]

When Sir Frederick Madden purchased the book on behalf of the British Museum in 1839, he noted that the signature offered "a sufficient resemblance to Shakespeare's signatures to warrant the conclusion that they are the same hand, although enough variation to preclude the idea of imitation."[56] After the acquisition "it was submitted to numerous competent judges, all of whom expressed a clear opinion in favour of the genuineness of the signature."[57]

This favorable opinion did not last, however. Thompson went on to reject the *Montaigne* signature, while granting that it bears "a practiced hand and one more expert than is usually to be found in such Shakespearian curiosities."[58] It is currently not in fashion to promote validation of the *Montaigne* signature, but, once again, it is impossible to scientifically prove or disprove the authenticity.

Robert Ellrodt sums up the lack of a clear-cut solution when he says: "The controversy over the alleged Shakespeare autograph in the British Museum copy of Florio's translation is inconclusive."[59] And perhaps the most insightful statement on the *Montaigne* comes courtesy of Frances A. Yates in *John Florio: The Life of an Italian in Shakespeare's England*: "Whether forged or genuine, it [the signature] probably represents a truth."[60] At minimum, something similar may soon also be said about the annotations in the copy of Baret in question: *The annotations are most definitely genuine, and, whether Shakespeare's or not, they represent a certain truth.*[61]

This assertion, however, bold as it may be, is ultimately unsatisfying for many of the most interested parties involved, as well as the public. What we are contending on the subject of the handwriting comes down to this: if the principal contention that paleographers have to stand on in refuting the extraordinary linguistic evidence in our copy of Baret is based upon the Italic irreconcilability with someone of Shakespeare's background, this reasoning is going to prove disingenuous. Irreconcilability of someone of Shakespeare's background and the works is, after all, the battle cry of what are termed anti-Stratfordians or anti-Shakespeareans. Why should the paleographer be able to say the same thing about the marginal hand in this copy of Baret for the sake of an easy dismissal, when books with Shakespeare's marginal notes are not available for comparison, and when we have in the example of signature "C" clear evidence that in the stylistic forming of letters, his hand managed alteration when restricted to small spaces? Shakespeare was nothing if not an exception to the rule, and undermining or reducing the linguistic evidence of our case may prove difficult, if not downright impossible.

In spite of this declaration of confidence, there is, aside from the Italic pickle, still another obstacle along paleographic grounds, and it is, not unreasonably, the most ominous problem of all. As soon as you make a claim that annotations could be in Shakespeare's own hand, people will want to see the annotations. And, as soon as they see them, whether expert or non-expert, there is bound to be disappointment. We contemplated not using our catalogue to visualize the book at all, leaving the website alone to carry the images, and trying to slowly overcome and chip away at the sheer impossibility of the implied suggestion by making the best argument that we ourselves could muster. This strategy would be to try to emphasize the argument and what was present in our Baret without the pressure that no set of pictures could ever live up to.

Whether in our book or another book yet to be contemplated as such, there are two certainties regarding any potential-to-be-argued, suddenly discovered, annotated book from Shakespeare's library. The annotations will not glow; quite the opposite, in fact – they will look ordinary. And there will no signs of great poetry; once again, just the opposite – they will sound ordinary. In truth, there should be no other way to conceive realistically of a book surviving that long without being noticed, if these ordinary qualities were not evident once studying the book commenced. Whether by reality or fantasy, the ordinary look and the unspectacular sound of the annotations would be a given. In some respects, how appropriate, how fitting is it that the man himself is still today so often attacked and demeaned by a certain persistent minority for being too ordinary?

Shakespeare on Handwriting

WHAT — one might be curious to know — does Shakespeare, himself, say on the subject? This is, after all, the writer who has something to say on *all* subjects, although without the commitment that would allow us to assess his opinions. The paleographic community continues to promote the consensus of Shakespeare's background — the Stratford grammar school education and how handwriting was taught there — being incompatible with an Italic hand. The surviving manuscript evidence, both authenticated (signatures) and strongly supported (Hand D), does nothing to disturb the idea that the English Secretary hand was his preferred choice. That said, no paleographer can deny, or makes an attempt to deny, that Shakespeare was keenly aware of many hands, in particular the increasingly popular Italic hand.

Only once does Shakespeare use the exact word *handwriting*:

☞ *Comedy of Errors*. Dromio of Ephesus (3.1.11–14; FF H3b)

Say what you wil sir, but I know what I know,
That you beat me at the Mart I haue your hand to show;
If yr skin were parchment, & ye blows you gaue were ink,
Your owne **hand-writing** would tell you what I thinke.

But he is far from quiet on the subject, and perhaps the fact that he writes plays wherein characters perform acts, and interpret letters received, centering on the question of a "true" or "false" hand, is indicative of just how conscious Shakespeare was of the importance of the appearance of handwriting, and how he understood that different hands would suit different conveyances and circumstances.

Consider here just a few of the "hands" of which Shakespeare speaks. He speaks of a court hand:

🖙 *2 Henry VI.* Butcher (4.2.93–94; FF n6)

> Nay, he can make Obligations, and write Court hand.

and a fair hand (i.e., neat hand):

🖙 *Merchant of Venice.* Lorenzo (2.4.12–14; FF P)

> I know the hand, in faith, in faith 'tis a faire hand
> And whiter than the paper it writ on,
> Is the fair hand that writ

and a martial hand:

🖙 *Twelfth Night.* Sir Toby Belch (3.2.39; FF Z1b)

> Go, write it in a martial hand,

and a Roman hand:

🖙 *Twelfth Night.* Malvolio (3.4.26; FF Zz)

> I thinke we doe know the sweet Romane hand.

Later in *Twelfth Night* (act 5, scene 1), Malvolio and Olivia have the following detailed and clever exchange built around the "true" author of a received letter:

🖙 *Twelfth Night.* Malvolio (5.1.327–41; FF Z4b–5)

> Lady you haue, pray you peruse that Letter.
> You must not now denie it is your hand,
> Write from it if you can, in hand, or phrase,
> Or say, tis not your seale, not your inuention:
> You can say none of this. Well, grant it then,
> And tell me in the modestie of honor,
> Why you haue giuen me such cleare lights of fauour,
> Bad me come smiling, and crosse-garter'd to you,
> To put on yellow stockings, and to frowne
> Vpon sir *Toby*, and the lighter people:
> And acting this in an obedient hope,
> Why haue you suffer'd me to be imprison'd,
> Kept in a darke house, visited by the Priest,
> And made the most notorious gecke and gull,
> That ere inuention plaid on? Tell me why?

🖙 *Twelfth Night.* Olivia (5.1.342–52; FF Z5)

Alas *Maluolio*, this is not my writing,
Though I confesse much like the Charracter:
But out of question, tis *Marias* hand.
And now I do bethinke me, it was shee
First told me thou wast mad; then cam'st in smiling,
And in such formes, which heere were presuppos'd
Vpon thee in the Letter: prethee be content,
This practice hath most shrewdly past vpon thee:
But when we know the grounds, and authors of it,
Thou shalt be both the Plaintiffe and the Iudge
Of thine owne cause.

Establishing the "true" scribe behind a given missive is a cause for concern and clarification elsewhere in the works, and *character* emerges as a key repetitive word. Consider *Hamlet*, when Claudius receives Hamlet's letter and wants to be certain of its author:

🖙 *Hamlet* (4.7.49–50; FF pp4)

LAERTES: Know you the hand?
CLAUDIUS: 'Tis *Hamlet's* Character,

The word *character* is slightly vague. It implies something more than *plausible*, if also less than a guarantee of *authentic*. The word pops up again in reference to a letter in *King Lear*, after Edmund is read a letter, presumably from Edgar:

🖙 *King Lear.* Gloucester (1.2.62; Q1608, scene 2, C1b)

You know the Caractar to be your brothers?

Shakespeare's knowledge of period hands and the ways in which he manages the nuances of handwriting and the problems of authenticating writing samples in his plays do not go unnoticed by paleographers, who regularly bring up with great abandon the scene when Hamlet alters his normal hand after intercepting his own death warrant and replacing it with one for Rosencrantz and Guildenstern:

🔖 *Hamlet*. Hamlet (5.2.30–38; FF pp6)

> Being thus benetted round with Villaines,
> Ere I could make a Prologue to my braines,
> They had begun the Play. I sate me downe,
> Deuis'd a new Commission, wrote it faire,
> I once did hold it as our Statists doe,
> A basenesse to write faire; and laboured much
> How to forget that learning: but Sir now,
> It did me Yeomans seruice: wilt thou know
> The effects of what I wrote?

Could a personal reference marker be present in this speech, which both acknowledges the sense of writing neatly and allows for the altering of hands to achieve a purpose?

There are numerous scenarios by which Shakespeare could have learned to form letters neatly in Italic. If Shakespeare did work as a proofreader to assist with gaining access to the books he deeply craved, he might well have been required to learn how to "write fair" – something he would not have been trained in at grammar school (as experts continue to stress). Later he could have "laboured much how to forget the learning." But, of course, we see even from certain elements in signature "C" that the learning to write in disconnected letters was never entirely lost.

The possibility that Shakespeare learned to write Italic simply because he wanted to is also not so far-fetched. A certain degree of vanity when it came to social status is one of the few character traits safely attributable to Shakespeare in the historical record. The attaining of a coat of arms on behalf of his father was important to Shakespeare. His success in applying for the arms earned a title that he would inherit – "gentleman" – and even gets the attention of his contemporaries, and one of his good pals (presumably) in particular. In *Every Man Out of His Humour*, Ben Jonson has a minor character parody Shakespeare's applied-for status, and his adopted motto, with what almost certainly was a referential jab, "not without mustard." The actual Shakespeare motto, once approved – chosen by son for father, and, by extension, for himself – "Non Sans Droit" (Not Without Right), secured for the Shakespeare family a certain social status that Shakespeare himself quite obviously relished.

There can be little doubt that Shakespeare, sensitive as he was to everything, social status included, was also keenly aware of the societal implications connected to styles of handwriting. This may have increased his own desire to dabble in learning to "write fair," or dabble in the "sweet Roman hand," even if he would never adopt such "neatness" for his writing hand, or in the variable formation of his signatures.

If Shakespeare did learn Italic, whatever the arguments as to how – whether through employment as a proofreader, through a sense of vanity in wanting to belong to a higher class, or simply out of curiosity to see letters on the page formed in different ways befitting of one who loved books and words – the instruction manuals themselves would not have been difficult to find, and he could have trained himself through their direct use. They were printed in connection with the same individuals who were responsible for printing a number of his well-known sourcebooks.

The previously introduced names Vautrollier and Field are located front and center when it comes to the introduction of handwriting books into circulation in late sixteenth century England. The first writing book printed in England was John de Beauchesne's: *A Booke containing divers sortes of hands, as well the English as French secretarie with the Italian, Roman, Chancelrie & Court Hands.* Thomas Vautrollier was the printer-publisher and chose this to be his first publishing project, but he did not stop there. "Writing books" became a sub-specialty. In 1582, Vautrollier published *The First Part of the Elementarie which entreateth chefelie of the right writing of our English tung by the educationalist Richard Mulcaster,* and in 1587, F. Clement's *The Petie Schole with an English Orthographie.* In this second book, two plates appear, one of Secretary examples and one of Italic examples, taken from *Newe Booke of Copies* (1574). Why should it be so improbable to imagine Shakespeare intrigued by writing manuals, and even possibly using them?

There is a fascinating story that may be relevant as well, involving a celebrated sixteenth-century calligrapher, Peter Bales, who is known for his book on handwriting, *The Art of New Brachygraphie.*[62] A brief account of Bales's life and exploits is colorfully documented in a multi-volume set, *The Curiosities of Literature*, by Isaac Disraeli that was first published between 1791 and 1823,[63] and his skills as a penman were known even to Holinshed, who relates that Bales presented Queen Elizabeth in 1575 with a miniature specimen of his work mounted in glass and set in a ring. Shakespeare would have read this account, no doubt, in Holinshed's *Chronicles*, a favorite among favorites.

In 1595, a famous contest of skill between Bales and a rival penman, Daniel Johnson, took place in London, with the winner awarded the prize of "the golden pen." Disraeli described the launch of the contest: "On Michaelmas day, 1595, the trial opened before five judges: the appellant and the respondent appeared at the appointed place, and an ancient gentleman was entrusted with 'golden pen.'"[64] The trial, or contest, apparently took place before a large crowd over multiple days and involved several disciplines (e.g., Italic; Secretary). The theatrical aspect would most certainly have appealed to Shakespeare, and there is no reason to think that, minimally, he heard about the contest, even if he did not personally witness Bales' "victory." In A. S. Osley's *Scribes and Sources: Handbook of the Chancery Hand in the Sixteenth Century*, Berthold Wolpe contributes a chapter highlighting the man who would assume the moniker "The Golden Pen": "It appears the skill of Bales was used by Sir Francis Walsingham and Sir Christopher Hatton for certain state activities, such as deciphering and copying secret correspondence. By intercepting letters and making changes or additions in forged handwriting, it was possible to compromise and set traps for their authors."[65] Wolpe then goes on to "wonder whether Shakespeare knew of these activities,"[66] and he, too, brings to the reader's attention the scene from Hamlet when the Prince does something similar by intercepting his own death warrant, sent by Claudius, and replacing it with the names Rosencrantz and Guildenstern.

Regardless of the interpretation and guesswork involved (and it remains just that), above all, let us not think that with a certain amount of practice and care, Shakespeare was fundamentally incapable of forming letters in Italic. The overriding question, already broached in the previous chapter, is whether Shakespeare should forever be categorically denied an ability to use both scripts based principally on his Stratford background. Does this not seem oddly in perverse harmony with someone who argues that a provincial boy from Stratford as author is incompatible with one of the great speeches in, say, *Henry V*? Given that marginal hands of the period are often acknowledged to be different, even radically different, from the writing hands of the same individuals, why should the possibility of variety in Shakespeare's marginal or book hand not be conceivable? As Jonathan Goldberg bluntly puts it on the subject of Shakespeare being able to use Italic, either for a signature or, by extension, a marginal annotation: "we do not know that he could not."[67]

One of the problems with a neat hand, where disconnected Italic letters are used, is that the personality or "character" of the annotator is hidden. As Goldberg puts it in his essay, "Hamlet's Hand": "the fair hand is legible, but its very legibility means that it cannot be owned as a mark of individuality."[68]

🖎 *Much Ado About Nothing*. Claudio (5.4.85–88; FF L)

And Ile be sworne vpon't, that he loues her,
For heres a paper written in his hand,
A halting sonnet of his owne pure braine,
Fashioned to *Beatrice*.

The whole of what we find written in our book, while lacking the dramatic discovery of a "halting sonnet," is unquestionably the product of *someone's* own pure brain, and the frequent efforts of this annotator's uncompromising and "characterless" hand are in the end revealing of "character" in a multitude of uncannily specific examples and tendencies.

Understandably, things bend heavily, even necessarily, under the burden of proof in the quest for *any* namable annotator, because we live in an age where an enormous amount of trust is placed in the ability to test and prove something scientifically. In the absence of scientific proof, evidence – no matter the strength – is often deemed unreliable, regardless of how it registers in the court of public opinion. It follows, then, that an inability to precisely test ink from the Elizabethan period[69] will make for a wobbly case in the quest for answers as to the exact age of the annotations in our Baret, let alone to the still more complicated determination of who has added the ink to the pages. Given the absence of annotated books from Shakespeare's library, we concede only that we are without a means for proper comparison.

Without a viable comparison, it could be argued that the road to defending Shakespeare as a plausible annotator will inevitably lead to a dead end no matter what our annotations demonstrate from a linguistic analysis. But the linguistic evidence is so substantial, and so much of what we find in the annotations from a personal perspective actually complements what others have long inferred. The details are, in fact, often so specific that it is startling. In other words, the linguistic and symbolic evidence and the prime candidate are a match, through and through, and all of it resides in a book that makes perfect sense. The last hurdle is in the paleography, where some revision along the lines of italic and secretarial variability would be required should the annotations ever plausibly – or close to definitively – come to be viewed as Shakespeare's own.

Shakespeare as Reader

I N ACT 5, scene 2, of *Hamlet*, the courier Osric rattles off technical terms relating to dueling prior to the duel between Hamlet and Laertes. Hamlet, frustrated, asks Osric, "What call you the carriages?" (5.2.118; Q1604, N2b). Before Osric can clarify that these are the hangers where the swords hang, Horatio chides him, snickering: "I knew you must be edified by the margent ere you had done" (5.2, p. 718, after 118; Q1604, N2b).[70] He's more or less saying that he knew Hamlet would at some stage need to look something up in the dictionary. James Black, in his paper *Edified by the Margent: Shakespeare and the Bible*, makes note of Horatio's aside: "It was precisely the Geneva Bible which Shakespeare had in mind when he wrote that line."[71]

Black is referring specifically to the preface in the Geneva Bible where the editors provide precise allusion to these words, telling the readers that for "good purpose and edification" they "have in the margent noted" certain things. This was the version printed for critical mass use, and the margins of this edition are heavily printed with marginalia. It has been frequently speculated that Shakespeare must eventually have owned his own copy of the Geneva Bible, as the allusions in the works following *Henry V* turn suddenly to this translation (see note 33).

But how curious is it that the information is located not in a book of the Bible itself, but in an editorial preface? Was Shakespeare so attentive a reader of prefaces? Could there be additional suggestive evidence in the works that he heeds the advice, or has gathered and stored information provided in the prefaces of other books?

In his *Alvearie*, the last paragraph of Baret's general preface reads: "Where you see *Vide*, it sendeth you to some such place there named, where you may find more concerning that Title, or word which you looke for, if you be not satisfied with the first. And this deuise I used for breuitie sake, because I would not write one thing twise, for increasing the volume and price of the booke in vaine. But if you see no *Vide*, then marke what English word is mentioned like in meaning to that which you seeke, and looke more in the Title thereof. Now, if Students desire anie more Phrases beside them which here we have gathered, they may themselves like diligent Bees here place such as they reade in good Authors, under their proper Titles, or in the margent of this Booke, for their owne private use against they shall neede."

Baret is telling the reader, particularly the student reader, how to find his way through the dictionary. There can be little doubt that our annotator read this preface closely, as it forms the fundamental approach to both how he engages with the text and what he supplies in "the margent of this Booke." Although the annotator's additional systematic use of the mute annotations are ultimately out of the scope suggested by Baret, the general prescriptions are followed most faithfully indeed.

Take this simple example of how the annotator uses "vide" in combining his annotations:

At the position S835–36, the annotator adds a slash to the definition: / ¶ Starke vide cold. Beside the word *cold*, he adds an English phrase and the French equivalent: it were a starke shame and ce seroit gra(n)d honte. If using *vide*, as Baret suggests, we trace back to the headword *cold*, we see that the annotator has engaged with the text, and a number of possibilities for using *cold*, at several intervals, including just below C776, where he underlines a portion of the printed text: *Think you that I am cold…that were a starck shame* (the French reckoning that one also sees at S835–36 appears just below).

As for Baret's *Starke vide cold*, the only time Shakespeare uses these two words together in a speech (Friar Laurence in *Romeo and Juliet*), it may or not be coincidental that the word *shame* also appears. And yet we observe, in the Baret text just above the underlined passage *that were a starck shame*, the following additional mute annotation, o **stiffe colde**. Baret has found, at least with this particular annotator, an energetic bee.

☞ *Romeo and Juliet*. Friar Laurence (4.1.103, 118; FF ff6)

Shall, **stiffe** and **starke**, and **cold**, appear like death,

. . .

And this shall free thee from this present **shame**,

Patricia Parker, while highlighting the *Alvearie* as one of several seminal dictionaries to study for learning more about Shakespearean language, notes that Baret urges that "words themselves be 'certain and sure messengers' and writings 'faithful and trustie interpreters' of 'such words, as were spoken and uttered by our voice' warns that the 'interpreter must not diminish any part of the meaning, nor adde any thing of his own braine,' just as the 'messenger' is not to 'alter any whit of his arrand, nor counterfait any kind of looke, countenance, or gesture, otherwise than the partie to whom he is sent, may plainely gather, and perfectly understand thereby, the full meaning, good will, and affection of him that sent the message.'"[72] "Such texts," writes Parker, "sound uncannily like Hamlet's instructions to the players not to add or to deviate from his script or Claudius's warnings to his ambassadors not to go beyond the 'scope' of his commission."[73]

Perhaps it sounds uncannily like Hamlet's instructions or Claudius's warnings to Professor Parker. To someone less familiar with *Hamlet*, these "texts" might sound like gobbledygook. What is interesting to see is where in Baret the "such texts" referenced by Parker in relation to *Hamlet* reside. They *all* reside in a single preface. The excerpted texts that Parker has located and quotes are all found in the body of prefatory comments in the preamble to letter "E" of the *Alvearie*. In our copy, the annotator has marked several of them and later transforms them into spoken annotations. If Patricia Parker is correct in hearing *Hamlet*, what an uncanny coincidence!

This is far from being a single occurrence where the prefatory comments that precede the entries under a given letter or a section of our Baret are marked by the annotator. How odd, especially given Parker's observation, that we should find numerous occasions when one sees, in these prefatory word salads on letters and pronunciation, not only the annotator's marks, but straightforward echoes (easily more visible than those Parker has identified) from the works.

These preamble texts are among those that are wholly unique to Baret, and, as such, cannot be played off as being shared, or spread, across the idiomatic range of the Elizabethan landscape. Another scholar who has observed and commented upon these odd contributions to letter reform is Jonathan Goldberg. Goldberg makes particular note of the acerbic tone that Baret exudes in the preambles: "In his dictionary, each alphabetical entry is preceded with a discussion of the letter….Consider his remarks on C: *'this letter troubles me worst of all & maketh me wonder howe it got this third place of honour'* . . . .By the time Baret gets into E, his violence for the letter is unrestrained; he would *'geld out many idle dumme E, ees . . . which signifie nothing.'*"[74]

Signifie nothing recalls, of course, the lines in *Macbeth*, and one of the most famous soliloquies in all of theater:

🢒 *Macbeth*. Macbeth (5.5.16–28; FF nn3b)

> She should haue dy'de heereafter;
> There would haue beene a time for such a word:
> To morrow, and to morrow, and to morrow,
> Creepes in this petty pace from day to day,
> To the last Syllable of Recorded time:

And all our yesterdayes, haue lighted Fooles
The way to dusty death. Out, out, breefe Candle,
Life's but a walking Shadow, a poore Player,
That struts and frets his houre vpon the Stage,
And then is heard no more. It is a Tale
Told by an Ideot, full of sound and fury
Signifying nothing.
Enter a Messenger.
Thou com'st to vse thy Tongue: thy Story quickly.

In the stage direction following "signifying nothing," a messenger enters. In Baret's commentary on letter "E" that Parker alludes to, the concept of the messenger ("certain and sure messengers") is of central importance. Macbeth's line following his soliloquy and the entrance of the messenger, rather less remembered, is "Thou comest to use thy tongue," and we have the word *tongtide* underlined in letter "E." Immediately following *signifie nothing*, the next line in Baret is: *What a monstrous absurditie is this*. That's not quite "tale told by an idiot," but it's in the ballpark. The fact that the entire discussion in letter "E" is swirling around sounds and words and tongues (albeit no mention of syllables) may have some also hearing Macbeth in addition to Hamlet upon future examinations.

We should note that the preambles are quite difficult to read, not only because of the density and arcane nature of the thoughts conveyed therein, but because of the typography. The lines are stacked one above the other in such a way that there is little breathing space, and the impressions themselves are somewhat dulled, although — for what it's worth — the impressions are of better quality than in the other three copies of Baret that we have acquired. This has made things easier on our annotator in his ability to access them, and pay attention to them he clearly has, much more so than one would expect.

It follows, then, if we are correct in accurately identifying the annotator who marked the text there and elsewhere, that

Shakespeare was an astonishingly careful reader; not only that, but he took heed of instructions, and followed them every bit as convincingly as he veered away linguistically in other capacities from convention. We anticipate some rebellion from those who will not want to imagine this attention to prefaces. People may prefer an image similar to the stereotypical Mozart, a playful, quirky fellow with an endless gift for variation, dibbling and dabbling, in Shakespeare's case with words, possessor of a raw gift where formal training was secondary – genius incarnate.

The truth is probably that Shakespeare represented both the showoff linguist and the serious, strictly raised and educated schoolboy. There is no question left to doubt by those who have constructed his most recent biographies: the days at the King's New School in Stratford were long and hard. Not only were they long and hard, a hallmark of the instruction was an immense attention to detail. The method he was trained in at school called for close readings, so why should he handle his dictionary any differently? One thing is for certain: the annotator of this quadruple dictionary is nothing if not a careful note-taker.

Becoming a Believer

THE MAIN BULK of our study will consist of examining a portion of the annotator's notes in combination with Baret's text, alongside selections from the works of Shakespeare. In spite of whatever gems are revealed, we must again address the problem that existed for us from the beginning, of which we were, and are, well aware; and that is a problem that no number of cleverly pieced together examples of possible pre-allusions (best case) or echoes (certainly the case) can solve.

Even among those who will be led to believe that Shakespeare not only consulted but actively used Baret, there is an inclination to imagine his copy not surviving because, well, books from Shakespeare's library have not survived.

Stephen Greenblatt wonders: "Why have scholars, ferreting for centuries, failed to find the books he must have owned – or rather, why did he choose not to write his name in those books, the way that Jonson or Donne or many of his contemporaries did?"[75] The phrasing of this question assumes that the ferreting performed by scholars has been thorough enough that if a book or books from Shakespeare's library had survived we would already know of them. For two booksellers in Manhattan to purchase, out of the blue, a heavily annotated book from the *library of all libraries*, on eBay... it's understandable that no one would give that a chance.

How could a book extensively written in by Shakespeare realistically survive entirely unnoticed to the present day? All along, we concluded this to be an enormous psychological barrier to overcome, particularly in light of the fact that the discovery was being claimed, not by a world's authority on Shakespeare with proximity to Stratford or the great libraries in England, but by a couple of rare booksellers in New York, who stumbled upon the book in question by making a purchase through the world's largest online auction site. Let us be the first to declare: the idea that we could be right is beyond ridiculous, it is almost unfathomable.

In the process of coming to grips with the problem ourselves, we have speculated and imagined the vehicle of eBay as akin to a great flood, which causes material to rise to the surface that had previously been hidden. This take on the machine that helped bring this book to us is without substantiation. It just feels right. An amateur paleontologist friend has discussed the obvious virtues of digging after the rains. In a similar sense, eBay can be seen as offering the advantage of exposing more books to a wider audience of potential buyers than ever before.

Seeing as how the antiquarian bookseller's job entails improving upon preexisting descriptions – and trying to find compelling storylines in the material offered for sale (to enable items to stand out from the enormous volume of antiquarian material available on the market) – in many respects, a rare bookseller is best positioned to take over and make the case for a lost book such as this one, even more so than a scholar. The drive to find new angles on incoming material fuels the imagination of the rare bookseller, and may account for why antiquarian booksellers routinely make discoveries with old books that had previously been overlooked. The fact that these discoveries are seldom newsworthy in a mainstream sense does not discredit the idea that the ferreting of old books to this day routinely brings attention to books that for centuries have been ignored.

On countless occasions, we have looked upon the pages of the copy of Baret's *Alvearie* that is in question and wondered: could this *really* be the book? Such an ordinary looking old book by the standards of antiquarian books, with features superficially so regular and uninspiring, that a comparison cannot help but be made with the annotator we have sensed – from early on – it *could* be. Had the seemingly ordinary boy from Stratford made use of this ordinary copy of a book printed in London, the title of which, many, many years later, a leading scholar became convinced he had often turned to?

As for the boy from Stratford, a strand of doubters would emerge during the nineteenth century that persists to the present day: no, not him; *that* guy, no way. This group remains on the outside of the scholarly Shakespeare community, one that has recognized and accepted – as do most people – that when it comes to human creativity and achievement, there are no adequate explanations for the sources from which we have seen it spring. How else to explain the results achieved by remarkable individual souls from humble backgrounds throughout history? On the grandest of scales, there is the boy from Stratford, doted upon by his protective mother, who goes on to create this massive body of work, the enthusiasm and awe for which shows no sign of ebbing.

As for our ordinary copy of this book from London, we hesitate and even cringe to think that it is this same strand of doubters that will desire to appropriate and reshape the handwritten annotations inside for the benefit of expounding upon the same tired conspiracy-driven tirades. We have elected to say very little regarding this group of naysayers, except to remind our readers that beyond the notable and direct allusions to Shakespeare by his contemporaries, the historical figures mentioned as alternatives to Shakespeare each fail miserably as a candidate one after the other.[76] Not only would we require a plausible explanation for how the proposed candidate led two lives at once (and produced two separate bodies of work), there would need to have been a deep and impossible-to-orchestrate conspiracy beginning in the early 1590s and carrying on beyond Shakespeare's lifetime (without benefit to anyone) over multiple generations and multiple circles.

We see the opportunity to silence this group once and for all – a gift, unnecessary from the standpoint of proving authorship of the greatest collection of literary works ever produced, but one that can function as something no less significant than a missing link in the annals of humanistic research and discovery: the Stratfordian argument sealed.

So why then should our efforts be met with such restraint? We believe we understand the basic reason. A copy of Baret belonging to a less remarkable individual than Shakespeare – given this particular book, all others, potential and actual – bears no threat, no weight. Any hypothetical survival that is plausible would require a similar amount of care and luck, since, as already noted, any book that old requires these things to survive. Yet the gap in interest between the Shakespeare copy and anyone else's copy is close to unbridgeable. An annotated copy owned by an unidentified language lover of the period – or even another writer of the period – might be interesting and would inspire, to some degree, specialized interest from librarians and collectors. Declaring the copy to have been Shakespeare's, beginning at some undefined juncture before he had fully begun to enjoy success as a writer, is to suddenly open up interest at a level beyond that of any other book. That is why, for Shakespeareans and paleographers alike, it would be such a terrifying pronouncement to make, and this is partly to explain why it has taken us so long to unveil the project. We felt as though we needed to protect the possibility, when the natural inclination of others would be to create distance from it, or even to destroy it.

We are in tune with the fact that those who make up the most accredited voices across the expanse of Shakespeare studies do not always see eye to eye. Assuming our report generates at least some notable attention, it will be interesting to see whether the strange copy of Baret's *Alvearie* that is in question overwhelmingly unites them or keeps them divided. It may or may not prove to be wishful thinking, but sustaining the division, in this case, remains the far more compelling result. We cannot imagine that support will immediately come pouring in from far and wide. But, likewise, we are of the opinion that our findings are, at minimum, strong enough to warrant keeping the status quo in regard to Shakespeareans interpreting the life, the works, and the discoveries (and this annotated dictionary is, if nothing else, a notable discovery) from different positions.

For some, the path to plausibility will be compelling only after the annotations are carefully scrutinized through computer-assisted stylometric analysis relative to the works of other period writers. But even those requiring a decisive victory in these calculations before being swayed may admit in advance of these studies that the annotator has left behind a trail fraught with improbable coincidence.

That this trail should contain allusions to what has been contested as "secret Shakespeare" and "apocryphal stories" – all of it ·buried in a period hand without a hint of funny business – makes a rejection of our hypothesis no less bizarre. If there were more, it would seem (if it doesn't already) to suggest an inexplicable cosmic joke. In addition to a select group of church memories evoked from definite early biblical translations into English, we know that the following held meaning for the annotator: the letters "W" and "S," the association of the Catholic IHS monogram with the yew tree, and the desire to increase a knowledge of French. The playful renderings of English and French on a single binder's leaf at the end allow for a unique opportunity at peeking into the mind of the annotator, as well as offering paleographic understanding that because of the large sample is more telling than what appears anywhere else. That this word gathering, alone and removed from the printed text, should yield for Shakespeare such remarkable textual and personal details is, on its own, enormously persuasive.

How, we wondered, could all of these marks have gotten there? Who else could have put them there? Once thing is certain: *someone* put them there.

Let us also be the first to admit that apart from making us true believers ourselves, the book was in some sense disappointing. Shouldn't there be more? Where are the signs of genius? Why not at least one combination somewhere that only *he* could have written? We console ourselves with the fact that written marginalia were generally reserved for comments on the immediate printed text at hand and were rarely used to begin or extend a creative idea intended for performance or publication. In our *Alvearie*, they developed into an expansive set of synonym relations among the words themselves, following the printed *vides* or the *vides* added by annotation, along with occasional use of the Latin and French indexes to extend these relationships. This trail of *vides* not only leads to word-by-word synonyms but, since so many of the Baret "definitions" of English words actually grew from usage examples extracted from the English translations of classical Latin authors, these provided abundant and unexpected word juxtapositions that the annotator noted with his many mute markers and that can then be found used throughout the Shakespeare canon.

Therefore, in looking at the annotations, aside from the buried personal markers, we found an intoxicating pool of linguistic echoes to consider when authorship emerged as a question. Naturally, we are intent upon sharing throughout this study the sum of what has provided for us the greatest boon. The more abundant and obscure the examples of Baret's language meeting Shakespeare's texts, seemingly born as a result of our annotator's dictionary play, the better our case. The full weight of what the annotations yield, we hope will be strong enough to quash – or at least blunt – the opinion that our argument is a circular one. There is bound to be some core group who feels it impossible that a specific annotator can ever be suggested, but we find it ill advised to dismiss for certain the most desirable of all candidates, and to argue the annotations being simply a collection of words and marks with no direct relation to Shakespeare. If – and this is a mighty big if, as our judgment alone will not be enough to challenge the public's interest – but if the body of annotations are ruled inseparable from Shakespeare and his works specifically, there really are only three possibilities: the annotator was familiar with the work, the annotator got lucky, or the annotator was Shakespeare.

In one of his two prefatory poems printed in the First Folio, Ben Jonson famously asks the reader to look, not upon the likeness of Shakespeare (and a much maligned likeness it has turned out to be) in the engraved frontispiece, but upon the words themselves. It is our hope that the currently held opinions that no books from Shakespeare's library have survived, and that his penmanship would have been of one style only, can similarly be brushed aside, in favor of looking directly upon the evidence provided by the annotations alongside and along with the printed text in our copy of John Baret's *Alvearie*, 1580.

The path by which we reached a level of confidence in being able to assert our case with real conviction was not without setbacks. At the same time, more often than not, we felt absorbed in a sort of fantasy world, feeling an incredible sense of gratitude that this book had found us, and that so much of it began to unfold so perfectly, with all its subtleties, and the wonder of the discoveries. It was difficult for each of us not to imagine himself as a character living in an unwritten Jorge Luis Borges story, possessed by the exact same purpose of trying to convince the world that the book discovered is the real thing. Not once have we ever lost sight of the fact that there is a fundamental problem shared by New York antiquarian bookseller and Borgesian character alike – a problem, for that matter, that anyone, real or imaginary, who finds Shakespeare's dictionary is faced with: no one is going to believe you.

However, in a Borges story that *has* been written, *Shakespeare's Memory*, the main character finds himself at the end of a most unexpected and unusual proposition that has been granted to him: whether or not to "accept Shakespeare's memory." After answering "yes" and gradually attaining the complete memory, the character realizes in time that he has "become Shakespeare," and he lives with both the blessing and the curse, until he decides that it is time to pass on "Shakespeare's memory" to another unsuspecting someone.

We have done what we can to expose, in these old neglected marks, a lost legacy of coincidences too abundant to suggest what we ourselves have often wondered: that we are mad to insist upon a personal connection between our book purchased on eBay and William Shakespeare. We are hopeful that this natural inclination to doubt will eventually subside, and that the story will end with the mightiest of candidates being seen as more likely than all others.

And to that effect, if one *were* to write this entirely as fiction – write a story about two booksellers who discover Shakespeare's dictionary and feel compelled to convince the world of it, all the while making it plausible that such an object could have survived for so long undetected, while at the same time providing the necessary clues throughout that the dictionary really had belonged to Shakespeare and was used by him during formative years to help shape his approach to language – well, then, one could invent no "newly uncovered" book more convincing than ours.

Part Two

The Evidence:
The Annotations as They Relate
to the Works – An Abridgment

Hamlet
The Narrative Poems
The Sonnets
The Early Comedies
The Early Histories
Falstaff
The Trailing Blank
Baret as Shakespeare's Beehive
What's in a Name?
"My Darling"

Hamlet

I N HIS JOURNAL letter to his brother George and wife Georgiana, with entries from 14 February 1819 to 3 May 1819, John Keats reached his famous understanding of Shakespeare on 19 February when he wrote, "Shakspeare led a life of Allegory; his works are the comments on it."[77] In a later entry written on 12 March in a lighter mood, having described his position in front of the fireplace – "I am sitting with my back to it with one foot rather askew upon the rug and the other with the heel a little elevated from the carpet"[78] – Keats added: "Could I see the same thing done of any great Man long since dead it would be a great delight: as to know in what position Shakspeare sat when he began *To be or not to be*," knowing full well that it was impossible to ever have the answer. As we became increasingly convinced that Shakespeare had authored the annotations in our copy of Baret, it was difficult to control the feeling experienced when examining the annotator's interaction with the text, as pieces of *Hamlet* would spring up from a marked page.

¶ **Poſſet.** Lac feruefactum in ceruiſiam aut vinum præcipitatum. Vulgò, Poſca,ę. ὀξύκρατον. Vide **wine.**
Poſſet curd. Lac feruefactum per ceruiſiam aut vinum concretum.

No seasoned reader of Shakespeare can look down at a Baret text under *posset* see next to it the word *curd*, and not think of *Hamlet* and the end of the first act, when the ghost of Hamlet's father – a role probably played by Shakespeare himself[79] – describes for his son how he was poisoned.

☞ *Hamlet.* Ghost (1.5.59–79; FF oo1b)

Briefe let me be: Sleeping within mine Orchard,
My custome alwayes in the afternoone;
Vpon my secure hower thy Vncle stole
With iuyce of cursed **Hebenon** in a **Violl,**
And in the **Porches** of mine eares did poure
The leaperous Distilment; whose effect
Holds such an enmity with bloud of Man,
That swift as Quick-siluer, it courses through
The naturall Gates and Allies of the body;
And with a sodaine vigour it doth **posset**
And **curd**, like **Aygre** droppings into **Milke,**
The thin and wholsome blood: so did it mine;
And a most instant **Tetter bak'd** about,
Most **Lazar-like,** with vile and loathsome crust,
All my smooth Body.
Thus was I, sleeping, by a Brothers hand,
Of Life, of Crowne, and Queene at once dispatcht;
Cut off euen in the Blossomes of my Sinne,
Vnhouzzled, disappointed, vnnaneld,
No **reckoning** made, but sent to my account
With all my imperfections on my head;

The twenty-one-line reenactment of the poisoning is filled with words and word combinations that our annotator has marked, added, and manipulated in his Baret, as is also the case in the ensuing exchange:

☞ *Hamlet.* Ghost (1.5.81–91; FF oo1b)

If thou hast nature in thee beare it not;
Let not the Royall **Bed** of Denmarke be
A **Couch** for Luxury and damned Incest.
But howsoeuer thou pursuest this Act,
Taint not thy mind; nor let thy Soule contriue
Against thy Mother ought; leaue her to heauen,
And to those **Thornes** that in her bosome lodge,
To **pricke** and **sting** her. Fare thee well at once;
The **Glow-worme** showes the Matine to be neere,
And gins to pale his vneffectuall Fire:
Adue, adue, *Hamlet:* remember me.

☞ *Hamlet*. Hamlet (1.5.92–95; FF 001b)

> Oh all you host of Heauen! Oh Earth; what els?
> And shall I couple Hell? Oh fie: hold my heart;
> And you my **sinnewes**, grow not instant Old;
> But beare me **stiffely** vp:

The proliferation of words covered by our annotator that we find emerging here and elsewhere in the works does not, by itself, suggest him to be Shakespeare, so much as the combination of everything that is in our Baret guides us toward eliminating both specific and general candidates from contention. This happy and admittedly self-serving conclusion is sure to face much stronger scrutiny than we are able on our own to supply. We have, in fact, done our best over six years to otherwise convince ourselves that the relationship between the annotations and the text might have *nothing* to do with Shakespeare. Following the full weight of what is presented in Part Two (our attempt to summarize the connections between the annotations in the Baret and the works), perhaps we will have convinced a fair number of our readers of why the plausibility of such a negation is remote at best.

Hamlet is the most famous of all Shakespeare creations, whether considered by play or by character, and the idea that this copy of Baret could be tied not only to the man himself, but possibly to the very time when *Hamlet* was written, strikes us as almost too large to fathom. It is, at least, somewhat easier to imagine the book in Shakespeare's hands while he was an impressionable student of literature, or a proofreader for the publisher Henry Denham, as we discovered along the way as previously speculated. But while writing *Hamlet*? Were we actually going to put forward the idea that this book was nearby, or even open, during a moment of composition? Just as Keats would never be able to see where Shakespeare was, or how he was positioned, when first putting "To be or not to be" to the page, we cannot with the most absolute certainty prove that Shakespeare did own and mark this particular copy, or conclude, if he did own it, whether an opened Baret remained integral to his working process during the composition of *Hamlet*, even if only for the forming of a single line.

What does appear irrefutable, when studying Baret in tandem with the play, is that portions of the *Alvearie* lodged in Shakespeare's head from having marked it in his memory, if not also with the aid of his quill. We previously referenced Patricia Parker's claim of "hearing Hamlet" in the prefatory remarks to letter "E" in Baret (our annotator's markings in our copy highlight adjacent wording in that same preface to letter "E"). That capacity requires clever means of deduction. With *posset* and *curd*, one does not need an advanced degree in linguistics or Shakespeare studies. It's right there and could not be more apparent: *Posset. Curd.* In our copy <u>curd</u> is underlined and appears as a spoken annotation under *crud* (vide curd). Posset is a spoken annotation under *sillibubbe*. So the involvement between the annotator and the text over these two words is in plain sight for anyone to notice, and the manipulation of the words is not confined to a single space in the text, but is in three separate locations involving both mute and spoken annotations, and this is a pattern that typifies the norm: a methodical massaging of the text through cross-referencing.

A slightly more discreet inclusion from this scene in *Hamlet* that demonstrates Shakespeare's comfort with Baret's synonyms follows closely the use of *posset* and *curd*. The stiffness Hamlet feels in the sinews and expresses to the audience when facing his father's ghost is a cramping, stubborn feeling, twice captured as such by Baret. Each time the annotator shows attention:

C1564. ¶ the Crampe
o   A kind of crampe, <u>stifnesse</u> in the **sinewes**, not able to **bow**.
S891. / ¶ To be Stiffe
o   To stand **stiflie**, or **stubbornlie** in a matter. The stiffenesse of
         sthe sinewes.

What helps to build a compelling case for Baret, and eventually for our annotator, is how consistently the *Alvearie* text enters the works time and time again. Hamlet links *stiffness* with *sinews* (as does Henry V in a very famous speech written one or two years earlier), and Claudius uses *sinews* with both *bow* and *stubborn*, each word appearing separately in one of the marked mute annotations that contains *sinews*.

☞ *Hamlet*. Claudius (3.3.70–72; FF pp1b)

Bow stubborne knees, and heart with strings of Steele,
Be soft as **sinewes** of the new-borne Babe,
All may be well.

One always has to worry that what looks like an individual use might in fact be an idiom or at least a common phraseology, and we do not deny that this will often bear out over the course of studying other writers of the period with frequent parallel combinations. But it is the near constant proliferation in Shakespeare of examples from Baret – examples simple and complex, commonplace and obscure – that should have scholars willing to champion the claim previously made by T. W. Baldwin, even aside from all the personal effects and other evidence shown to this particular copy that makes the case for authorship so intriguing.

The annotator often will highlight seemingly the most mundane word combinations or pairings, and some may argue these examples especially to be trivial – a detriment in making significant pronouncements as a result of the broad scope of what has been uncovered. But consider the language lover that has marked this book, whether you want to keep this person nameless or attach to him a particular famous name. The marking of a simple, straightforward pairing of words is exactly befitting of someone who is captivated by their potential power. Why else place a little circle here:

P40. ¶ Pale of colour
o   A **pale redd**

Only a passionate lover of language would bother to mark such a thing. Shakespeare combines *red* with *pale* thirteen times, almost half of the occurrences taking place in the narrative poems. Once he does so in *Hamlet* (1.2.230; FF nn6):

HAMLET: **Pale**, or **red**?

This line comes during the exchange with Horatio over the appearance of his father's ghost. Consider the two preceding lines (1.2.227–29; FF nn6):

HAMLET: What, lookt he **frowningly**?
HORATIO: A **countenance** more in sorrow then in anger.

The annotator who has paid attention to *pale red* has also paid attention to the qualities of countenances:

F1159. / ¶ to **Frowne** and lowre
   o With an **heauie, sad, frowning, lowring, soure**, or displeasant **countenaunce**.

Baret frequently offers such a cluster of words for his readers to consider, and in Shakespeare we often see, especially in the early works, the clustering of the suggested words in a single verse or speech.

🐌 *Comedy of Errors*. Adriana (5.1.45–46; FF I)
   This weeke he hath beene **heauie, sower sad**,
   And much different from the man he was:

🐌 *Venus and Adonis* (st. 31, 181–86)
   And now Adonis with a lazie sprite,
   And with a **heauie**, darke, disliking eye,
   His **lowring** browes ore-whelming his faire sight,
   Like mistie vapors when they blot the skie,
      Sowring his cheekes, cries, fie, no more of loue,
      The sunne doth burne my face I must remoue.

On their own, annotations such as these and the verbal parallels in Shakespeare may be written off as trivial, but the sheer mass of them is to be reckoned with, especially if the end result for Shakespeare is considerably greater than for other premodern authors.

The notion of "hair standing on end" has been cited in *Hamlet* as a Shakespeare original, although he actually first makes use of the expression in *Richard III*. In *Hamlet* he does so twice, with Hamlet's mother and his dead father's ghost each taking memorable spins with it:

☞ *Hamlet.* Gertrude (3.4.112–13; FF pp2)
> Your bedded **haire**, like life in excrements,
> Start vp, and **stand an end**.

☞ *Hamlet.* Ghost (1.5.18–20; FF oo)
> Thy knotty and combined lockes to part,
> And each particular **haire** to **stand an end**,
> Like Quilles vpon the **fretfull Porpentine**:

The father's ghost usage includes the word *porcupine*, a singular occurrence in Shakespeare. The annotator has noted Baret's take on the porcupine, as well as the suggestion that is printed in Baret that hair can be made both to stare or stand on end.

> P576./ ¶ a **Porcupine**, a beast so called, that casteth prickes from him at men, as it were arrowes
> S835./ ¶ his **haire Stareth**, or **standeth** on end

Shakespeare likes it both ways, as he so often does, making use of it staring and standing:

☞ *Julius Caesar.* Brutus (4.2.331; FF ii3b)
> That mak'st my blood cold, and my **haire** to **stare**?

Gertrude's ongoing depiction of her son's madness swells mightily in act 3, scene 4, where one could almost literally code from one line to the next bits of Baret that are annotated in our copy. Hamlet compares his newly crowned stepfather to a mildewed ear of corn, and we find, marked in our Baret, *mildew* in exactly that sense:

M354. / ¶ **Mildew on corne**

🖝 *Hamlet*. Hamlet (3.4.63–64; FF pp2)

Heere is your Husband, like a **Mildew'd eare**
Blasting his wholsom breath. Haue you eyes?

The annotator frequently will take a piece of Baret from a mute annotation underlining and turn it into a spoken annotation (most of the spoken annotations are formed in this way). From there, we see an echo into a Shakespeare text. Take the example of the marginal addition spred rankly (R37–38) added in the margin alongside *rank*. *Rankly* is underlined where it appears in the text under *grow* (G587) with the word *spread* in the sample sentence. *Rankly* is used only once in Shakespeare, in the first act of *Hamlet* by the father's ghost, and this returns us to our start, as these lines immediately precede the speech from where we began with *posset and curd*:

🖝 *Hamlet*. Ghost (1.5.36–40; FF oo)

       so the whole eare of Denmarke,
Is by a forged processe of my death
Rankly abus'd: But know thou Noble youth,
The Serpent that did sting thy Fathers life,
Now weares his Crowne.

In the Baret bath that is act 3, scene 4, hovered over by his mother and his father's ghost, Hamlet uses *rank* together with *spread*.

🖝 *Hamlet*. Hamlet (3.4.138–43; FF pp2)

It will but skin and filme the Vlcerous place,
Whil'st **ranke** Corruption **mining** all within,
Infects vnseene. Confesse your selfe to Heauen,
Repent what's past, auoyd what is to come,
And do not **spred** the **Compost** on the Weedes,
To make them **ranke**.

We find here two additional words of interest, *mining* and *compost*. These are "peculiar" usages[80] (words occurring one time only in Shakespeare) for which the annotator has provided multiple annotations in his Baret. *Compost* is especially interesting:

C973. **Compendiously**, adds to compesse or dung stercoran

This spoken annotation in the margin is a cross-reference to the Baret definition at D1361 of *To dung or <u>compesse</u>. Stercoro, ras, pen. Cor. Pliny*. The word <u>compesse</u> (underlined) was an obsolete form of *compost*.

Other "peculiar" words from *Hamlet* marked in our Baret include *mining*, *winch*, and *puppets*. At M186 in Baret, we find: *The match of a lamp, the <u>weeke</u> of a candle.*

☞ *Hamlet*. Claudius (4. 7, p. 718, after 96; Q1604, L4b)[81]

There liues within the very flame of loue
A kind of **weeke** or snufe that will abate it.

This is Shakespeare's only usage of *wick*, and receives in the *OED* an early usage citation under section "b. collectively, without article, as the name of a substance." Claudius's lines were not included in the First Folio, but are retained in most modern editions and are taken from the "good" 1604 quarto, where *weeke* is spelled exactly as in Baret where it is found underlined in our copy. Creating a poetic twist on a commonplace word is at the heart of Shakespeare's approach to language.

Baret receives a citation in many critical editions of Hamlet for the peculiar usage of "stithy": "Baret in his *Alvearie* of 1580 writes *stithie*, and refers to anvil, which he renders 'Incus . . . without bellowes, anvils, and stithees, sans **enclumes** et soufflets.'"[82] The annotator has marked with a slash the entry for *stithy* and added enclumes after the *vide anvil*, thereby noting the inclusion of the French word under *anvil*. As for the usage of *stithy*, it is no great surprise that the lines include another echo from Baret marked by our annotator:

G313. / ¶ a **Goast**, an image in mans **imagination**

🖝 *Hamlet*. Hamlet (3.2.80–82; FF oo6)

It is a damned **Ghost** that we haue seene:
And my **Imaginations** are as foule
As Vulcans **Stythe**.

At B1368 we see: *To make a great stream of a small brook.* The annotator underlines the whole of this text as well as underlining *withie bowes* at B1400: *Browse made for beastes of withie bowes.* *Withie* is an archaic usage for *willow* and does not appear in Shakespeare. *Willow*, however, is used dramatically eleven times, most of the usages belonging to Desdemona, but also famously by Gertrude in *Hamlet* as she recalls the drowning of Ophelia:

🖝 *Hamlet*. Gertrude (4.7.138–39; FF pp4b)

There is a **Willow** growes aslant a **Brooke**,
That shewes his hore leaues in the glassie **streame**:

The annotator frequently appreciates "rare words"[83] that wind up appearing in *Hamlet*, such as *scullion, offal, pickaxe, survivor*, and *redeliver*. And he makes interesting use, in multiple senses, of favorite words such as *scant* and *gage*. At B98, *bang or beate with a cudgell*, the annotator underlines *cudgell* and puts a slash in the margin next to *bang*. Shakespeare was the first to use *cudgel* as a verb (the noun existed, in archaic forms, since the ninth century or earlier). *Cudgel* in *1 Henry IV* has the literal meaning "to beat with a cudgel," but in *Hamlet* it takes the figurative meaning of "racking one's brain": "Cudgell thy braines no more about it" (First Clown, 5.1.56; FF pp5).

The search for linguistic alternatives is a trademark of the annotator, who has closely followed the guidelines set forth in the preface of his Baret. Consider the marginal spoken annotation at K1:

castrell vide kastrell vide hauke

Variability of both species name and spelling are contained

here. Hamlet mentions the hawk in a frequently quoted line from act 2, scene 2:

🪶 *Hamlet* (2.2.380–1; FF oo4)

> I am but mad North, **North-West**: when the
> **Winde** is Southerly, I know a **Hawke** from a Handsaw.

Among the observations we have noted is that the spelling of *hawk* in the second quarto of 1604 matches the spelling, *hauke*, found in our margin.

🪶 *Hamlet* (2.2.380–1; Q1604, F2b)

> I am but mad North **North west**; when the **wind** is Sou-
> therly, I knowe a **Hauke**, from a **hand saw**.

The proverbial underlined phrase in our Baret, *chalk from cheese*, holds essentially the same meaning that Hamlet extends when he declares that he knows a hawk from a handsaw (or, to use the parlance of our own time, his ass from his elbow).

Even the Northwest wind from these lines has not escaped our annotator:

N176. ¶ Northward, or Northern
o The **Northwest** wind.

The echoes from these mute annotation combinations ripple throughout the play: *delicate + tender; form + fashion; dirge + mirth;* the *Alvearie* contains a lively buzzing drone of *Hamlet,* and our annotator has vociferously marked so much of it, but with no signs anywhere – a total absence of character names, names of works, lines from the works – that this could even remotely be conceived of as a Shakespeare reader aiming at a better under-standing of the texts through Baret.

The modern reader may be less familiar with some of the pe-riod associations in Baret that echo in Shakespeare:

H401. / ¶ **Herbingers** that appoint lodging for a Princes **traine**

The elements are not pasted directly together, true enough, but shall Horatio's inclusion of them in the first scene of the play be tossed off as pure coincidence?

☞ *Hamlet.* Horatio (1.1, p. 716, after 106; Q1604, B2b)[84]

> A moth it is to trouble the mindes eye:
> In the most high and palmy state of Rome,
> A little ere the mightiest *Iulius* fell,
> The graues stood tennatlesse, and the sheeted dead
> Did squeake and gibber in the Roman streets
> As starres with **traines** of fier, and dewes of blood
> Disasters in the sunne; and the moist starre,
> Vpon whose influence *Neptunes* Empier stands,
> Was sicke almost to doomesday with eclipse.
> And euen the like precurse of feare euents
> As **harbindgers** preceading still the fates
> And prologue to the *Omen* comming on
> Have heauen and earth together demonstrated
> Vnto our Climatures and countrymen.

The annotator's phrase dead corse in our margin lands squarely in act 1:

☞ *Hamlet.* Hamlet (1.4.32–37; FF oo)

> What may this meane?
> That thou **dead Coarse** againe in compleat steele,
> Reuisits thus the glimpses of the Moone,
> Making Night hidious? And we fooles of Nature,
> So horridly to shake our disposition,
> With thoughts beyond thee; reaches of our Soules,

The annotator adds arras to the margin after previously noting and marking *arras* in the Baret text. Could there be a stronger Shakespeare word to find in the margin? It feels almost too labored and familiar to go into Polonius hiding behind the arras, but the connections are also subtle. Arras was a town in France that specialized in tapestries, or arras hangings, the same sort that are featured in *Hamlet* as well as in early comedies and in scenes involving Falstaff. Shakespeare likely lodged in a room with arras hangings,[85] so a plausible personal connection is also there. The annotator further adds personality to the page when repeatedly concerning himself with games such as *tennis* (vel tennice), *blindman buf* and *hoodwinke* (blindman buf v. hood-winke), and the underlined *hoodmanblind*. These games are ones that Shakespeare likely would have played during childhood.[86]

H597./ ¶ the **Hoodwinke** play, or hoodmanblinde, in some places called the blindmanbuf

☞ *Hamlet.* Hamlet (3.4.70–71; FF pp2)

. . . . What diuell was't,
That thus hath cousend you at **hoodman-blinde?**

Whether or not we are correct in identifying the annotator, the printed capital "S" in the Baret text that the annotator imitates is formed completely outside of the paleographic realm of either italic or secretarial, and must be construed (along with the likewise imitated "W"s) as being nothing if not a personal effect. The printed capital "S" occurs most notably with the spoken annotation beginning shuffled.

S397–98. Adds shuffled togither by ignorance

Here, one can plainly see how the annotator has done his best to imitate to ornate "S" as it appears at the headwords under "S" in Baret. He is not especially good at it, but he tries. The fragment that is added after shuffled – togither by ignorance – appears in the Baret prologue to letter "A," where the annotator has brought our attention. Both the Baret prefatory "A" text and the annotation read *togither*, not *together*.

Shuffle or, *shuffled*, total four usages in Shakespeare, most famously in "To be or not to be":

🖝 *Hamlet*. Hamlet (3.1.66–70; FF 005)

             . . . To dye to sleepe,
To sleepe, perchance to Dreame; I, there's the rub,
For in that sleepe of death, what dreames may come,
When we haue **shufflel'd** off this mortall coile,
Must giue vs pawse.

Ignorance (37 times) is a commonly used word, including three usages in *Hamlet*, one by Hamlet himself almost immediately following his use of *shuffled* in the soliloquy.

🖝 *Hamlet*. Hamlet (3.1.147–49; FF 005b)

you gidge, you amble, and you lispe, and nickname
Gods creatures, and make your Wantonnesse, your **Ignorance**.

This raises an intriguing issue of proximity alliance that we will be exploring throughout our efforts to compare selections from the works to the annotated Baret. In a pattern that started to emerge late in our analysis, neighboring word usages outside of the primary definitions – or unrelated within the definition – frequently suggested themselves to be related to the annotator's keen eye for memory, or, if you prefer, his memory's keen eye.

Consider one of the instances within the other letter ("W") where the annotator has imitated the majiscule letter as printed in Baret, for no apparent reason other than what can only be personal meaning:

W191. a Whip vide scourge, adds whipsawe

The effort to copy the "W" is as obvious as it was with the "S." Shakespeare does not use *Whipsaw*, but he does use the same sense of "whip" with the same sense of "saw" together one time. It occurs in act 3, scene 2, of *Hamlet*, when Hamlet is addressing the players.

☞ *Hamlet.* Hamlet (3.2.1–14; FF 005b)

Speake the Speech I pray you, as I pronounc'd
it to you trippingly on the Tongue: But if you mouth it,
as many of your Players do, I had as liue the Town-Cryer
had spoke my Lines: Nor do not **saw** the Ayre too much
your hand thus, but vse all gently; for in the verie Torrent,
Tempest, and (as I say) the Whirle-winde of
Passion, you must acquire and beget a Temperance that
may giue it Smoothnesse. O it offends mee to the Soule,
to see a robustious Pery-wig-pated Fellow, teare a Passion
to tatters, to verie ragges, to split the eares of the
Groundlings: who (for the most part) are capeable of
nothing, but inexplicable dumbe shewes, & noise: I could
haue such a Fellow **whipt** for o're-doing Termagant: it
outHerod's Herod. Pray you auoid it.

This may seem like a stretch upon first glance, but let us more closely examine the annotator who has whipsawed his way between mute and spoken annotations using *vide* and proximity.

Whipsawe, in accordance with the pattern, comes from an underlining, as does the spoken annotation phrase he whipped or rushed in, which the annotator enters into the upper margin above the same location, W191. The Baret regions from where these texts have been pulled are spread out:

B657. A **whipsawe**, wherewith timber is sawed, a bush sieth or bille to cut bushes, or a forrest bille.

G410. **He whipped** or rushed in.

But if we look at the mute annotation just below where the annotator has entered whipsawe, just prior to W192, we see the really compelling evidence:

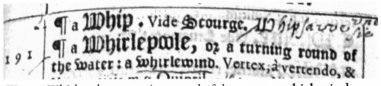

W191. a Whirlpoole, or turning round of the water: a **whirlewind**.

Now look at Hamlet's lines again:

☞ *Hamlet.* Hamlet (3.2.1–14; FF 005b)

> Speake the Speech I pray you, as I pronounc'd
> it to you trippingly on the Tongue: But if you mouth it,
> as many of your Players do, I had as liue the Town-Cryer
> had spoke my Lines: Nor do not **saw** the Ayre too much
> your hand thus, but vse all gently; for in the verie Torrent,
> Tempest, and (as I say) the **Whirle-winde** of
> Passion, you must acquire and beget a Temperance that
> may giue it Smoothnesse. O it offends mee to the Soule,
> to see a robustious Pery-wig-pated Fellow, teare a Passion
> to tatters, to verie ragges, to split the eares of the
> Groundlings: who (for the most part) are capeable of
> nothing, but inexplicable dumbe shewes, & noise: I could
> haue such a Fellow **whipt** for o're-doing Termagant: it
> outHerod's Herod. Pray you auoid it.

Do we require more? How about right below at W192?

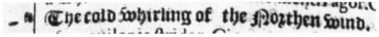

☞ *Hamlet.* Horatio

> These are but wild and **whirling** words, my lord. (1.1.137)
> These are but wild and **hurling** words, my Lord. (FF 001b)
> These are but wild and **wherling** words, my Lord. (Q1603, D1r)
> These are but wilde and **whurling** words my Lord. (Q1604, D4r)

☞ *Hamlet.* Hamlet (5.2.96; FF pp6)

> No, beleeue mee 'tis very **cold**, the **winde** is **Northerly**.

The entire zone, if you will, of this copy of Baret's *Alvearie* contains echoes of *Hamlet*, echoes that we must imagine were formed and stored well before the composition of the lines that contain them, but perhaps there is also the possibility that he glanced at this area over the course of the polishing phases.

In his book *Forgetful Muses: Reading the Author in the Text*, Ian Lancashire references the image clusters discussed by Caroline Spurgeon in her book *Shakespeare's Imagery and What It Tells Us*.[87] "One such network," he writes, "associated human greed and flattery with fawning dogs....Spurgeon believed that clusters of repeating words, infused by a powerful emotion, created this semantic web in [Shakespeare's] long-term memory."[88] The image clusters that Lancashire notes in Spurgeon he admits are "well supported by references from Shakespeare's works."[89]

The *fawn flatter dog* cluster is one to which Baret gives serious weight, and our annotator has exploited it almost to the point of obsession, by marking his ink to the page repeatedly.

F651. o **Flattering**, or **fawning** with faire lookes and wordes.
F651. o A smell feast, which followeth bellicheere, a **flatterer**.
F651. o With faire and pleasant wordes, **flatteringly**.
F651. o **Flatterie**, the **fawning** of a **dogge**, properly.
F651. o Like a **flatterer**, **flatteringly**.
F128. / to **Faune**, or **flatter**, adds fawning
F128. o A **fauner**, or **flatterer**.
F128. o The **fauning** of **dogges**.
F128. o To **faune** upon.

🖎 *Hamlet*. Hamlet (3.2.54–60; FF 004b–005)
Nay, do not thinke I **flatter**:
For what aduancement may I hope from thee,
That no Reuennew hast, but thy good spirits
To feed & cloath thee. Why shold the poor be **flatter'd**?
No, let the Candied tongue, like absurd pompe,
And crooke the pregnant Hindges of the knee,
Where thrift may follow **faining**?

🖎 *Hamlet*. Hamlet (Q1604, G4V)
Nay, doe not thinke I **flatter**, (Q1604, G4v)
For what aduancement may I hope from thee,
That no Reuenew hast, but thy good spirits

To feede and clothe thee, why should the poore be **flatterd**?
No, let the candied tongue, licke absurd pompe,
And crooke the pregnant hindges of the knee,
Where thrift may follow **fauning**; . . .

We hazard a guess that this example may be seen as positively weak relative to many of the others that we have, and will raise some impatience, and this is no knock on Lancashire's choice. We were drawn to his book largely because of his own serious involvement in pre-Renaissance dictionaries. What we came to realize is just how much more intricate the image clusters are inside our Baret, and how tenaciously the annotator navigates over the text throughout, all the while leaving an amazing trail of Shakespearean echoes and personal fingerprints.

As we have stressed, especially intriguing are these instances when the annotator's echoes to Shakespeare's texts are infused with the annotator's personal markers, such as with "W" and "S." The monograms beside the variant spellings of *yew*, already introduced, are another such case. Let us take a look at a specific instance of a spoken annotation next to the monogram:

U/V44. / ¶ Ugh tree vide Yew, adds IHS monogram, and arbor and a viage

The annotator's a viage is Middle English for "a voyage." The term was already becoming archaic in Shakespeare's time (see the *OED* entry for *voyage*). The *Middle English Dictionary*'s definition "c" lists the figurative sense for *viage* as "going to heaven."[90] It appears exactly in this sense in the second, or "good," quarto of *Hamlet*, uttered by Claudius, as he anticipates Hamlet's death.

☞ *Hamlet*. Claudius (3.3.24–26; Q1604, I)
Arme you I pray you to this speedy **viage**,
For we will fetters put about this feare
Which now goes too free-footed.

👉 *Hamlet*. Claudius (3.3.24–26; FF pp)

> Arme you, I pray you to this speedie **Voyage**;
> For we will Fetters put vpon this feare,
> Which now goes too free-footed.

In the First Folio, *viage* is changed to *voyage*, but the debate continues as to which is preferable, with a strong argument in favor of the word *viage* as printed in the second quarto. For starters, the word *voyage* does appear later in the second quarto, again from Claudius, this time when he has learned that Hamlet has not died.

👉 *Hamlet*. Claudius (4.7.60–67; FF pp4)

> To thine owne peace: if he be now return'd,
> As checking at his **Voyage**, and that he meanes
> No more to vndertake it; I will worke him
> To an exployt now ripe in my Deuice,
> Vnder the which he shall not choose but fall;
> And for his death no winde of blame shall breath,
> But euen his Mother shall vncharge the practice,
> And call it accident:

The difference between *voyage* here and *viage* earlier in the second quarto relates directly to the sequence of events, with Claudius using *viage* in a figurative sense when he expects Hamlet to die, and then using *voyage* after he has learned that Hamlet has not died. It appears that the folio editor's change from *viage* to *voyage* was an early attempt at modernization, and one that alters the author's intention of Claudius gravely anticipating for Hamlet a speedy trip, or *viage*, to heaven.

Furthermore, to argue against Shakespeare's intended choice of *viage* in the second quarto would be to ignore how incredibly unlikely the substitution would have been had the text properly read *voyage*. In early English literature the word was more readily used, and Shakespeare would have been familiar with it from Chaucer's *Canterbury Tales*, where it appears ten times. The figurative sense of "going to heaven" that Claudius implies in the second quarto is also found in Chaucer:

☞ "The Parson's Prologue" (48–51)

> [And] Iesu for his grace wit me sende
> To shewe yow the wey in this **viage**
> Of thilke parfit glorious pilgrymage
> That highte Ierusalem celestial.[91]

Our annotation a viage is inserted alphabetically, and yet one must additionally acknowledge the intriguing possibility of a symbolic connection suggested by the neighboring IHS monogram.

Another of the most archaic annotations we located in relation to *Hamlet* is the word *brood*.

☞ *Hamlet*. Claudius (3.1.165–68; FF 005b)

> Loue? His affections do not that way tend,
> Nor what he spake, though it lack'd Forme a little,
> Was not like Madnesse. There's something in his soule?
> O're which his Melancholly **sits** on **brood**,

This last line is essential to the understanding of Hamlet's character and the inward focus that is at the heart of the play.

A58. / ¶ **Abrooding**, or **sitting abroode**, adds couuée

These annotations are among the first to appear in the book, but the annotator's interest is not there exhausted. Similarly related mute annotations are also found among the many subsidiary definitions under the L40 headword definition *to **Laie**:*

> L55. I feare not a whit if all the matter *laie* in your hands.
> To lie at rest, to be *laid* along.
> A **henne** past *laieing*, or **brood**.
> To *laie* up straw together in a rike, or cocke.
> L56. To *laie* bodies along vpon the ground.

Each of these underlinings gives birth to a spoken annotation from which we can find a Shakespearean echo, none more powerful than the idea that one of these texts may have been linked to Hamlet's restless pathos: Hamlet sitting and brooding like a hen.

In closing our condensed summary of what we find relating to *Hamlet*, we return to another of the most analyzed speeches in the play, Hamlet's first soliloquy, with its well-known first two lines:

🖝 *Hamlet.* Hamlet (1.2.129–30; FF nn6)

Oh that this too too solid Flesh, would melt,
Thaw, and **resolue** it selfe into a Dew:

In a 1902 issue of *The Atlantic Monthly*, a William Burnet Wright added his name to the already long list of those wanting a word on the matter. Wright spends much time on the soliloquy, wondering, "How can flesh melt? It can burn, shrivel, change into gases; but melt it cannot."[92] He then turns the reader's attention to another unusual pairing – that of *thaw* with *resolve* in the next line, and offers assistance by asserting that *resolve* and *dissolve* were interchangeable in Elizabethan English.

That much is true; in fact, under *dissolve* in Baret, it says: *to dissolve, or melt*. The annotator has left no trace here, perhaps finding the text not unusual enough to mark. Shakespeare combines *dissolve* and *melt* in a verse or a speech six times, including in the narrative poems, *Venus and Adonis* and *Rape of Lucrece*, which we will examine in our next chapter. But consider again here the opening two lines of Hamlet's first soliloquy, this time with an amended text, one that selects *dissolve* over *resolve itself*:

🖝 *Hamlet.* Hamlet (1.2.129–30; FF nn6)

Oh that this too too solid Flesh, would melt,
Thaw, and **dissolve** into a Dew:

Not as good. The full definition in Baret under the headword for *thawe* reads *to Thawe, or resolue that which is frozen*. This is followed by Latin, Greek, and French equivalents, before the entry ends with *Vide Relent*. Following Baret's direction in his preface, a careful reader would arrive at:

R161. ¶ to **Relent**, or dissolue as ice that *thaweth* doth, to *thawe*. Vide *melt*.

Although our annotator has left no annotation at this position, we are drawn to one particular combination out of twenty-four from the canon involving *relent* and its variants:

☞ *Rape of Lucrece* (st. 262, 1828–34)

Couragious Romaine, do not steepe thy hart
In such **relenting dew** of Lamentations,
But kneele with me and helpe to beare thy part,
To rowse our Romaine Gods with inuocations,
That they will suffer these abhominations.
 (Since Rome her self in thē doth stand disgraced,)
 By our strong arms frō forth her fair streets chaced.

Relenting dew. What an odd juxtaposition! And how strange is it to encounter, once more, the verbal choice of *dew*, much as we stumble upon it when we trace *relent* back to T144 in Baret where we find *thaw* married to *resolve*.

Thaw and *resolve* are combined only on that one occasion in *Hamlet*. But Shakespeare did well with it; other writers contemporary to him may or may not have made the connection, but Shakespeare holds ownership of the pairing as it stands today. And, had Mr. Wright looked into a copy of Baret, he might have seen this:

But not every copy of Baret has had an annotator, and not every annotator would have marked the line with a slash as our annotator has, one of so many annotations to appear in our book that youth and observation copied there.

The Narrative Poems

A S THE ANNOTATIONS are studied together with Shakespeare's works, one question that emerges is whether we see the concentration of definitions and examples from Baret, Baldwin's noted "varied synonyms," echoing evenly throughout the concordance, or in various time frames or works more than in others. Through patient and repetitive study, absent the computer-aided analysis that eventually will be sought out, we have concluded that the early works achieve the best results, followed by the early middle works through *Hamlet* and *Troilus and Cressida*, then the late middle works, and finally the last works. Only in the very late works does the influence seem to trail off considerably.

The narrative poems, *Venus and Adonis* and *Rape of Lucrece*, are among the most valuable of Shakespeare's works to consider for the purposes of our study, not only because they fall early in the chronology but also because of the personal connections Shakespeare had to their publisher, Richard Field. The relationship with Field, coupled with the fact that theaters were closed at the time (due to an outbreak of plague), may have left Shakespeare with a heightened interest in the print versions relative to what he showed for his plays. What is generally agreed upon is that we are left with finished texts that are probably as accurate as any that exist in the canon.

Characterizing our book's annotations as a whole, they do not seem to reveal, at quick glances, a single particular interest on the part of the annotator. It looks like a miscellany of symbols and various word scribbles and nothing more, and will presumably look that way at first perusals even to those most accustomed to studying annotated books of the period. As our own cataloguing of the annotations advanced, we were amazed at the array of dedication across the linguistic spectrum. Given that the attention to subject matter is invariably broad across the entire dictionary, we are allowed an advantageous peek into the language of the day that a specialist's narrow lens would not capture.

That said, to view the complete catalogue of both the added words and the printed words that are highlighted is to shed light on some telling themes that became apparent among the wide expanse of the annotator's interests. A mass of annotations deal with natural history: animals, plants, herbs, and so forth. The treatment, not only in number but also in detail, strikes us as markedly out of line with what one would almost certainly find in other annotated premodern dictionaries where a generalist interest was on display. Shakespeare, who was of the country in both background and spirit, calls upon an outpouring – even an excess – of natural history in his works, relative to other writers of his day.[93]

Shakespeare's near constant allusions to nature did not alone, of course, make him a more serious contender to be the annotator, but as other evidence began to fall into place, the weight of the natural history became intriguing.

René Weis has written that "it is one thing to read about the dive-dapper 'peering through a wave' and ducking in when 'being looked on' – and what an extraordinary image that is for the callow Adonis to use in *Venus and Adonis* – but to see a little grebe or dive-dapper on a pond or in a still corner of the Avon endows the image, and indeed the creature, with a particular kind of imaginative life. The only way Shakespeare could have learned to distinguish ducks from grebes, to know that one of the dive-dapper's characteristics is its extreme shyness, was through patient bird-watching on the river, through living close to nature in a way few do today."[94]

The annotator is anything but shy in declaring his interest in the divedapper in our copy of Baret, working over, almost to the point of obsession, the various printed entries relating to the little bird. Look at this cluster of annotations culled from four separate locations:

D667. / ¶ a Didapper, a douker bird.

D1019. / ¶ a Dobchicke bird: otherwise called a Dowker, a Diuer, or a Didapper.

D1116. to Douk...vide dine ([sic]; adds frustra [Latin, error]), adds douker bird and plongeon

D1334. Adds to duke or dive and plonger urinari

The Little Grebe, or Dabchick, was known locally as dobchicke or dobchicken, divedapper being the familiar name. The annotator repeatedly makes note of both the bird and a chief behavioral characteristic alluded to by Weis, its propensity for ducking and diving under the water. Yet another cluster of annotations is found concentrated within two entries, D993 and D994.

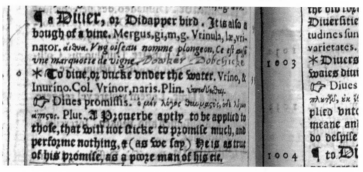

D993. / ¶ a Diuer, or Didapper bird, adds Dowker and Dobchicke
D994. o To diue, or ducke under the water...diues promissis...A Prouer-be aptly to be applied to those, that will not sticke to promise much, and performe nothing (as we say) he is as true of his promise, as a poore man of his eie.

Many will notice how the neighboring Baret text, *to diue, or ducke under the water*, is echoed in Shakespeare's recollection of the divedapper. The annotator marks this subsidiary definition with a little circle, just below the use of a slash at *a Diuer, or Didapper bird*. Directly in between these two Baret entries he adds the spoken annotations dowker and dobchicke, two variations on the divedapper name, with lines connecting them to the printed text, *to diue, or ducke under the water*. But the really remarkable textual evidence lies buried in the underlining of the proverb (an English translation from Plutarch) that completes the entry at D994. The underlined Baret word that echoes at the start of the stanza in *Venus and Adonis* where the divedapper makes its appearance is *promise* (ushered forth in Baret by the Latin that precedes it, *diues promissis*). As we look now at these lines from the poem, which, for Weis, illustrate so sensitive an observation that Shakespeare could only have made it through personal experience, we cannot help but argue that it is anything but coincidental that the word *promise* is leading the way, thereby suggesting that personal experience and the use of his Baret have come together to produce a dazzling moment of poetry.

☞ *Venus and Adonis* (st. 15, 85–90)

Vpon this **promise** did he raise his chin,
Like a **diuedapper** peering through a waue,
Who being lookt on, **ducks** as quickly in:
So offers he to giue what she did craue,
   But when her lips were readie for his pay,
   He winks, and turnes his lips another way.

In one short series of exchanges between the annotator and the text – an exchange that involves spoken and all three primary mute annotation types – the stanza is illuminated. It is our conclusion that the annotator took to this book while hard at work in London, but as is common throughout Shakespeare, his memories have taken him back to Stratford.

A large number of annotations help to paint hunting scenes of the period, scenes with which Shakespeare must have been personally familiar, involving deer, rabbits, birds, and the cries of hounds. One cannot help but think of the story, often thought to be apocryphal, of Shakespeare and Thomas Lucy, involving Shakespeare's poaching of a deer, told in several separately formulated seventeenth-century accounts. These accounts were only vaguely familiar to us, but we felt inclined to pursue further background on the matter, particularly in light of what was discovered (and will later be discussed in some detail) on the trailing blank. In the twentieth century, doubt arose over whether the game park at Charlecote would even have had deer. But according to Jonathan Bate, the story has come back into favor in recent years "when it was noted that Charlecote did have a warren or small game park, where there would have been rabbits, hare, pheasant, and roe deer."[95] René Weis has suggested that "for all we know, the roes of Charlecote may be the reason why Shakespeare used 'fleeter than the roe' and 'the fleet-foot roe' in *Taming of the Shrew* and *Venus and Adonis*."[96]

In *Venus and Adonis*, Shakespeare goes beyond mention of "the fleet-foot roe" to describe further aspects of the hunt, combining language found in these two long underlined Baret phrases marked by our annotator:

A20. He will hold or keep him at abbay
C267. The dere should hunt the houndes

The *OED* mentions the *Alvearie* for its definitions surrounding "barking" and "abay":

1. Barking, baying of dogs upon their prey; especially when they have run it down, and are closing round it. to stand at abay, said of the dogs: to stand barking round.

J. Baret Aluearie, 1580: "Abbay is a French woorde, and signifieth barking against something. For when the Dere is utterly wearied and out of breath, then is he faine (setting himselfe to some hedge, tree, etc.) to stande at defiance against all the houndes barking rounde about him, and to defende himselfe with his hornes, as it were at the sworde poynt, as long as he is able. Hereupon we say commonly of men at variance: He will holde or keepe him at abbay."

{ 105 }

2. to be at abay, said of the hunted animal when the dogs 'stand at abay' round him, or have reduced him to desperation; hence, to be in extremities, to be in straits so as to have nowhere to turn, to be in desperation. (Now at bay.)

Shakespeare frequently taps into these definitions in early works:

☞ *Taming of the Shrew*. Tranio (5.2.57–58; FF T6b)
'Tis well sir that you **hunted** for your selfe:
'Tis thought your **Deere** does hold you **at a baie**.

☞ *Midsummer Night's Dream*. Hippolyta (4.1.111–14; FF O1b)
I was with Hercules and Cadmus once.
When in a wood of Creete they **bayed** the Beare
With **hounds** of Sparta; neuer did I heare
Such gallant chiding.

In two separate stanzas from *Venus and Adonis* we find these echoes along with the echo of another mute annotation, ostensibly separated from the others, a little circle connecting the words *fear* and *timorous* that Shakespeare recalls as being emblematic to the hunted.

F270. o **Fearefulnesse**, bashfulnesse, **timorousnesse**.

☞ *Venus and Adonis* (st. 147, 877–82)
By this **she heares the hounds are at a bay**,
Whereat she starts like one that spies an adder,
Wreath'd vp in fatall folds iust in his way,
The **feare** where of doth make him shake, & shudder,
    Euen so the **timerous yelping** of the **hounds**,
    Appals her senses, and her spirit confounds.

☞ *Venus and Adonis* (st. 113, 673–78)
But if thou needs wilt **hunt**, be rul'd by me,
Vncouple at the **timerous** flying hare,
Or at the foxe which liues by subtiltie,
Or at the Roe which no incounter dare:
    Pursue these **fearfull** creatures o're the downes,
    And on thy wel breathd horse keep with thy **hoūds**

❦ 106 ❧

This additionally noted annotation that marks a verbal link between *fear* and *timorous* may seem trivial, but Shakespeare's desire and ability to enter into the lives and capture the perspective of all his creations, whether great or small, sympathetic or dubious, human or otherwise, is here on display. No writer ever displayed this skill on par with Shakespeare, and Baret's *Alvearie* would clearly have been a useful tool in helping him to hone his talents.

The barking dogs and fleeing deer may ring throughout *Venus and Adonis*, but the theme of hunting is not restrictive to deer and hounds alone in either Shakespeare or the margins. The "earth-delving conies" also receive attention.

C1734. / ¶ Cullars, or <u>robbars</u> drawnen out of **a flocke of sheepe**
C1744. ¶ a Cunnie
C1745. o A cunnie <u>garth</u>, a <u>warren.</u>
C1746. A cunniehole, adds cunniegree
G98. Adds a cunnie garth

☞ *Venus and Adonis* (st. 115, 685–90)

Sometime he runnes among **a flocke of sheepe**,
To make the cunning hounds mistake their smell,
And sometime where **earth-deluing Conies** keepe,
To stop the loud pursuers in their yell:
  And sometime sorteth with a heard of deare,
  Danger deuiseth shifts, wit waites on feare.

This stanza seems likewise to be drawn from personal experience. Nonetheless, one has to wonder, would the *flocke of sheep* have made the verse had that text not lain in such close proximity to *cunnie hole*, thereby lodging inside the mind of the reader/ annotator turned poet?

This raises again a most revealing concern: textual proximity in Baret mirroring textual proximity in Shakespeare. It is something we see over and over again, such as in this instance with *wax* and *boar*.

B1152. / ¶ Braune of a wilde bore
o To **waxe** or be hard fleshed, or brauned like a **bore.**

☞ *Venus and Adonis* (st. 69, 409–14)

I know not loue (quoth he) nor will not know it,
Vnlesse it be a **Boare**, and then I chase it,
Tis much to borrow, and I will not owe it,
My loue to loue, is loue, but to disgrace it,
    For I haue heard, it is a life in death,
    That laughs and weeps, and all but with a breath.

☞ *Venus and Adonis* (st. 70, 415–20)

Who weares a garment shapelesse and vnfinisht?
Who plucks the bud before one leafe put forth?
If springing things be anie iot diminisht,
They wither in their prime, proue nothing worth,
    The colt that's backt and burthend being yong,
    Loseth his pride, and neuer **waxeth** strong.

These words, appearing in back-to-back stanzas in *Venus and Adonis*, beg us to consider whether the reverberation in the mind of the poet could account for their being found in succession. Another example of possible reverberation is observed in the Baret text that falls under *hovering*:

H674. / ¶ Houering, and readie to commit a **murder**
o To <u>houer</u> over a thing, to buy it.
    The **Eagle** houereth or <u>soreth</u> high.

☞ *Venus and Adonis* (st. 9, 49–54)

He burnes with bashfull shame, she with her teares
Doth quench the maiden burning of his cheekes,
Then with her windie sighes, and golden heares,
To fan, and blow them drie againe she seekes.
    He saith, she is immodest, blames her misse,
    What followes more, she **murthers** with a kisse.

☞ *Venus and Adonis* (st. 10, 55–60)

Euen as an emptie **Eagle** sharpe by fast,
Tires with her beake on feathers, flesh, and bone,
Shaking her wings, deuouring all in hast,

Till either gorge be stuft, or pray be gone:
   Euen so she kist his brow, his cheeke, his chin,
   And where she ends, she doth anew begin.

Why should the word *murders* be so quickly followed by the image of an eagle? Only the full body of evidence yielded in this annotated dictionary would even suggest the possibility that an echo was felt in the mind of the poet during composition, but, if there are merits of our argument, the juxtaposition may be valid in being born through close association with Baret.

Acutely demonstrating an awareness of sights, smells, and sounds throughout his Baret, the nameless annotator, at minimum, shares with Shakespeare a close skill of observation. He acknowledges the baying of the hounds, and when he enters into the margin shrich owle arix, the echo of "night's hearld," the owl from *Venus and Adonis* shrieking "'Tis very late," may have existed also on a personal level.

The pastoral and the botanical examples are often archaic usages: the annotator and Shakespeare share an interest in *mead*, an Elizabethan word for *meadow*, and *brakes*, a period usage for *fern*. The spoken annotation barrow hillock contains two words used separately and one time only: *barrow*, by Falstaff, and *hillocks* in *Venus and Adonis*, a particularly sublime example of Shakespeare's feel for natural history:

☞ *Venus and Adonis* (st. 40, 235–40)
   Witin this limit is reliefe inough,
   Sweet bottome grasse, and high delightfull plaine,
   Round rising **hillocks, brakes** obscure, and rough,
   To shelter thee from tempest, and from raine:
      Then be my deare, since I am such a parke,
      No dog shal rowze thee, though a thousand bark.

No aspect of natural history is too small to consider for either poet or annotator, each of whom shows an uncanny interest in the glow-worm.

G279. / ¶ a Globerd, or gloworme, adds a gloe worme vide luisant
G298. Adds gloworme or globerd and gloe

🖙 *Venus and Adonis* (st. 104, 619–24)

On his bow-backe, he hath a battell set,
Of brisly pikes that euer threat his foes,
His eyes like **glow-wormes** shine, when he doth fret
His snout digs sepulchers where ere he goes,
  Being mou'd he strikes, what ere is in his way,
  And whom he strikes, his crooked tushes slay.

The natural history echoes we locate within *Rape of Lucrece* lack the quantity of those found within the earlier poem, but they are by no means absent:

L479. ¶ **Lime,** to take **birds** with
o To **lime birdes.**

🖙 *Rape of Lucrece* (st. 13, 85–91)

This earthly sainct adored by this deuill,
Little suspecteth the false worshipper:
"For vnstaind thoughts do seldom dream on euill.
"**Birds** neuer **lim'd**, no secret bushes feare:
So guiltlesse shee securely giues good cheare,
  And reuerend welcome to her princely guest,
  Whose inward ill no outward harme exprest.

D1277–78. ¶ Dronkenesse, adds a drone bee

🖙 *Rape of Lucrece* (st. 120, 834–840)

If COLATINE, thine honor laie in me,
From me by strong assault it is bereft:
My Honnie lost, and I a **Drone-like Bee,**
Haue no perfection of my sommer left,
But rob'd and ransak't by iniurious theft.
  In thy weake Hiue a wandring waspe hath crept,
  And suck't the Honnie which thy chast Bee kept.

The continual links between the annotations and the long narrative poems stretch well beyond natural history. We have referenced the biblical annotations as among the most significant of the spoken annotations for several reasons, none more critical than the fact that they have all been born out of the annotator's memory and do not appear in Baret. One of these annotations carries a whiff in *Venus and Adonis:*

B581. The blood shal bespring my clothes IS. 63

🖙 *Venus and Adonis* (st. 195, 1165–70)
By this the boy that by her side laie kild,
Was melted like a vapour from her sight,
And in his **blood** that on the ground laie spild,
A purple floure **sproong vp**, checkred with white,
   Resembling well his pale cheekes, and the **blood**,
   Which in round drops, **vpō** their whitenesse stood.

The wording in the annotation explicitly comes from the translation of the Great Bible (1539) and Bishops' Bible (1568), and not the Geneva Bible (1560) or the King James Bible (1611), both of which use *sprinkled* and conclude the line with *garments* and not *clothes.* Our annotator has not copied the line out of a printed Bible, as it is close to the Great Bible and Bishops' Bible translations but not exact. It reinforces the very critical point that we have and will continue to argue and emphasize throughout: the biblical annotations installed in the margins are memories specific of hearing the Great Bible and Bishops' Bible being read in church. This is essential information when considering the dating of the annotations. In lieu of the inexact science that is paleography, a calculation for the annotations being from a time after Shakespeare already takes a hit on the basis of the biblical associations alone.

Robert Nares discusses, in his early book on archaic and proverbial language in Shakespeare, the many alternate usages of *gage.*[97] Our annotator demonstrates, in multiple spoken and mute annotations, that he is laboring through this understanding.

The spoken annotation at P199, upon a pawn sur gage, lands neatly in that last line of one of the seven-line stanzas of *Rape of Lucrece:*

☞ *Rape of Lucrece* (st. 193, 1345–51)

When, seelie Groome (God wot) it was defect
Of spirite, life, and bold audacitie,
Such harmlesse creatures have a true respect
To talke in deeds, while others saucilie
Promise more speed, but do it leysurelie.
  Even so this patterne of the worne-out age,
  Pawn'd honest looks, but laid no words to **gage.**

If the annotations have unifying principles that tie them all together, it is the notion of alternate usages, and the pleasure in seeking word combinations. Regarding pawn sur gage, one need only to look at act 4, scene 2, of *Richard II*, where we find *gage* is used eight times and *pawn* twice (there are also earlier usages of both words in the same play), to see the utility that Shakespeare found for that particular pairing.

Another example of word association between the Baret text and Shakespeare can be seen with the word *pensive*. Shakespeare uses *pensive* and its variants five times. In *Rape of Lucrece*, the spelling of *pensiveness* is deliberately shortened because of the length of the following line (see original text). Note also the use of *sorrow* in the same line and its appearance in Baret.

P250–51. ¶ **Pensive**. Vide Sorrowe, adds pensiuenesse

☞ *Rape of Lucrece* (st. 214, 1492–98)

Here feelingly she weeps TROYES painted woes,
For sorrow, like a heauie hanging Bell,
Once set on ringing, with his own waight goes,
Then little strength rings out the dolefull knell,
So LUCRECE, set a worke, **sad** tales doth tell
  To pencel'd **pensiuenes** & colour'd **sorrow**, (row,
  She lends them words, & she their looks doth bor-

Pensiveness, with its one use, is another "peculiar" word. However, it also occurs in the anonymous play *Arden of Feversham* (1592), which, because of its language, its advanced approach to characterization, and its timing in relation to Shakespeare's early career, has long been thought to have possibly been written by Shakespeare, at least in part. The recent chronology that appears with the Royal Shakespeare Company editions of the plays, edited by Jonathan Bate and Eric Rasmussen, places *Arden of Feversham* at the head of the listing of Shakespeare's works with its range of dates given as 1589–91 together with a "?" and the added phrase: "possible part authorship."[98] We find a suggestive point in *Arden of Feversham* that supports this when comparing the anonymous author's use of *pensiveness* with Shakespeare's use in *Lucrece*. Note the same occurrence of *sad* in the preceding lines.

☞ *Arden of Feversham*. Mosby (3.5; Q1592, E4)

> But here she comes, and I must flatter her –
> – How now, Alice? what **sad** and passionat?
> Make me pertaker of thy **pensiuenes**:
> Fyre diuided burnes with lesser force.

Word couplings in the margin are occasionally phrased precisely as they are in Shakespeare. The word *moe* may seem distinctly modern, but it was an Elizabethan word representing quantity (as well as an animal sound, as shown in the Baret text definition) with the added spoken annotation prefaced by *many* to indicate the "quantity" meaning.

M441. ¶ to make a **Moe** like an ape, adds many moe

☞ *Rape of Lucrece* (st. 212, 1478–84)

> Why should the priuate pleasure of some one
> Become the publicke plague of **manie moe**?
> Let sinne alone committed, light alone
> Vppon his head that hath transgressed so.
> Let guiltlesse soules be freed from guilty woe,
>> For ones offence why should so many fall?
>> To plague a priuate sinne in generall.

(The phrase is also found in *Richard III* and *King John*.)

Located just ahead at M427, the annotator adds make moane.
This coupling is used precisely in *Merchant of Venice* and *Midsummer Night's Dream*. Several times in the narrative poems and in other early works, Shakespeare squeezes the two words into a single line. Twice he does so in *Rape of Lucrece*:

🔖 *Rape of Lucrece* (st. 140, 974–80)

Disturbe his howres of rest with restlesse trances,
Afflict him in his bed with bedred grones,
Let there bechaunce him pitifull mischances,
To **make** him **mone**, but pitie not his **mones**:
Stone him with hardned hearts harder then stones,
  And let milde women to him loose their mildnesse,
  Wilder to him then Tygers in their wildnesse.

The spoken annotation is inserted just above its neighboring word, *Mocke*.

M427. Mocke.
o A mocker, one that **laugheth** other **to scorn**.

Three separate mute annotations, under *mock*, *laughter*, and *delude*, each attest to this interest at the notion of expressing "laughter to scorn":

🔖 *Venus and Adonis* (st. 1, 1–6)

Even as the sunne with purple-colourd face,
Had tane his last leaue of the weeping morne,
Rose-cheekt Adonis hied him to the chace,
Hunting he lou'd, but loue he **laught to scorne**:
  Sick-thoughted Venus makes amaine vnto him,
  And like a bold fac'd sutor ginnes to woo him.

To help make the best case for Baret, it is useful to cross-reference the texts from where the annotator has appropriated his spoken annotations. In the case of make moane the words lie in a heavily negotiated cluster under *complain:*

C974. ¶ to Complaine
o A cõplaining, lamenting, or moane making.
o A secrete accuser, or complayner, a tell' tale, a picke shanke.

❦ 114 ❧

C974. to Complaine, to bewaile, to **make moane**, to finde himself **grieved**....A complainte, <u>moaning</u>, or bewayling when one findeth himself **grieved** with a thing. A complaynt, a <u>moane</u> making, a lamentable expressing of a thing, that one is **grieved** with.

The association of *make moan* with *grief* is bound up here in this word salad, and one notices the proximity that follows in the second usage from *Rape of Lucrece:*

🔖 *Rape of Lucrece* (st. 159, 1107–13)

The little birds that tune their mornings ioy
Make her **mones** mad, with their sweet melodie,
"For mirth doth search the bottome of annoy,
"Sad soules are slaine in merrie companie,
"**Griefe** best is pleas'd with **griefes** societie;
　"True sorrow then is feelinglie suffiz'd,
　"When with like semblance it is simpathiz'd.

Make moan is also textually incorporated in *Venus and Adonis*, with echoes – literal and figurative – of grief.

🔖 *Venus and Adonis* (st. 139, 829–34)

And now she beates her heart, whereat it grones,
That all the neighbour caues as seeming troubled,
Make verball repetition of her **mones**,
Passion on passion, deeply is redoubled,
　Ay me, she cries, and twentie times, wo, wo,
　And twentie ecchoes, twentie times crie so,

There are further examples of words clusters shared between the two poems:

D69. /¶ to **Dasell** the **sight** with glistring **brightnesse**

🔖 *Rape of Lucrece* (st. 54, 372–78)

Looke as the faire and fierie pointed Sunne,
Rushing from forth a cloud, bereaues our **sight**:
Euen so the Curtaine drawne, his eyes begun
To winke, being blinded with a greater light.
Whether it is that shee reflects so **bright**,
　That **dazleth** them, or else some shame supposed,
　But blind they are, and keep themselues inclosed.

🦢 *Venus and Adonis* (st. 178, 1063–68)

Vpon his hurt she **lookes** so **stedfastly,**
That her **sight dazling,** makes the wound seem three,
And then she reprehends her mangling eye,
That makes more gashes, where no breach shuld be:
 His face seems twain, ech seuerall lim is doubled,
 For oft the eye mistakes, the brain being troubled

The above example also incorporates:

S864. o to **looke stedfastlie.**

Many of Baret's servings are often no more than simple couplings, but the annotator gobbles up these couplings, and so does Shakespeare. An example that appears in both long poems occurs with *proud* and *disdain.*

D822. o **Proud disdainfulnesse.**

🦢 *Venus and Adonis* (st. 127, 757–62)

What is thy bodie but a swallowing graue
Seeming to burie that posteritie,
Which by the rights of time thou needs must haue,
If thou destroy them not in darke obscuritie?
 If so the world will hold thee **indisdaine,**
 Sith in thy **pride,** so faire a hope is slaine.

🦢 *Rape of Lucrece* (st. 6, 36–41)

Perchance his bost of Lucrece Sou'raigntie,
Suggested this **proud** issue of a King:
For by our eares our hearts oft taynted be:
Perchance that enuie of so rich a thing
Brauing compare, **disdainefully** did sting
 His high picht thoughts that meaner men should
 That golden hap which their superiors want. (vant,

Sometimes in a single mute annotation we find the entire sample sentence essentially retranscribed into verse.

B1502. ¶ a **Burden:** a lode
B1504. o The bodie **burdeneth** or **lodeth the mind** with **vices.**

☞ *Rape of Lucrece* (st. 105, 734–35)
> Shee beares the **lode** of **lust** he left behinde,
> And he the **burthen** of a guiltie **minde**.

Echoes can also result from two mute annotations merging together. Consider how these two separately marked annotations work together as sublime agents to formulate the echo that is heard in *Venus and Adonis* around the words *foul, canker,* and *rust.*

> F992. ¶ to be **Foule,** vncleanlie, sluttish, or filthie
> o **foulnesse, or rustinesse** of the teeth.

> C56./¶ a **Canker:** a worme that creepeth vpon herbes, and commonly eateth coleworts

> C57. o **Cankred, or rustie.**

☞ *Venus and Adonis* (st. 128, 767–68)
> **Foule cankring rust,** the hidden treasure frets,
> But gold that's put to vse more gold begets.

Textual proximity between a spoken annotation and the printed text is again seen on this occasion with *wanton* and *dally*:

> D27. to **dallie**: to plaie the **wanton** foole, adds dalliance flatterie

☞ *Venus and Adonis* (st. 18, 123–28)
> Ouer my Altars hath he hong his launce,
> His battred shield, his vncontrolled crest,
> And for my sake hath learnd to sport, and daunce,
> To toy, to **wanton, dallie,** smile, and iest,
>   Scorning his churlish drumme, and ensigne red,
>   Making my armes his field, his tent my bed.

Other occurrences involve annotations working in conjunction with a removed *vide* related text (alphabetically speaking) and its conjoining text.

> W187–88. ¶ **Whet.** vide Sharpe, adds whetstones

Baret's *vide* sends us to the definition of Sharpe at S314, at the bottom of the sub-definitions:

I will quicken, or **sharpen** you: I will be a **whetstone** to you.

☞ *Troilus and Cressida*. Thersites (5.2.77; FF ¶¶5)

Now she **sharpens**: well said **Whetstone** –

A less literal echo is heard in *Venus and Adonis* in this stanza, which also contains *tusk* and *flank*, products of additional mute annotations that appear in Baret and are found in Shakespeare only in *Venus and Adonis*.

☞ *Venus and Adonis* (st. 15, 85–90)

Tis true, tis true, thus was Adonis slaine,
He ran vpon the Boare with his **sharpe** speare,
Who did not **whet** his **teeth** at him againe,
But by a kisse thought to persuade him there.
  And nousling in his **flanke** the louing swine,
  Sheath'd vnaware the **tuske** in his soft groine.

Archaic usages and "rare words" abound in the narrative poems:

D419. /¶ the **Dent**, or <u>notch</u> in a <u>leafe</u>
D420. o **Dented, or notched. With dent of sword**, adds dint

☞ *Venus and Adonis* (st. 59, 353–54)

His tender cheeke, recieues her soft hands print,
As apt, as new falne snow takes any **dint**.

The phrase "dint of sword" is later found in its entirety in *2 Henry IV*.

At C247, the annotator adds two mute little circles at subsidiary definitions for *cavil*, and between them, the spoken words caueling quastions. All usages of *cavil* are found in early works.

C247. ¶ a **Cauillour**:
o A captious **cauill**.
o Subtill **cauillations**.

☞ *Rape of Lucrece* (st. 147, 1025–26)

In vaine I **cauill** with mine infamie,
In vaine I spurne at my confirm'd despight,

𝕝𝕖 *Rape of Lucrece* (st. 157, 1093–94)

Thus **cauils** shee with euerie thing shee sees,
True griefe is fond and testie as a childe,

The linguistic juxtapositions and associations in Baret that echo in *Venus and Adonis* and *Rape of Lucrece* are so many that a reduction may increase the sense that the examples are trivial. But verbal dexterity is enhanced through the use of options, whether idiomatic sayings or pairing of synonyms, and no writer takes advantage of the dexterity, or seems as obsessed with it, as Shakespeare.

Here are just a few additional mute annotations where verbal parallels are found within the narrative poems:

Y22. ¶ **Yeeld**
o By **yeelding** thou shalt **ouercome.**

𝕝𝕖 *Venus and Adonis* (st. 149, 889–94)

This dismall crie rings sadly in her eare,
Through which it enters to surprise her hart,
Who **ouercome** by doubt, and bloodlesse feare,
With cold-pale weakenesse, nums ech feeling part,
   Like soldiers when their captain once doth **yeeld,**
   They basely flie, and dare not stay the field.

P503. / ¶ he **Plight** her his **faith** and trueth, or made her promise, xc.

𝕝𝕖 *Rape of Lucrece* (st. 242, 1690)

Shall **plight** your Honourable **faiths** to me,

B232. ¶ **Batter**
o To batter walles.
o The wall is battered.

𝕝𝕖 *Rape of Lucrece* (st. 67, 463–64)

His hand that yet remaines vppon her brest,
(Rude Ram to **batter** such an Iuorie **wall**:)

☞ *Rape of Lucrece* (st. 104, 722–23)

> Shee sayes her subiects with fowle insurrection,
> Haue **batterd** downe her consecrated **wall**,

M5. ¶ **Mad, <u>wood</u>,** out of his wit, furious

☞ *Venus and Adonis* (st. 54, 323–24)

> As they were **mad** vnto the **wood** they hie them,
> Outstripping crowes, that striue to ouerfly them.

S299. / ¶ water **Shallower** and **deeper**. Vide **Foorde**, adds vel fourd

☞ *Rape of Lucrece* (st. 190, 1329–30)

> **Deep** sounds make lesser noise thē **shallow foords**,
> And sorrow ebs, being blown with wind of words.

But no example shall, we suspect, resonate so powerfully as this text:

> Lucrece willinglie killed her selfe in punish=
> ment of vnwilling adulterie and rape. Obla-

It's right there on the page, and the annotator has located it at K58 and marked it with his mute underlining *and rape.* The Baret text effectively sums up the plot of the entire poem in a single line.

The Sonnets

RANCIS MERES wrote, as early as 1598: "As the soule of *Euphorbus* was thought to live in *Pythagoras:* so the sweete wittie soule of *Ovid* lives in mellifluous & hony-tongued Shakespeare, witnes his *Venus and Adonis,* his *Lucrece,* his sugred *Sonnets* among his private friends, &c."⁹⁹

We have attempted to show some of the connections between what has been annotated in our copy of Baret's *Alvearie* 1580 and the texts of the earlier printed longer poems, and now hope to make an even stronger impression in turning to the "hony-tongued" Shakespeare's sonnets. In 1599, a year after Meres alludes to these "sugred sonnets" circulating among private friends, William Jaggard published *The Passionate Pilgrime,* a slender, well-received volume containing twenty poems, with William Shakespeare listed as the author. The first three we know are by Shakespeare; two other poems, including a sonnet, are also by Shakespeare. In some of the other fifteen poems, authorship has been determined, but not in all of them. Only in 1609, after Shakespeare most likely sold his sonnets to a well-established publisher, Thomas Thorpe, was a complete sonnet sequence published for the first time. To what extent Shakespeare authorized the publication remains unresolved.¹⁰⁰ One may assume that Shakespeare himself played a significant role in organizing the 154-poem sequence. If there is a parallel between the publication of the sonnets, and his two long narrative poems, *Venus and Adonis* and *Rape of Lucrece,* it is that the theaters were again shuttered because of plague, and the timing likely afforded Shakespeare the opportunity to finish the poems as he desired them to be finished, readjust the sequence, and bring the whole of it to a publisher.[101]

The sonnets are considered to have two main sequences (the first considerably longer than the second), and even within the sequences there are regular turns from one sonnet to the next that suggest a fairly careful arrangement. So much is placed on the relative lack of interest Shakespeare demonstrated for seeing his plays properly into print that it can inaccurately be assumed that he looked at all publications in the same manner. In a 1612 work, *An Apology for Actors*, Thomas Heywood goes so far as to insinuate that Shakespeare had been "might offended" by the 1599 publication of *The Passionate Pilgrime* and that the book was published under his name solely "altogether unknown to him."[102]

While we do not intend to assert ourselves as historians, nor elaborate in such a way as to pose as such, this background debate is helpful in understanding what makes our annotations relating to the sonnets so special. Perhaps most importantly for our purposes, after Thomas Thorpe in 1609, Shakespeare's sonnets were not reprinted until John Benson's highly edited and flawed 1640 edition. Then, for sixty-nine more years, through the tumultuous political periods of Civil War, Interregnum, Restoration, and Glorious Revolution, which also affected the language and literary culture, there was no printed edition of Shakespeare containing any of his poems until midway through the reign of Queen Anne in 1710, when Charles Gildon edited a volume of poems to supplement Nicholas Rowe's edition of the plays, though adhering to John Benson's revisions. In 1711 Bernard Lintott published his two-volume edition containing *Venus & Adonis*, *The Rape of Lucrece*, and *The Passionate Pilgrime*, together with the sonnets, which he restored to the original Thorpe sequence. This suggests the clear traces between our annotations and the sonnets to be of even greater intrigue, in all but eliminating the idea that someone could have been working from a printed text, or else was very familiar with the printed text, and then made the annotations in our copy of Baret.

The other very interesting factor is the length of time from the onset of the composition to the conclusion. Most scholars feel that the "dark lady" sequence (127–54) was "essentially complete by 1599."[103] Regarding the main sequence, that of the "fair youth," composition likely ran from at least the early 1590s (if not earlier) through 1603–04, when the theaters were closed for plague once again. What this adds up to, even by the most conservative of estimates, is a time frame of composition that minimally runs between ten and twelve years. We will never be able to say over what exact time frame our book was annotated, although if we are correct regarding authorship, the trailing blank dates from around 1598, and the book was likely acquired at least ten years before that, when the annotations may have started off within some professional discipline. There is a great amount of overlap between these suggested time frames, perhaps accounting for the tremendous number of echoes we find. But, just to remind our readers, this is not to imply that one will find poetry in our annotations – quite the opposite, in fact. There is, however, poetry to be found in the Baret text, if you know where to look.

Can you turn a mute little circle into a sonnet? It appears as if Shakespeare could.

F968. ○ **Forsworne, perjured, false, that hath broken his oth.**

☞ *Shake-speares Sonnets.* Sonnet 152

In louing thee thou know'st I am **forsworne**,
But thou art twice **forsworne** to me loue **swearing**,
In act thy bed-vow **broake** and new faith torne,
In vowing new hate after **new loue** bearing:
But why of two **othes breach** doe I accuse thee,
When I **breake** twenty: I am **periur'd** most,
For all my vowes are **othes** but to misuse thee:
And all my honest faith in thee is lost.

For I haue **sworne** deepe **othes** of thy deepe kindnesse:
Othes of thy loue, thy truth, thy constancie,
And to inlighten thee gaue eyes to blindnesse,
Or made them **swere** against the thing they see.
  For I haue **sworne** thee faire: more **periurde** eye,
  To **swere** against the truth ſo foule a lie.

The theme of Sonnet 152 can be said to echo another mute annotation, this time a slash:

A703. /¶ an Attonement, a **louing** againe after a **breache** or falling out

The verbal affinities are so strong, it is almost as if Shakespeare challenged himself to compose a sonnet based upon the text marked with a little circle. Before you try this at home, all jesting aside, this tells us something profound about language. It is, after all, there for the taking. There are kernels to be had in marked and unmarked sample sentences in Baret that can grow into sonnets. But it is not done easily, nor can just anyone do it.

Sonnet 152 is a version of one of the three *Passionate Pilgrime* poems that had first appeared in the 1598 quarto of *Love's Labour's Lost*. In the play, Berowne is the speaker, and this is the version of his sonnet to Rosaline in act 4, scene 2:

☞ *Love's Labour's Lost*. Berowne (4.2.106–19; Q1598, E1b)
  If Loue make me forsworne, how shall I sweare to loue?
  Ah neuer fayth could hold, yf not to beautie vowed.
  Though to my selfe forsworne, to thee Ile faythfull proue.
  Those thoughts to me were Okes, to thee like Osiers bowed
  Studie his byas leaues, and makes his booke thine eyes.
  Where all those pleasures liue, that Art would comprehend.
  If knowledge be the marke, to know thee shall suffise.
  Well learned is that tongue, that well can thee commend.
  All ignorant that soule, that sees thee without wonder.
  Which is to mee some prayse, that I thy partes admire,
  Thy eie *Ioues* lightning beares, thy voyce his dreadful thūder
  Which not to anger bent, is musique, and sweete fier.
  Celestiall as thou art, Oh pardon loue this wrong,
  That singes heauens prayse, with such an earthly tong.

The sonnet also bears thematic and linguistic similarity to another *Passionate Pilgrime* poem that is a version of what is found in the play, that sonnet being Longaville's to Maria in act 4, scene 3.

☞ *Love's Labour's Lost* (4.3.57–70; Q1598, E3)
> Gainst whom the world cannot holde argument,
> Perswade my hart to this false periurie?
> Vowes for thee broke deserue not punishment.
> A Woman I forswore, but I will proue,
> Thou being a Goddesse, I forswore not thee.
> My Vow was earthly, thou a heauenly Loue.
> Thy grace being gainde, cures all disgrace in mee.
> Vowes are but breath, and breath a vapoure is.
> Then thou faire Sunne, which on my earth doost shine,
> Exhalst this vapour-vow in thee it is:
> If broken then, it is no fault of mine:
> If by mee broke, What **foole** is not so wise,
> To loose an oth, to winn a **Parradise**?

It ends with the echo of a proverbial phrase, common at the time. One can find the phrase printed in a copy of Baret under *paradise*. In our copy, the proverb is underlined by the annotator:

> P92. ¶ **Paradise**, a place of joie… <u>To bring one into a fooles paradise, to make glad in vaine.</u>

The three poems from *Love's Labour's Lost* that are in versions printed in *The Passionate Pilgrime* are all a little silly. As Duncan-Jones has written, "In the theatre, it seems, Shakespeare almost invariably presents the writing of love poetry in general, and sonnets in particular, as ridiculous."[104] Over time, however, the poetry of the sonnets has endured – some sonnets more than others, certainly; but of the whole, there can be no denying what may properly be viewed at this point as a mystique. To suggest that verbal echoes are contained in this marked text of Baret, and that Shakespeare could have made those marks, is to partially upset the mystique.

According to Duncan-Jones, "Sir John Suckling is the only early 17th century writer that can be shown to have read the 1609 quarto attentively and appreciatively."[105] Half a dozen verbal reminiscences are in his *Brennoralt* – which contains these lines:

Shee's gone. Life's like a Dials hand hath stolne
From the faire figure e're it was perceiv'd

The lines we see here are "echoing two of Shakespeare's tenderest lines about the fair youth"[106] from Sonnet 104:

☞ *Shake-speares Sonnets.* Sonnet 104 (9–10)

Ah yet doth beauty like a Dyall hand,
Steale from his figure, and no **pace** perceiu'd,

The first two printed entries under the letter "P" in Baret define *pace*, and this is how they look in our copy:

P1. / a **Pace** in going, a step.
P2. To go a <u>stalking</u>, or **stealing pace**, softly.

The quotation cited in Baret is "suspenso graduire" from Terence. It may be interesting to know that in the Golding translation of Ovid we find "with stealing pace dooth creepe." Looking back on Suckling's poem, wherein the echo is cited in the two lines from *Brennoralt*, we notice that *stealing* has been replaced with *stolne*, and the word *pace* is absent.

Is it possible that the memory flicker from underlining *stealing pace* is the echo our annotator required in writing these tender lines about the fair youth in Sonnet 104? Perhaps Shakespeare was remembering Ovid, or both Ovid and Baret, but the underlined text in Baret is compelling. The annotator may simply have found it pleasing in itself, or it could have been the planted seed that eventually found purchase in Sonnet 104.

That the echoes should run even into Baret's preambles, where Shakespeare's attention was obviously drawn, will further the debate.

Consider the preface to letter "B" and the mute annotation we witness there: *And the cause thereof may seeme to be either ignorant printers and their correctours, when printing began first to be used, taking one letter for an other, being written in divers **ragged** hands....*

☞ *Shake-speares Sonnets.* Sonnet 6

Then let not winters **wragged hand** deface,
In thee thy summer ere thou be distil'd:
Make sweet some **viall**; treasure thou some place,
With beautits treasure ere it be selfe kil'd:
That vse is not forbidden vsery,
Which happies those that pay the willing lone;
That's for thy selfe to breed an other thee,
Or **ten times** happier be it ten for one,
Ten times thy selfe were happier then thou art,
If ten of thine ten times refigur'd thee,
Then what could death doe if thou should'st depart,
Leauing thee liuing in posterity?
　Be not **selfe-wild** for thou art much too faire,
　To be deaths conquest and make wormes thine heire.

Ragged hands sounds somehow mundane, and yet the "wragged hand" in the opening lines to Sonnet 6 is anything but common-place-sounding among the poetry of the period. We were unable to locate any echo of "ragged hand" among Shakespeare's contemporaries. Helen Vendler notes "ragged hand" as being "odd."[107]

Other echoes of Baret in Sonnet 6 include the phrase *ten times* — a seemingly trivial inclusion in our discussion, but the little circles at T126 and D1092 propose it otherwise, as do several other sonnets that contain the coupling.

T126.　o　**Ten times...**
D1092.　o　**Ten times double.**

Sonnet 6 also contains the word *vial*, for which we have a spoken annotation, and the hyphenated *self-willed*, for which we have the key word entry **selfewill** with a slash.

"Ragged hand" is not the only text suggestive of the individual prefaces to letters in Baret. In the preface to letter "E," specific texts referenced by Patricia Parker as bearing the uncanny qualities one hears in *Hamlet*,[108] the annotator has shown great interest, underlining words such as *arrand* and *tongtide* (this word appears in the preface just after the lines drawn from it by Parker). Our annotator has added mine arrand vide handle in the margin back in letter "A." Under *handle*, we find the word *arrand* underlined as part of the definition: *I have handled the matter well or done mine arrand trimly*. The word is a Shakespeare favorite, used many times, including a Falstaff usage. *Tongue-tied* is another word loved by Shakespeare. He uses it in four sonnets and many of the early plays and some later plays.

The preface to letter "E" reads: *But what a monstrous absurditie is this, that E being naturally a sounding vowell and giveth power to other words to speake, should now be so* <u>*tongtide*</u>. Compare this sentence from Baret with these lines from *1 Henry VI*:

꙰ *1 Henry VI*. Richard (Gloucester) (2.4.25–30; FF k6)
Since you are **tongue-ty'd,** and so loth to **speake,**
In dumbe significants proclayme your thoughts:
Let him that is a true-borne Gentleman,
And stands upon the honor of his birth,
If he suppose that I haue pleaded truth,
From off this Bryer pluck a white Rose with me.

Further on in the preface to letter "E," we find the following text with underlining:

<u>**weede out**</u> of our writings a great number of superfluous letters

This text contains another favorite Shakespeare word, *superfluous*. The overall meaning of the text, and its underlined portion, may bear a connection to Sonnet 76, where the poet worries about "dressing old words new."

Why is my verse so barren of new pride?
So far from variation or quicke change?
Why with the time do I not glance aside
To new found methods, and to compounds strange?
Why **write** I still all one, euer the same,
And keepe inuention in a noted **weed**,
That euery word doth almost fel my name,
Shewing their birth, and where they did proceed?
O know sweet loue I alwaies **write** of you,
And you and loue are still my argument:
So all my best is **dressing old words new**,
Spending againe what is already spent:
  For as the Sun is daily new and old,
  So is my loue still telling what is told,

A couple of prefaces apart from letter "E" where *tongtide* is underlined, in the preface to letter "C," the annotator has underlined *miscalling*.

☞ *Shake-speares Sonnets.* Sonnet 66

Tyr'd with all these for restfull death I cry,
As to behold desert a begger borne,
And needie Nothing trimd in iollitie,
And purest faith vnhappily forsworne,
And gilded honor shamefully misplast,
And maiden vertue rudely strumpeted,
And right perfection wrongfully disgrac'd,
And strength by limping sway disabled,
And arte made **tung-tide** by authoritie,
And Folly (Doctor-like) controuling skill,
And simple-Truth **miscalde** Simplicitie,
And captiue-good attending Captaine ill.
  Tyr'd with all these, from these would I be gone,
  Saue that to dye, I leaue my loue alone.

Is it not odd to find them so close together in a sonnet, and marked among so spare a group of markings in the two nearby prefaces in Baret?

In the preface to letter "D," the annotator has underlined *lispingly at the tongues end*. *Tongue's end* is used once in Shakespeare:

🖛 *Love's Labour's Lost.* Boy (3.1.10–11)

No my compleat master, but to Iigge off a tune at the **tongues end**, (FF L4b)
No my complet Maister, but to Iigge off a tune at the **tongues ende**, (Q1598, C3b)

Also in *Love's Labour's Lost*, the word *lisp* is combined with the "honey-tongued Boyet."

Verbal echoes for Shakespeare must have been roused by many things: the prodigious memory, first and foremost, containing details from what he had read and what he had witnessed firsthand, his childhood observations, and his extraordinary ear for words and what one could do with them. It does not seem so far-fetched to imagine Baret's dictionary as the perfect supplemental tool, and to forgive the multitude of years that have elapsed since these annotations were first written but never noticed. How else to explain the heaping embarrassment of riches that are the echoes from the annotated text in Baret into the sonnets? Considering our space limitation, these are necessarily a weakened reduction of all of our Baret annotations that are traceable to the sonnets.

T246. o **Tillage**: **husbandrie.**

🖛 *Shake-speares Sonnets.* Sonnet 3 (5–6)

For where is she so faire whose vn-eard wombe
Disdaines the **tillage** of thy **husbandry**?

C1269. ¶ a **Coping**, adds accouplement

🖛 *Shake-speares Sonnets.* Sonnet 21 (5)

Making **a coopelment** of proud compare

One wonders, in the case of Sonnet 23, whether Shakespeare himself is to be identified as the "unperfect actor."

M27. ¶ a **Maime**

o Lacking some principall **part**: lame: maimed: **vnperfect**.

F539. / ¶ a **Fine**, or forfet
o A letter trimly and learnedly **written**, or penned **finely**.
o **Finenesse of witte**.

B1502. ¶ a **Burden**: a lode
o To grieue: to **burden**: to lode.
o Burdeinous: **chargeable**: very heauie.

☞ *Shake-speares Sonnets*. Sonnet 23
As an **vnperfect** actor on the stage,
Who with his feare is put besides his **part**,
Or some fierce thing repleat with too much rage,
Whose strengths abondance weakens his owne heart;
So I for feare of trust, forget to say,
The perfect ceremony of loues right,
And in mine owne loues strength seeme to decay,
Ore-charg'd with **burthen** of mine owne loues might:
O let my books be then the eloquence,
And domb presagers of my speaking brest,
Who pleade for loue, and look for recompence,
More then that tonge that more hath more exprest.
    O learne to read what silent loue hath **writ**,
    To heare wit eies belongs to loues **fine wiht**.

The word *lame* in the mute annotation at M27 is echoed in Son-net 37 and also in Sonnet 89. There are several other annotations, spoken and mute, related to *lame* and *halt*. Notice how the web of mute annotations in this particular set of instances seems to clearly connect *maime* with "unperfect actor."

In another instance, consider how the interaction between *stealing* and *trifles*, *thievery* and *falsehood* informs Sonnet 48:

P343. / ¶ to **Picke** out,
o A picker, or petie briber, that **stealeth** and picketh small **trifles**.

T145. ¶ a **Theefe**
o **Theeuish**: a great piker: naturallie giuen to **stealing**.
o Theeuishlie: with an intent, or affection to **steale**.

O80. nooseled in **falshood**

☞ *Shake-speares Sonnets.* Sonnet 48

How carefull was I when I tooke my way,
Each **trifle** vnder truest barres to thrust,
That to my vse it might vn-vsed stay
From hands of **falsehood**, in sure wards of trust?
But thou, to whom my iewels **trifles** are,
Most worthy comfort, now my greatest griefe,
Thou best of deerest, and mine onely care,
Art left the prey of euery vulgar **theefe**.
Thee haue I not lockt vp in any chest,
Saue where thou art not, though I feele thou art,
Within the gentle closure of my brest,
From whence at pleasure thou maist come and part,
   And euen thence thou wilt be **stolne** I feare,
   For truth prooues **theeuish** for a prize so deare.

In the next in the sequence, Sonnet 49, we see a great example of legal language contained in a mute annotation entering a sonnet.

D925. o A **caster** of an accompt: an **auditor**: a disputer: a reasoned.

☞ *Shake-speares Sonnets.* Sonnet 49 (1–4)

Against that time (if euer that time come)
When I shall see thee frowne on my defects,
When as thy loue hath **cast** his vtmost summe,
Called to that **audite** by aduis'd respects,

In Sonnet 53, the language of the mute annotations is explicitly contained in imagery involving shadows and imitations, and also the notion of "disguised" and "counterfeit" with painting.

P237. ¶ **Peinting**
o Coloured, **peinted**, disguised.
o To print with a **counterfaite** colour.

E485. ¶ an **Expressing**, or representing
o To make like: to expresse, or deuise the forme or likenesse of.
o A **shadowing**: also an **imitation**, or expressing of another thing, somewhat to the likenesse and nature of the same.

What is your substance, whereof are you made,
That millions of strange **shaddowes** on you tend?
Since euery one, hath euery one, one shade,
And you but one, can euery **shaddow** lend:
Describe *Adonis* and the **counterfet**,
Is poorely **immitated** after you,
On *Hellens* cheeke all art of beautie set,
And you in *Grecian* tires are **painted** new:
Speake of the spring, and foyzon of the yeare,
The one doth **shaddow** of your beautie show,
The other as your bountie doth appeare,
And you in euery blessed shape we know.
  In all externall grace you haue some part,
    But you like none, none you for constant heart.

The next sonnet in the sequence brings us to the familiar theme of fading beauty, echoed in a number of mute annotations:

F37. ¶ **Fairenesse** of weather: quietnesse
F46. The floures that shewe **fairest** to the eie, do sonnest **vade** and wither
    away.
U/V1. Adds vade vide fairenesse and flestive
F15. / ¶ to **Fade**, or be withered: to faile
A312. o **Wantonly**: with wanton intisings and alluring.

Oh how much more doth beautie beautious seeme,
By that sweet ornament which truth doth giue,
The Rose lookes **faire**, but **fairer** we it deeme
For that sweet odor, which doth in it liue:
The Canker bloomes haue full as deepe a die,
As the perfumed tincture of the **Roses**,
Hang on such thornes, and play as **wantonly**,
When sommers breath their masked buds discloses:
But for their virtue only is their show,
They liue vnwoo'd, and vnrespected **fade**,
Die to themselues. Sweet **Roses** doe not so,
Of their sweet deathes, are sweetest odors made:
  And so of you, beautious and louely youth,
    When that shall **vade**, by verse distils your truth.

The odd pairing of *patience* and *sufferance* highlights Sonnet 58.

P4. o **Patience: sufferance**.

H51. A Proverbe aptly to be applied to those, which do passe their life with great **pleasure**, and much quietnesse, having (as we saie) Fortune at a **becke**.

C372. / ¶ a **Charter** or letters **patents** of a prince

☞ *Shake-speares Sonnets*. Sonnet 58
> That God forbid, that made me first your slaue,
> I should in thought controule your times of **pleasure**,
> Or at your hand th' account of houres to craue,
> Being your vassail bound to staie your leisure.
> Oh let me suffer (being at your **beck**)
> Th' imprison'd absence of your libertie,
> And **patience** tame, to **sufferance** bide each check,
> Without accusing you of iniury.
> Be where you list, your **charter** is so strong,
> That you your selfe may priuiledge your time
> To what you will, to you it doth belong,
> Your selfe to pardon of selfe-doing crime.
>   I am to waite, though waiting so be hell,
>   Not blame your pleasure be it ill or well.

The brilliant lines from Sonnet 62 contain the spoken annotation chopt, spelled as such in the original 1609 quarto:

C505. ¶ to **Choppe**, or cut of, adds chopt

P834. / ¶ **Puke** colour between russet and blacke, adds tanne

L697. o Loue of ones selfe: **selfe loue**: selfe liking.

☞ *Shake-speares Sonnets*. Sonnet 62 (9–12)
> But when my glasse shewes me my selfe indeed
> Beated and **chopt** with **tand** antiquitie,
> Mine owne **selfe loue** quite contrary I read
> Selfe, so **selfe louing** were iniquity,

Three sonnets, numbers 68, 74, and 75, combine to hold our interest because of the echoes found in a tightly intertwined set of annotations. The first thing to consider regarding the annotations added or marked is the wide range of points in the dictionary from which they are drawn:

F487–88. Adds he hath filcheth his possessive vide interest

F677. ¶ a **Fleece** of wooll, adds to fleec vide onterest

S374–75. Adds a shorne sheepe vide interest

I205. ¶ Interest, or the borowing of vsurie monie wherwith to pay my debt. And when he hath thus **filched** and **fleeced** his *Possessive*, so long till he hath made him as ruch as a newe **shorne** sheepe, then he will turne him to commons into Ludgate: where for his Ablatiue case, he shall have a Datiue cage, crauing and crying at the <u>grate</u>, your worships charitie for the Lordes sake.

C1734. / ¶ **Cullars**, or <u>robbars</u> drawen out of a flocke of **sheepe**

R355. Adds robbars or cullars

Within the entry for *interest* Baret includes a long quotation translated from Latin, which seems to consist of an elaborate mnemonic for recalling various cases in grammar, and includes the translated phrase: *And when he hath thus filched and fleeced his Possessive, so long till he hath made him as rich as a newe shorne sheepe,* where *filched*, *fleeced*, and *shorne* have been underlined in the text. One can see the annotator hard at work, and almost begin to follow his mind.

Falstaff and Iago each use forms of *filched*, and there are usages for *interest* in the *fleeced* sense in *Richard III* and *Venus and Adonis*. And look at how the terminology cluster is essential in these three sonnets. *Shorn, fleece,* and *robbing* are combined in Sonnet 68. *Filching* and *interest* appear back-to-back in Sonnets 74 and 75.

☞ *Shake-speares Sonnets.* Sonnet 68

Thus is his cheeke the map of daies out-worne,
When beauty liu'd and dy'ed as flowers do now,
Before these bastard signes of faire were borne,
Or durst inhabit on a liuing brow:
Before the goulden tresses of the dead,

The right of sepulchers, were **shorne** away,
To liue a scond life on second head,
Ere beauties dead **fleece** made another gay:
In him those holy antique howers are seene,
Without all ornament, it selfe and true,
Making no summer of an others greene,
Robbing no ould to dresse his beauty new,
 And him as for a map doth Nature store,
 To shew faulse Art what beauty was of yore.

☞ *Shake-speares Sonnets.* Sonnet 74

Bvt be contented when that **fell** arest,
With out all bayle shall carry me away,
My life hath in this line some **interest**,
Which for memoriall still with thee shall stay.
When thou reuewest this, thou doest reuew,
The very part was consecrate to thee,
The earth can haue but earth, which is his due,
My spirit is thine the better part of me,
So then thou hast but lost the **dregs** of life,
The pray of wormes, my body being dead,
The coward conquest of a wretches knife,
To base of thee to be remembred,
 The worth of that, is that which it containes,
 And that is this, and this with thee remaines.

☞ *Shake-speares Sonnets.* Sonnet 75

So are you to my thoughts as food to life,
Or as sweet season'd shewers are to the ground;
And for the peace of you I hold such strife,
As twixt a **miser** and his wealth is found.
Now proud as an inioyer, and anon
Doubting the **filching** age will steale his treasure,
Now counting best to be with you alone,
Then betterd that the world may see my pleasure,
Some-time all ful with feasting on your sight,
And by and by cleane starued for a looke,
Possessing or pursuing no delight
Saue what is had, or must from you be tooke.
 Thus do I **pine** and **surfe**t day by day,
 Or **gluttoning** on all, or all **away**,

There is no shortage of additional annotations echoed in the sonnets just referenced. They include the spoken annotation a miser niggard, which is echoed not only here but in several sonnets from early in the sequence dealing with the need for procreation as a message to the self-absorbed youth.

L497. /¶ to **Linger**

L499. o He **pineth away** with a lingring consumption.

P379. /¶ to **Pine**, or <u>weare</u>, and wither **away**

D1196. ¶ **Dregges**: <u>lize</u>: grounds of any thing

L559. /¶ **Liuerwort,** adds lize dregges

S276–77. Adds setlings or dregges of oile

F379. /¶ a **Fell**, or sheeps skinne, adds fell felon

Let us return to one of the core annotations relating to this cluster of three sonnets, as it may prove most revealing regarding a generally accepted editorial change in the last line of a sonnet later in the sequence:

C1734. **Cullars**, or <u>robbars</u> drawn out of a flocke of **sheepe**

R355. Adds robbars or cullars

🖙 *Shake-speares Sonnets.* Sonnet 99

The forward violet thus did I **chide**:
Sweet **thief**, whence didst thou **steal** thy sweet that smells,
If not from my love's breath? The purple pride
Which on thy soft cheek for complexion **dwells**
In my love's veins thou hast too grossly dy'd.
The lily I condemned for thy hand,
And buds of marjoram had **stol'n** thy hair;
The roses fearfully on thorns did stand,
One blushing shame, another white despair;
A third, nor red nor white, had **stol'n** of both,
And to his **robbery** had annexed thy breath;
But, for his **theft**, in pride of all his growth
A vengeful **canker** eat him up to death.
    More flowers I noted, yet I none could see,
    But sweet, or **colour** it had **stol'n** from thee.

The forward violet thus did I **chide**,
Sweet **theefe** whence didst thou **steale** thy sweet that smels
If not from my loues breath, the purple pride,
Which on thy soft cheeke for complexion **dwells**?
In my loues veines thou hast too grosely died,
The Lillie I condemned for thy hand,
And buds of marierom had **stolne** thy haire,
The Roses fearefully on thornes did stand,
Our blushing shame, an other white dispaire:
A third nor red, nor white, had **stolne** of both,
And to his **robbry** had annext thy breath,
But for his **theft** in pride of all his growth
A vengfull **canker** eate him vp to death.
　More flowers I noted, yet I none could see,
　But sweet, or **culler** it had **stolne** from thee.

The original version published in 1609 printed *culler* – subsequently changed to *colour* in almost every modern edition.

More flowers I noted, yet I none could see,
But sweet, or **colour** it had stolne from thee.

Booth[109] points out that *sweet* is used first as an adjective and then as a noun (for perfume) in the opening lines. Its meaning in the last line is the problem. We have read it over carefully, trying to map out, line by line, what the sonnet is really saying. Perhaps our spoken annotation robbars or cullars will be determined to be the key.

We also noted that our biblical annotation, "blood be sprung upon his clothes," as used in *Venus and Adonis*, is in a six-line stanza that compares a white flower that has turned to red, but purple is also cited, just as in Sonnet 99.

Images of the canker worm and the juxtaposition of *stealing* and *thievery* are likewise echoed in mute annotations.

C56. / a **Canker**: a worme that creepeth upon herbes, and commonly eateth coleworts.

T145. Theefe.

o **Theevish**: a great piker: naturallie given to stealing.

o Theeverie, an inclination to theft and **stealing**.

One of the sonnets where we see an intriguing example of the proximity speculation already referenced in highlighting the longer poems is Sonnet 71.

Just above the Baret definition at M427:

¶ to Mocke, to jest at, to laugh to scorne, to delude

The annotator adds the words make moane, *moane* here being an alphabetical insertion, and we have seen that in both *Venus and Adonis* and *Rape of Lucrece* the annotator uses the two words in close proximity. But in Sonnet 71 there is also the echo of *mock*, suggestive to us that the annotator has retained a visual memory in addition to the linguistic echo and used it in the important closing couplet:

Lest the wise world should look into your **moan**,
And **mock** you with me after I am gone.

The annotations relating *warning* and *remembrance*, *love* and the *world* are also intriguing here:

W71. o A **warner**, one that putteth in **remembraunce**.

B565. Beside.....To **love** himselfe more then all the **world** doeth beside.

🖝 *Shake-speares Sonnets.* Sonnet 71

Noe Longer mourne for me when I am dead,
Then you shall heare the surly **sullen** bell
Giue **warning** to the **world** that I am fled
From this vile **world** with vildest wormes to **dwell**:
Nay if you read this line, **remember** not,
The hand that writ it, for I loue you so,
That I in your sweet thoughts would be forgot,
If thinking on me then should make you woe.
O if (I say) you looke vpon this verse,
When I (perhaps) compounded am with **clay**,
Do not so much as my poore name reherse;
But let your **loue** euen with my life decay.
  Least the wise **world** should looke into your **mone**,
  And **mocke** you with me after I am gon.

At times the combination of verbal echoes comes from the last words one would think of with relation to love poetry. *Charter* and *patent* combine in Sonnet 87.

C372. /¶ a **Charter** or letters **patents** of a prince

P186. /¶ letters **Patents**

☞ *Shake-speares Sonnets*. Sonnet 87 (1–8)

Farewell thou art too deare for my possessing,
And like enough thou knowst thy estimate,
The **Charter** of thy **worth** giues thee releasing:
My bonds in thee are all determinate.
For how do I hold thee but by thy granting,
And for that ritches where is my **deseruing**?
The cause of this faire guift in me is wanting,
And so my **pattent** back againe is sweruing.

Sonnet 113 offers the slightly awkward combination of *the heart* and *effectually*.

I269. ¶ the Inwardes of man, or beast

I274. o Very inwardly, from the bottome of **the hart**, very **effectuously**.

☞ *Shake-speares Sonnets*. Sonnet 113 (1–8)

Since I left you, mine eye is in my minde,
And that which gouernes me to goe about,
Doth part his function, and is partly blind,
Seemes seeing, but **effectually** is out:
For it no forme deliuers to **the heart**
Of bird, of flowre, or shape which it doth lack,
Of his quick obiects hath the minde no part,
Nor his owne vision houlds what it doth catch:

In Sonnet 122, *score* and *tally:*

S103. ¶ a **Score**, or **tallie** of wood, wheron a number of things deliuered, is marked

☞ *Shake-speares Sonnets*. Sonnet 122 (9–12)

That poore retention could not so much hold,
Nor need I **tallies** thy deare loue to **skore**,
Therefore to giue them from me was I bold,
To trust those tables that receaue thee more,

In Sonnet 136, *number* and *reckoning:*

R94. ¶ to **Reckon: number, or tell:**
○ A **reckoning,** or rehearsing. All things **reckoned,** or well **accompted** after they haue told their cardes. A shot, or **reckoning.**

At C78, the annotator adds / cardes vide reckon. (This is an example of the annotator's frequent use of a slash mark in a spoken annotation, similar to the mute slashes that mark head-word definitions throughout the text.) The *vide* association here of *cards* and *reckon* is placed with five Baret definitions of *card*, C74 to C78, as in relation to weaving, rather than as a game of *cards*.

N209. ¶ **Number,** recken, or cast

N210. ○ A **numbring, reckening,** a rehearsing.

☞ *Shake-speares Sonnets.* Sonnet 136 (7–14)
In things of great receit with ease we prooue.
Among a **number** one is **reckon'd** none.
Then in the **number** let me passe vntold,
Though in thy stores account I one must be,
For nothing hold me, so it please thee hold,
That nothing me, a some-thing sweet to thee.
  Make but my name thy loue, and loue that still,
  And then thou louest me for my name is *Will*.

Our annotator loved playing with variation on *frowning* and *louring*. He either wrote Sonnet 149 in part because of his appreciation for those two words, or would have presumably been impressed to see them coupled in a sonnet.

L722–23. **Lowre**
○ A **lowring, or frowning.**

F1159. / to **Frowne and lowre.**
○ Sowrenesse, **lowring,** crabbed looking: crooked: **frowning.**

F1159. **Frowne**
○ With an heauie, sad, frowning, lowring, soure, or displeasant countenaunce.

☞ *Shake-speares Sonnets.* Sonnet 149 (5–8)

Who hateth thee that I doe call my friend,
On whom **froun'st** thou that I doe faune vpon,
Nay if thou **lowrst** on me doe I not spend
Reuenge vpon my selfe with present mone?

There are annotations linking *falsehood* and *forgery, fire* and *brand:*

☞ *Shake-speares Sonnets.* Sonnet 137 (5–8)

If eyes corrupt by ouer-partiall lookes,
Be anchord in the baye where all men ride,
Why of eyes **falsehood** hast thou **forged** hookes,
Whereto the iudgement of my heart is tide?

F898. ¶ to **Forge**
o To vse **falshood**, or **forging** of a crime.

C1537. ¶ carpenters **Craft**
C1549. o A craftie beguiler: a **false** deceiuer: a subtile knaue, that hath
long practised **falshood**, an old craftie foxe.

D179. ¶ Deceiue: to beguile
D191. o Colourable deceit: **falshood.**

O80. <u>nooseled **in falsehood**</u>

☞ *Shake-speares Sonnets.* Sonnet 153

Cvpid laid by his **brand** and fell a sleepe,
A maide of *Dyans* this aduantage found,
And his loue-kindling **fire** did quickly steepe
In a could vallie-fountaine of that ground:
Which borrowd from this holie **fire** of loue,
A datelesse liuely heat still to indure,
And grew a seething bath which yet men proue,
Against strang malladies a soueraigne cure:
But at my mistres eie loues **brand** new **fired,**
The boy for triall needes would touch my brest,
I sick withall the helpe of bath desired,
And thether hied a sad distemperd guest.
  But found no cure, the bath for my helpe lies,
  Where *Cupid* got new **fire; my mistres** eye.

☞ *Shake-speares Sonnets*. Sonnet 154

The little Loue-God lying once a sleepe,
Laid by his side his heart inflaming **brand**,
Whilst many Nymphes that vou'd chast life to keep,
Came tripping by, but in her maiden hand,
The fayrest votary tooke vp that **fire**,
Which many Legions of true hearts had warm'd,
And so the Generall of hot desire,
Was sleeping by a Virgin hand disarm'd.
This **brand** she quenched in a coole Well by,
Which from loues **fire** tooke heat perpetuall,
Growing a bath and healthfull remedy,
For men diseasd, but I **my Mistrisse** thrall,
   Came there for cure and this by that I proue,
   Loues **fire** heates water, water cooles not loue.

F445. A **fire brand**, a <u>cresset light</u>, adds a firebrande

O24. **Firebrandes** of sedition: things that maintaine, and giue occasion of sedition.

H37–38. o A **firebrand** halfe burned.

The annotations do not reveal (quite to the relief of scholars, we imagine) any great secrets regarding the "dark lady," but we do see that our annotator has paid attention to *dun* as color, and a text where *tread* and *maistresse* are combined.

D1366. / ¶ **Dunne**, or darke colour

D1374. / ¶ **Duskish**, and blacke, adds duskie dunne

T343. ¶ to **Tread** vnder foote, <u>to stampe</u> down, <u>to trample</u> or go vpon, to despise
o The Usher, or **tread**er that goeth before his maister, or **maistresse**.

T326–27. / ¶ to Trample. vide **Tread**, adds conculcare

☞ *Shake-speares Sonnets*. Sonnet 130

My Mistres eyes are nothing like the Sunne,
Currall is farre more red, then her lips red,
If snow be white, why then her brests are **dun**:
If haires be wiers, black wiers grow on her head:
I haue seene Roses damaskt, red and white,

❦ { 143 } ❦

But no such Roses see I in her cheekes,
And in some perfumes is there more delight,
Then in the breath that from **my Mistres** reekes.
I loue to heare her speake, yet well I know,
That Musicke hath a farre more pleasing sound:
I graunt I neuer saw a goddesse goe,
My Mistres when shee walkes **treads** on the ground.
  And yet by heauen I thinke my loue as rare,
  As any she beli'd with false compare.

Sonnet 115 is the first of two sonnets that link *altering* with *mind*.

A325. ¶ To Alter:

A326. o **Changed: altered**

A327. o Alienation, or **altering**: withdrawing of the **minde** from the friendship or any man: delyuerance of possession to an other.

🙶 *Shake-speares Sonnets.* Sonnet 115 (5–12)
But **reckening** time, whose milliond accidents
Creepe in twixt vowes, and **change** decrees of Kings,
Tan sacred beautie, blunt the sharp'st intents,
Diuert strong **mindes** to th'course of **altring** things:
Alas why fearing of times tiranie,
Might I not then say now I loue you best,
When I was certaine ore in-certainty,
Crowning the present, doubting of the rest:

Depending upon the course of developments related to this annotated copy, we now come to the annotation that may elicit the biggest "wow" of all.

Two words: let, impediment (L333).

333 ✳ **Let, impediment: hinderaunce. Impedimen-**
tum, tij & Præpedimentum, neut. gen. Obstácu-
lum, li, neut. gen. Plaut. ἀνακοπή, ἐμπόδισμα, κώλυμα.

Let seems to have had a much different main meaning then, which now only exists for a "let" in a tennis serve. This exact meaning, as expressed in Baret, of *let* as an impediment or obstruction, a hinderance, ties in the first and last words of that famous opening phrase in Sonnet 116.

Let me not to the marriage of true **mindes**
Admit **impediments**, loue is not loue
Which **alters** when it **alteration** findes,
Or **bends** with the remouer to remoue.
O no, it is an euer fixed marke
That lookes on **tempests** and is neuer shaken;
It is the star to euery wandring **barke**,
Whose worths vnknowne, although his higth be taken.
Lou's not Times foole, though rosie lips and cheeks
Within his **bending sickles compasse** come,
Loue alters not with his breefe houres and weekes,
But beares it out euen to the edge of doome:
   If this be error and vpon me proued,
   I neuer writ, nor no man euer loued.

L325. ¶ to **Let**: to hinder
L326. o If the **Mariners** would haue **letted** me, that is, geuen me licence, libertie, or leaue, xc.

B1255. /¶ a **Brigantine**, or **barke**

T118. ¶ **Tempestuous** xc troublous weather
o A great **tempest** of wind especiallie on the sea: a trouble, or ruffling in a Commonweale.

B656. /¶ a **Bille**: <u>an hooke: a sieth: **a sickle**</u>. ...

O74. Things so old, that they <u>be out of **compasse** of our memorie</u>.

B1044. to **Bowe**, to **bende**.
B1056. o A bowing or **bending**: the **chaunge** or **altering** of the tune of the voice in pronuntiation.

The echo cluster is made richer still by the mention of *mariners* in the Baret text, and *wandering bark* in the poem. And the annotator seems fascinated with things that bend, change, and alter. Of course, the real romantic question is whether this copy of Baret could have caused a flicker in the mind between *let* and *impediment* and helped, in so doing, to trigger one of the most celebrated lines in English poetry.

Other than in Booth's *Shakespeare's Sonnets*,[110] which always gives every sense and meaning of a sonnet's word composition, we cannot find any reference to *let* being brought up as a synonym for *impediment* as Baret is using it here. But how marvelous it would be to imagine future Sonnet 116 references to Baret tied to the little circle at L333 in one particular copy purchased on eBay, with or without an authorship attribution.

The Early Comedies

OW DID Shakespeare remember so much? Anyone who has carefully studied Shakespeare's works has been led to consider this question. To some extent, Shakespeare himself must have been in awe of his own capacity for memory, whether through the penny of his own observation or through the nourishment offered by the books he read.

The annotator marks two entries that express an archaic usage appearing several times in Shakespeare on the subject of memory:

> H199. ¶ **the Harte**: not only read, but also <u>cunned</u> by harte
> C1743. /¶ to **Cunne**, or learn perfectly. a booke worthie to be cunned by heart

The annotator liked these examples; he seems to have felt the desire to "con" large portions of Baret by heart.

☛ *Love's Labour's Lost.* Boyet (5.2.89–99; Q1598, G2v)

> Vnder the coole shade of a Siccamone,
> I thought to close mine eyes some halfe an houre:
> When lo to interrupt my purposed rest,
> Toward that shade I might beholde addrest,
> The King and his companions warely,
> I stole into a neighbour thicket by,
> And ouer hard, what you shall ouer heare:
> That by and by disguis'd they will be heere.
> Their Heralde is a prettie knauish Page:
> That well **by hart hath cond** his embassage,
> Action and accent did they teach him there.

It is often speculated that in instances where Shakespeare borrows large portions of text (a most famous example is the *ye elves* speech in *Tempest* taken from Golding's *Ovid*), the correlating passages could not have been installed in his mind so precisely, so that one is led to reason that the sourcebooks were likely open on his desk at the time of composition.[111] There are similar instances from earlier in the canon with passages from Holinshed. More often than not, one imagines that with his astonishing memory he carried into the writing process countless snippets from the books he read. How else to account for the proliferation of echoes from various sourcebooks that permeate his poems and plays? As we turn to parallels found within the early comedies, we hope to identify a number of these occasions where the Baret text may have been the instigator, and our copy the precipitator.

Let us begin with an example from one of the earliest plays, where critical editions have already long cited Baret for a word usage. It involves a pairing in a speech that could justifiably be explained away as an example of minor consequence in the search for textual echoes. The word is *tents*, and the speech falls in act 2, scene 1, of *Taming of the Shrew:* "Tents were hangings, tentes, French, probably so named from the tenters upon which they were hung, tenture de tapisserie signified a suit of hangings."[112] Baret shows that a canopy was sometimes a tester, "a canopy properly that hangeth aboute beddes to keepe away gnattes, sometimes a tent or pavilion, some have used it for a testorne to hange over a bed."

Turning to our particular copy of Baret, we are pleased to find that our annotator does give attention in two places to the proposed variants: *tent, tester, canopy.*

T130. ¶ **a Tent**, or pauillion. Vide Booth, and <u>Testerne</u>
T136–37. / ¶ a Testerne to hang over a bed. Vide **Canopie.**

The marking of the *vide* associations of *tent* to *testern* to *canopie* is established in the record. Applied to *Taming of the Shrew*, Gremio's speech looks like this:

First, as you know, my house within the City
Is richly furnished with plate and gold,
Basons and ewers to laue her dainty hands:
My hangings all of tirian tapestry:
In Iuory cofers I haue stuft my crownes:
In Cypres chests my arras counterpoints,
Costly apparell, **tents,** and **Canopies,**
Fine Linnen, Turky cushions bost with pearle,
Vallens of Venice gold, in needle worke:
Pewter and brasse, and all things that belongs
To house or house-keeping: then at my farme
I haue a hundred milch-kine to the pale,
Sixe-score fat Oxen standing in my stalls,
And all things answerable to this portion.
My selfe am strooke in yeeres I must confesse,
And if I die to morrow this is hers,
If whil'st I liue she will be onely mine.

In spite of the Baret citation, one might reasonably ask if this is even relevant, worthy of entering a serious discussion, when a sourcebook, let alone authorship, is suggested to be at stake. Do things change if the rest of the speech contains throughout even stronger — far more explicit — echoes of what the annotator also marks in this copy? Included are the following:

F1211. ¶ to **Furnish**
o A **house** verie well and **richlie furnished.**

I57. ¶ an **Imbroderer**
o To worke **tapestrie,** or **hangings** with diuers colors:

D322. ¶ oh **Deintie** gentleman !
o Minionly: trimly: gaily: costely: finely, and **costly apparelled: dein-tily:** netely.

C532. / ¶ **Cypres**, a kinde of fine **lynnen** clothe, a sayle of a shippe, the skirtes of a coate

E390. / ¶ an **Ewer**

N55. ¶ **Needle**
o A garment of **needle worke**, or embrodered.

H690. ¶ an **House**
o To **stand**, or be as **cattle** in a stable, or **stall**: to be housed, as beastes are.

M356. ¶ Milke.
M360. o A **milke paile**.

A514. Adds arras

P328. ¶ **Pewter**, or tinne.
o A Pewterer; adds to trailing blank pewter

What looked like a minor echo with tents and canopies now becomes a vibrant soup of wordplay, courtesy of Baret's *Alvearie*:

☛ *Taming of the Shrew*. Gremio (2.1.342–58; FF T)
First, as you know, my **house** within the City
Is **richly furnished** with plate and gold,
Basons and **ewers** to laue her **dainty** hands:
My **hangings** all of tirian **tapestry**:
In Iuory cofers I haue stuft my crownes:
In **Cypres** chests my **arras** counterpoints,
Costly apparell, **tents**, and **Canopies**,
Fine **Linnen**, Turky cushions bost with pearle,
Vallens of Venice gold, in **needle worke**:
Pewter and brasse, and all things that belongs
To house or house-keeping: then at my farme
I haue a hundred **milch**-kine to the **pale**,
Six-score fat **Oxen standing** in my **stalls**,

And all things answerable to this portion.
My selfe am strooke in yeeres I must confesse,
And if I die to morrow this is hers,
If whil'st I liue she will be onely mine.

Put aside for a moment whether our annotator actually did write Gremio's colorful speech that takes place in act 2, scene 1, of *Taming of the Shrew*, wherein, despite being "struck in years," Gremio attempts to justify that he is worthy of Bianca by reeling off his qualifications. The suggestion, based upon the dynamic (and very specific) word associations offered by Baret that the annotator has marked and examined, is that a healthy portion of Gremio's assets were registered, so that, theoretically, if he *wanted* to piece together the speech, he was off to a fine start.

There are other speeches in the early comedies where we see similarly powerful results alongside the annotated Baret. In *Comedy of Errors*, Stephen Greenblatt cites Adriana's long speech in act 2, scene 2, for being the most telling in all of Shakespeare on the spousal relationship from the woman's perspective.[113]

🖝 *Comedy of Errors.* Adriana (2.2.122–32; FF H3)

How comes it now, my Husband, oh how comes it,
That thou art then estranged from thy selfe?
Thy selfe I call it, being strange to me:
That vndiuidable Incorporate
Am better then thy deere selfes better part.
Ah doe not teare away thy selfe from me;
For know my loue: as easie maist thou fall
A drop of water in the breaking gulfe,
And take **vnmingled** thence that drop againe
Without addition or diminishing,
As take from me thy selfe, and not me too.

U/V138. ¶ to **Unfetter**, to shake off anie thing that letteth, to **vnmingle**, or ridde one from another

U/V182–83. Adds vnmingle

Arguably the pivotal word in the entire speech, *unmingled*, is right there in our margin, after being first located in the text and underlined. On its own, what this reveals is limited. However, when we consider the annotation together with one of the longest continuous sequences of Baret text that the annotator underlines...

W209. A **faire harlot** is aptlie compared vnto **sweete** wine **mingled** with deadlie **poison.**

¶ Whoredome: adulterie: deflowring of a
virgine. Stuprum, pri,n.g.Cic. μοιχεία.Paillardise,
coupて auec femmes marieez, ou non. & Stuprôſus, ſa,
ſum. Val. μοιχείας, μιςὸς **Given to whoredome, or
adulterie.** Vide **Iduoutrie,** and **Harlot.**
**A faire harlot is aptlie compared vnto ſwœte
ſwine mingled with deadlie poiſon, &c.** Formoſa
ſcorta mulſo læthalibus venenis temperato opti-
mè comparantur:quòd adferent quidem initiô vo-
luptatem,ſed quam perpetuus dolor conſequatur.
Diogenes.

2 0 9

...and then go back to the speech in full, the depth of the revelation may change:

☞ *Comedy of Errors*. Adriana (2.2.113–49; FF H3)

    I, I, *Antipholus*, looke strange and frowne,
    Some other Mistresse hath thy **sweet** aspects:
    I am not *Adriana*, nor thy wife.
    The time was once, when thou vn-vrg'd wouldst vow,
    That neuer words were musicke to thine eare,
    That neuer obiect pleasing in thine eye,
    That neuer touch well welcome to thy hand,
    That neuer meat **sweet**-sauour'd in thy taste,
    Vnlesse I spake, or look'd, or touch'd, or caru'd to thee.
    How comes it now, my Husband, oh how comes it,
    That thou art then estranged from thy selfe?
    Thy selfe I call it, being strange to me:
    That vndiuidable Incorporate

Am better then thy deere selfes better part.
Ah doe not teare away thy selfe from me;
For know my loue: as easie maist thou fall
A drop of water in the breaking gulfe,
And take **vnmingled** thence that drop againe
Without addition or diminishing,
As take from me thy selfe, and not me too.
How deerely would it touch thee to the quicke,
Shouldst thou but heare I were licencious?
And that this body consecrate to thee,
By Ruffian Lust should be contaminate?
Wouldst thou not spit at me, and spurne at me,
And hurle the name of husband in my face,
And teare the stain'd skin of my **Harlot** brow,
And from my false hand cut the wedding ring,
And breake it with a deepe-diuorcing vow?
I know thou canst, and therefore see thou doe it.
I am possest with an **adulterate** blot,
My bloud is **mingled** with the crime of lust:
For if we two be one, and thou play false,
I doe digest the **poison** of thy flesh,
Being **strumpeted** by thy contagion:
Keepe then **faire** league and truce with thy true bed,
I liue distain'd, thou vndishonoured.

The words are dispersed and the speech is long, but *fair, mingled, harlot, poison,* and *sweet* are all in one mute annotation (located in Baret under *Whoredom: adulterie*) and are all in one speech, a significant speech. We hazard a safe guess that it is unlikely that this Baret text has ever previously been referenced in relation to Adriana's speech, and yet this cluster can hardly seem trivial if one fails to find among premodern writers a single other example of the words all appearing in the same speech. (*Strumpted* is also highlighted, as the annotator marks *harlot vide strumpet* – echoed similarly in *Richard III*.)

If this evidence in favor of Baret is not on its own compelling enough, consider Adriana's next speech of consequence, a moment later:

W155. o The **Vine** lodeth & weigheth downe the **elme**

𝕺| **𝕿𝖍𝖊 𝖁𝖎𝖓𝖊 𝖑𝖔𝖉𝖊𝖙𝖍 & 𝖜𝖊𝖎𝖌𝖍𝖊𝖙𝖍 𝖉𝖔𝖜𝖓𝖊 𝖙𝖍𝖊 𝖊𝖑𝖒𝖊.**

☞ *Comedy of Errors.* Adriana (2.2.171–83; FF H3)

> How ill agrees it with your grauitie,
> To counterfeit thus grosely with your slaue,
> Abetting him to thwart me in my moode;
> Be it my wrong, you are from me exempt,
> But wrong not that wrong with a more contempt.
> Come I will fasten on this sleeue of thine:
> Thou art an **Elme** my husband, I a **Vine:**
> Whose weaknesse married to thy stranger state,
> Makes me with thy strength to communicate:
> If ought possesse thee from me, it is drosse,
> Vsurping Iuie, Brier, or idle Mosse,
> Who all for want of pruning, with intrusion,
> Infect thy sap, and liue on thy confusion.

A cluster of annotations conceivably, enticingly, has been suggested to relate to schoolboy memories, and an echo identified in *Midsummer Night's Dream:* "Even in Ovid's Latin a schoolboy could find obscene possibilities in the *rima tenuis,* Shakespeare's 'crannie hole or chink'… and Shakespeare locates suitable double entendres in the business, like Thisbe's words to the wall, *My cherry lips have often kissed thy stones.*"[114] Having not had the opportunity to view this particular copy of Baret when they constructed this analysis, one can only imagine the authors being delighted at seeing three mute annotations around the word *chink*, and a spoken annotation in Latin, rima – the key connecting "dirty" word. Bracketed are usages for each word in Shakespeare:

C483. /¶ to **Chinke** [five], or cleaue: to open, chappe, or gape
R353. /¶ to **Riue** [six] vide **Chinke**, Chap, Cleaue

R330. /¶ a **rift**. Vide Chinke; adds rima

🖙 *Midsummer Night's Dream*. Snout (as Wall) (5.1.154–63; Q1600, H)

In this same enterlude it doth befall,
That I, one *Flute* (by name) present a wall:
And such a wall, as I would haue you thinke
That had in it a **cranied hole or chinke**:
Through which the louers, *Pyramus*, and *Thisby*,
Did whisper often, very secretly.
This **lome**, this **roughcast**, and this stone doth showe,
That I am that same **wall**: the truth is so.
And this the **cranie** is, right and sinister,
Through which the fearefull louers are to whisper.

The fabric of the speech becomes more textured (or more thrilling, depending upon one's position) when we identify the echo of another seemingly ordinary little circle echoing in an earlier scene in the play when Bottom and the actors are facing the problem of how to represent a wall:

C166. ¶ a **Cast**, or <u>throwe</u>
o The **plaistering**, parietting or **rough casting** of **walles**.

L587–88. / ¶ **Lome**, or dawbing earth mingled with chaffe, or strawe

🖙 *Midsummer Night's Dream*. Bottom (3.1.61–66; Q1600, D2)

Some man or other must present **wall**: and let him
haue some **plaster**, or som **lome**, or some **rough cast**, about
him, to signifie **wall**; or let him holde his fingers thus: and
through that **crany**, shall *Pyramus* and *Thisby* whisper.

Whether or not this is *the* copy of Baret that Shakespeare had as his own, will it take away from some of the deity aspect often endowed upon him, will some feel cheated that "rough-cast" – which appears three times in the works, each time in *Midsummer Night's Dream* – was buried in a line in Baret, a high-lighted line that seems to lodge in Shakespeare's head, much the same as did the obscene possibilities from his schooldays having to do with *rima tenuis*, cranny holes, and chinks?

In *Two Gentlemen of Verona*, we see an instance – one of many from this copy of Baret – where a cluster of words from a double mute annotation is essentially appropriated directed into the text.

☞ *Two Gentlemen of Verona*. Duke (3.1.68–79; FF C3)

No, trust me, She is peeuish, **sullen**, **froward**,
Prowd, **disobedient**, **stubborne**, lacking duty,
Neither regarding that she is my childe,
Nor fearing me, as if I were her father:
And may I say to thee, this pride of hers
(Vpon aduice) hath drawne my loue from her,
And where I thought the remnant of mine age
Should haue beene cherish'd by her child-like dutie,
I now am full resolu'd to take a wife,
And turne her out, to who will take her in:
Then let her beauty be her wedding dowre:
For me, and my possessions she esteemes not.

A fifth word highlighted in the speech, *proud,* is found in a cluster of little circles under *froward*. The headword *selfewill* is used four times: *Rape of Lucrece, Romeo and Juliet, Troilus and Cressida,* and Sonnet 6.

There are no uniquely Shakespearean lines in our margins, it has already been duly noted. But there are occasions when the annotator seems to have formulated unique Shakespeare word combinations out of this particular copy of Baret, by remembering the printed text and his corresponding spoken annotations:

D1. **Dace:** a little fish, adds menuise (minnows)
M306. Adds menues or little fish

Under the definition of *base,* we find the mute slash and the single-word underlining:

B198. / ¶ a **Base** fish.

☞ *Love's Labour's Lost*. Ferdinand (1.1.241–43; FF L2b)

> . . . There did I see that low spiri-
> ted Swaine, that **base Minow** of thy myrth,

Curiously, we find in a line from Marlowe's *Edward II*, a similar pairing – not in meaning, but certainly in sound: "The gloz-
ing head of thy **base minion** thrown." *Love's Labour's Lost* was
written not long after *Edward II*, and it is tempting to speculate
the birth of Shakespeare's "base minnow" through the combination of hearing Marlowe and this copy of Baret's *Alvearie*.

The slash mark at ***Dace****: a little fish* is also of note, as it represents a "peculiar" or one-time usage, the single occurrence coming by way of Falstaff, ever-present throughout this particular
copy of Baret:

☞ *2 Henry IV*. Falstaff (3.2.320–22; FF gg1b)

> If the young
> **Dace** be a Bayt for the old Pike, I see no reason, in the Law
> of Nature, but I may snap at him

Our annotator seems to have taken an interest in all things,
small and lowly fish included. Preceding *dace* in the dictionary
is *cuttledace*, and it, too, has a slash. Shakespeare does not use
cuttledace, but he does use *dace* as we have just seen, and he also
uses *cuttle*. Whereas the previous example was Falstaff, *cuttle* is
directed at Falstaff by Doll Tearsheet:

☞ *2 Henry IV*. Doll Tearsheet (2.4.125–26; FF g5)

> By this Wine, Ile thrust my Knife in your mouldie
> Chappes, if you play the sawcie **Cuttle** with me.

The fertile ground that is Baret's *Alvearie* has led the annotator to an exploration of minutia and archaic terminology relating
to the natural world, and he takes full advantage, marking, for
example, diseases in horses such as *fashions* and *bots*, each of which
is used in this ridiculously detailed speech on horses:

☞ *The Taming of the Shrew*. Biondello (3.2.43–61; FF T2)

Why *Petruchio* is comming, in a new hat and
an old ierkin, a paire of old breeches thrice turn'd; a
paire of bootes that haue beene candle-cases, one buck-
led, another lac'd: an olde rusty sword tane out of the
Towne Armory, with a broken hilt, and chapelesse: with
two broken points: his horse hip'd with an olde mo-
thy saddle, and stirrops of no kindred: besides possest
with the glanders, and like to mose in the chine, troubled with the Lampasse, **infected with the fashions**, full
of Windegalls, sped with Spauins, raied with the Yel-
lowes, past cure of the Fiues, starke spoyl'd with the
Staggers, **begnawne with the Bots**, Waid in the backe,
and shoulder-shotten, neere leg'd before, and with a
halfe-chekt Bitte, & a headstall of sheepes leather, which
being restrain'd to keepe him from stumbling, hath been
often burst, and now repaired with knots: one girth six
times peec'd, and a womans Crupper of velure, which
hath two letters for her name, fairely set down in studs,
and heere and there peec'd with packthred.

Shakespeare does not use *flittermouse* for "bat," but he does
once call upon *reremice* to do the job. The annotator notes:

B225./ ¶ **Batte**, flittermouse, or **reremouse**.
R251. Adds reremouse vespertilio

☞ *Midsummer Night's Dream*. Titania (2.2.1–8; Q1600, C3)

Come, now a Roundell, and a Fairy song:
Then, for the third part of a minute hence,
Some to kill cankers in the musk rose buds,
Some warre with **Reremise**, for their lethren wings,
To make my small Elues coates, and some keepe backe
The clamorous Owle, that nightly hootes and wonders
At our queint spirits: Sing me now a sleepe:
Then to your offices, and let mee rest.

These are not speeches typical of Shakespeare's contemporaries, and it is difficult to conceive of another fellow writer
showing the interest in natural history that our annotator dem-

onstrates. We shall be quite interested to see attempts at parceling out the natural history annotations in this copy of Baret relative to the usages found in the works of other premodern writers.

Twice in *Midsummer Night's Dream* we locate specific Baret citations for natural history terms where the text receives attention from the annotator.

R419. Adds rudder beast vide dewlap

In a reference to the three Shakespeare usages, Baret is consistently cited: "In an old dictionary (Baret's *Alvearie*) we find: 'the **Dewlap** of a rudder-beast, **hanging** downe **vnder** the necke.'"[115]

🖝 *Midsummer Night's Dream*. Theseus (4.1.118–23; Q1600, F4b)

> My hounds are bred out of the *Spartane* kinde:
> So flew'd, so sanded: and their heads are hung
> With eares, that sweepe away the morning deawe,
> Crooke kneed, and **deawlapt, like** *Thessalian* **Buls**:
> Slowe in pursuit; but matcht in mouth like bels,
> Each **vnder** each.

🖝 *Midsummer Night's Dream*. Puck (2.1.46–49; Q1600, B3b)

> And sometime lurke I in a gossippes bole,
> In very likenesse of a rosted crabbe,
> And when she drinkes, against her lips I bob,
> And on her withered **dewlop**, poure the ale.

The one other usage is in *Tempest*, far removed in the chronology, where the echo of the *hanging dewlap* from Baret's *Alvearie* is heard again.

🖝 *Tempest*. Gonzalo (3.3.43–46; FF B)

>   . . . when wee were Boyes
> Who would beleeue that there were Mountayneeres,
> **Dew-lapt, like Buls**, whose **throats** had **hanging** at 'em
> Wallets of flesh?

Continuing with the natural history theme and moving to botany, there are three usages of *woodbine* in the works, two in *Much Ado About Nothing* and one in *Midsummer Night's Dream:*

☞ Tatiana (4.1.41–44; Q1600, F3a–b)

So doth the **woodbine,** the sweete **Honisuckle,**
Gently entwist: the female Iuy so
Enrings the barky fingers of the Elme.
O how I loue thee! how I dote on thee!

"Baret, in his *Alvearie*, 1580, enforces the same distinction that Shakespeare thought it necessary to make...*Woodbin that beareth the Honie-suckle.*"[116]

H582. / ¶ **Honiesuckle herbe.** Vide **woodbine.**
W368. / ¶ **Woodbin** that beareth the **Honiesuckle**

We see here that both mentions of woodbine in Baret's *Alvearie* do receive attention from our annotator. Johnson indicates in a textual note the likelihood of Baret being responsible for the mistake, implied by the lines from *Midsummer Night's Dream*, but, if not, he speculates, "perhaps Shakespeare made a blunder."[117] Could the blunder have been born out of *this* copy of Baret?

Among the many birds that our annotator scrawls into the margin is the chattering bird that is a Shakespeare favorite, the chough.

☞ *Midsummer Night's Dream.* Puck (3.2.19–24; Q1600, D4)

When they him spy;
As wilde geese, that the creeping Fouler eye,
Or russet pated **choughes,** many in sort
(Rysing, and cawing, at the gunnes report)
Seuer themselues, and madly sweepe the sky:
So, at his sight, away his fellowes fly,

Holinshed speaks of the "greediness of the *corvorant* genera-tion" in his *Chronicles*, and at C1285, the annotator offers this al-ternate spelling and also underlines *cormorant* and most of the rest of the subsidiary definition:

C1285. ¶ **Cormorant,** adds a coruorant
o **Cormorant** or greedie deuourer of meat.

The opening lines of *Love's Labour's Lost:*

☛ King Ferdinand (1.1.1–7; Q1598, A2)

Let Fame, that all hunt after in their lyues,
Liue registred vpon our brazen Tombes,
And then grace vs, in the disgrace of death:
When spight of **cormorant deuouring** Time,
Thendeuour of this present breath may buy:
That honour which shall bate his sythes keene edge,
And make vs heires of all eternitie.

Richard II follows *Love's Labour's Lost* in the most recent chronologies.

☛ John of Gaunt (2.1.36–39; Q1597, C3b)

He tires betimes that spurs too fast betimes
With eagre feeding foode doth choke the feeder,
Light vanitie insatiate **cormorant**,
Consuming meanes soone praies vpon it selfe:

Additional annotations relating to *meat* have Shakespearean parallels:

V45. 0 A **victualing** house, or tauerne, where **meate** is eaten out of due season.

☛ *Two Gentlemen of Verona.* Speed (2.1.162–65; FF B6b)

I, but hearken sir: though the Cameleon Loue
can feed on the ayre, I am one that am nourish'd by my
victuals; and would faine haue **meate**: oh bee not like
your Mistresse, be moued, be moued.

M213. / ¶ a Meal, or a **repast of meate**

☛ *Taming of the Shrew.* Katherina (4.3.9–15; FF T4)

Am staru'd for **meate**, giddie for lacke of sleepe:
With oathes kept waking, and with brawling fed,
And that which spights me more then all these wants,
He does it vnder name of perfect loue:
As who should say. if I should sleepe or eate
'Twere deadly sicknesse, or else present death.
I prethee go, aud get me some **repast**,

Under the entry for *a Dere* (D456) we find the phrase *A young fallowe deere called a pricket*.

P710. Adds a pricket deer

☞ *Love's Labour's Lost*. Holfernes (4.2.52–62; Q1598, E)

I wil somthing affect the letter, for it argues facilitie.
The prayfull Princesse pearst and **prickt**
a prettie pleasing **Pricket,**
Some say a Sore, but not a sore,
till now made sore with shooting.
The Dogges did yell, put ell to Sore,
then Sorell iumps from thicket:
Or **Pricket**-sore, or els Sorell,
the people fall a hooting.
If Sore be sore, then el to Sore,
makes fiftie sores o sorell:
Of one sore I an hundred make
by adding but one more l.

Pricket is found only in this one scene in *Love's Labour's Lost*, where it is used six times as a repetitive tag throughout the dialogue between the pedant Holofernes, Sir Nathaniel, and Dull. Park Honan, in his biography *Shakespeare: A Life*,[118] makes use of recent discoveries in contemporary Stratford and Warwickshire records to note although the statutes provided severe punishments for poaching deer, these punishments were known, in practice, to be seldom enforced, and he makes the claim that "just because it involved outwitting the park-keeper, and a good deal of self control and silent skill, deer-poaching appealed to the intelligent young." He cites this early play where Shakespeare "would celebrate deer-killing and grammar-school pedantry in the same scene."

The argument for Baret as definitive sourcebook is partially based on this ongoing pattern we locate in the early works, where a disproportionate number of twists on words, and specific examples of word usage, appear in the works that are printed in Baret, often worded more closely than previously identified sources. The alignment between the annotator's copy and the Shakespeare texts only serves to advance the discussion to the question of authorship, especially as the pieces are examined in their entirely along with the personal trail left behind. Regardless to what extent our authorship proposal is defended or denied, some of the Baret usages are most intriguing on their own, and might have otherwise remained buried. The fun that Shakespeare had with Baret's synonyms is palpable. Take this example from the very early play, *Taming of the Shrew*:

F1116. /¶ to **Frette** and **fume**

☞ *Taming of the Shrew*. Hortensio (2.1.148–53; FF S6b)

> Why no, for she hath broke the Lute to me:
> I did but tell her she mistooke her **frets**,
> And bow'd her hand to teach her fingering,
> When (with a most impatient diuellish spirit)
> **Frets** call you these? (quoth she) Ile **fume** with them:
> And with that word she stroke me on the head,

We locate archaic spoken annotations in the margins found in the same play. At Y42, the annotator adds ywis just before the last headword definition in the Baret text. This is the annotator's final spoken annotation to be found in the dictionary text – and is as antiquated a Shakespearism as one could hope to find in the margin. According to C. T. Onions in his book *A Shakespeare Glossary*, *ywis* was "often spelt 'I wis' and erroneously understood as = I know."[119] The meaning is closest to "certainly" or "assuredly," and we find in Shakespeare four results, including:

☞ *Taming of the Shrew*. Katherine (1.1.61–65; FF S4)

> I'faith sir, you shall neuer neede to feare,
> **I-wis** it is not halfe way to her heart:
> But if it were, doubt not, her care should be,
> To combe your noddle with a three-legg'd stoole,
> And paint your face, and vsxe you like a foole.

In the other Shakespeare usages (*Richard III*, *Pericles*, and *Merchant of Venice*), *ywis* was also represented as *I wis* and *I'wis*.

Another spoken annotation involving an antiquated word that is found in *Taming of the Shrew* links sith with because:

S453–54. Adds sith that give gemman and because

Sith and *because* were essentially synonymous, and *sith* could be used as either adverb or preposition, but neither use is recorded in the *OED* after 1600. Shakespeare has it both ways, and once, in *Taming of the Shrew*, Shakespeare uses *sith* and *because* in the same speech:

☞ *Taming of the Shrew*. Tranio (1.1.208–15; FF S4b)

So had you neede:
In breefe Sir, **sith** it your pleasure is,
And I am tyed to be obedient,
For so your father charg'd me at our parting:
Be seruiceable to my sonne (quoth he)
Although I thinke 'twas in another sence,
I am content to bee *Lucentio*,
Because so well I loue *Lucentio*.

In *Love's Labour's Lost*, the landscape is dotted with echoes from the spoken and the mute annotations:

L74. o The **house** ringeth with **mourning** and **lamenting**.

☞ *Love's Labour's Lost*. Princess of France (5.2.799–802; Q1598, I4b)

I wilbe thine: and till that instance shutt
My wofull selfe vp in a **mourning house**,
Rayning the teares of **lamentation**,
For the remembraunce of my Fathers death.

C166. ¶ a **Cast**, or throwe
C10. o By the craft I have **cast away** twenty pounds vpon the **singing wench**.

☞ *Love's Labour's Lost*. Costard (5.2.668–70; Q1598, I3)

Faith vnlesse you play the honest *Troyan*, the poore
wench is cast away: shee'falss quicke, the childe bragges in her
bellie already: tis yours.

While it is disappointing that the wench is not singing above, let it be duly noted that *wench* and *sing* are combined in this scene in a speech by Berowne and earlier in the play in a speech by Moth. Both speeches contain a host of additional mute and spoken annotations; the speeches are little *Alvearies* unto themselves.

From the same scene, *cog* is used for cheating at dice. Note the spoken annotation and the exchange in the play:

C740. ¶ a **Cognisance**, adds to cogge or foist a die

☞ *Love's Labour's Lost* (5.2.232–35; Q1598, G4b)

BIRON: Nay then two treyes, an if you grow so nice
    Methegline, Wort, and Malmsey; well runne, **dice**:
    There's halfe a dozen sweets.
PRINCESS OF FRANCE: Seventh sweet, adieu:
    Since you can **cog**, I'll play no more with you.

Comparisons with other premodern writers will help to determine how many of these echoes are commonplace and which ones are obscure. A certain amount of guesswork goes into imagining the following two examples as being particularly obscure:

I/J105. o **Fame** going **abrode** and increasing.

☞ *Love's Labour's Lost*. Princess of France (2.1.20–24; FF L3b)

You are not ignorant all-telling **fame**
Doth noyse **abroad** *Nauar* hath made a vow,
Till painefull studie shall out-weare three yeares,
No woman may approach his silent Court:

P494. o A plentifull **wit** to **deuise**.

☞ *Love's Labour's Lost*. Armado (1.2.173–75; FF L3)

Assist me some extemporall god of Rime, for I am sure I
shall turne Sonnet. **Deuise Wit**, write Pen, for I am for
whole volumes in folio.

The additional verbal parallels with *Two Gentleman of Verona* include an instance of legal terminology (one of many selections from in and outside our margins testifying to the annotator's interest in law). *Spokesman* has been underlined at A706, the definition of *Atto*rney. Then, the annotator adds it as part of a spoken annotation above S746.

> A706. ¶ the **Attorney** or proctour on the defendantes part: a <u>spokesman</u>: a patrone: he that in trouble and perill defendeth.

> S746. ¶ a **Sponge,** adds a spokesman an atornay

🖝 *Two Gentlemen of Verona.* Speed (2.1.137; FF B6b)
> To be a **Spokes-man,** from Madam Silvia.

In addition to this "peculiar" usage of *spokesman* in *Two Gentlemen of Verona*, *attorney* is used seven times in the plays, and once in *Venus and Adonis*.

The annotator also likes insults and offers *lubber* and *lout* as options:

> D1032. /¶ a **Dolt,** adds lubber or lout

🖝 *Two Gentlemen of Verona* (2.5.40–41; FF C2)
> LAUNCE: A notable **Lubber**: as thou reportest him to bee.
> SPEED: Why, thou whorson Asse, thou mistak'st me,

🖝 *Two Gentlemen of Verona* (4.4.64–65; FF C6)
> PROTEUS: For 'tis no trusting to yond foolish **Lowt**;
> But chiefely, for thy face, and thy behavior,

From the same play we see the enticing little flips and echoes:

> R358. /¶ **Robin redbrest**

🖝 *Two Gentlemen of Verona.* Speed (2.1.17–19; FF B5)
> Marry by these speciall markes: first, you haue
> learn'd (like Sir *Protheus*) to wreath your Armes like a
> Male-content: to rellish a Loue-song, like a *Robin*-**red-**
> **breast**:

> P385. **Pinning,** adds to pin together and establ pour le bestial. pinfold

> P620. /¶ a **Pownd,** or <u>pinfold</u> for cattell.

🖝 *Two Gentlemen of Verona.* Proteus (1.1.111–13; FF B5)
> PROTEUS: You mistake; I meane the **pound, a Pinfold.**

SPEED: From a **pound** to a **pin**? **fold** it ouer and ouer,
'Tis threefold too little for carrying a letter to your louer

I/J336. ¶ a **Juggler**, he that **deceiueth**, or deludeth by Legier de main
o To **juggle**, or **dazell** the **eies**.

Juggle and *eyes* are combined twice, both times in *Comedy of Errors*.

☞ *Comedy of Errors*. Antipholus of Syracuse (1.2.97–103; FF H2)
They say this towne is full of cosenage:
As nimble **Iuglers** that **deceiue** the **eie**:
Darke working Sorcerers that change the minde:
Soule-killing Witches, that deforme the bodie:
Disguised Cheaters, prating Mountebankes;
And manie such like liberties of sinne:
If it proue so, I will be gone the sooner:

Dazzle in the mute annotation has been changed to *deceive* in the speech (used in the headword definition of *juggler* just above), but the meaning and essence of the little circle have been preserved.

The annotator adds a connective line between the printed words *Gods* and *Yield*.

2 1   ¶ **Yeaſt**, oʒ,**Gods good**. Vide **Barme**.ſpʋn̄
2 2   ¶ to **Yeeld** himſelfe to another , to become

☞ *Comedy of Errors*. Antipholus of Syracuse (3.2.39–40; FF H4)
Are you a **god**? would you create me new?
Transforme me then, and to your powre Ile **yeeld**.

The simple combinations remain present, demonstrating the ongoing desire for variation and choice.

Anchor in the text is related to measurement: *Ancher*, *A Dutch liquid measure*.

A370. / ¶ an **Ancher**, adds anchor vide measurably

In a sequentially early spoken annotation, the annotator's *vide* sends us here:

M223. ¶ **Measurably.** Vide Meanlie.

M242. o To **measure**, or iudge the <u>shoot anchor</u> of all goodnesse, by his owne **commodities**.

Measure and *commodities* are combined in this sense in *Comedy of Errors*:

☞ *Comedy of Errors*. Antipholus of Syracuse (4.3.1–11; FF H5b)

> There's not a man I meete but doth salute me
> As if I were their well acquainted friend,
> And euerie one doth call me by my name:
> Some tender monie to me, some inuite me;
> Some other giue me thankes for kindnesses;
> Some offer me **Commodities** to buy.
> Euen now a tailor cal'd me in his shop,
> And show'd me Silkes that he had bought for me,
> And therewithall tooke **measure** of my body.
> Sure these are but imaginarie wiles,
> And lapland Sorcerers inhabite here.

The annotator continually makes note of odd words (to the modern ear) and expressions found in Baret. What's curious is how often these have but a single usage in Shakespeare — a pattern that is in total keeping with Shakespeare's frequent demonstration of reaching for a certain verbal choice one time and one time only.

> F1100. My **backe freends,** or such as be out with me, & beare me a grudge, or owe me small good will.

☞ *Comedy of Errors*. Dromio of Syracuse (4.2.37–38; FF H5b)

> A **back friend**, a shoulder-clapper, one that countermãds
> The passages of allies, creekes, and narrow lands:

The play is filled with other examples from Baret following in this pattern:

> M327. / ¶ a **Mermaide**. **Siren**,

☞ *Comedy of Errors*. Antipholus of Syracuse (3.2.45–47; FF H4)

> Oh traine me not sweet **Mermaide** with thy note,
> To drowne me in thy sister floud of teares:
> Sing, **Siren**, for thy selfe, and I will dote:

> H273. o One verie **Headie** through **rage** &d furie.
> H276. o **Headie rashnesse** and affection.

F1205. o **Furiously, madly, outrageously**.

☞ *Comedy of Errors*. Antipholus of Ephesus (5.1.215–18; FF I1b)

My Liege, I am aduised what I say,
Neither disturbed with the effect of Wine,
Nor **headie-rash** prouoak'd with **raging** ire,
Albeit my wrongs might make one wiser **mad**.

B186. o A **barrayne witte**.

☞ *Comedy of Errors*. Adriana (2.1.90; FF H2b)

Are my discourses dull? **Barren** my wit,

W44. / ¶ **Wanne**. Vide **Pale**.

☞ *Comedy of Errors*. Luciana (4.4.109; FF H6b)

Aye me poore man, how **pale** and **wan** he looks.

This last example, how wan and pale it must look! But we have chosen to end this chapter with that example to emphasize that the annotator, whoever he was, does not care. There is no plan to leave a traceable path. *Wan vide pale* receives attention simply because you can say it both ways. The annotator is obsessed with saying it both ways, and Shakespeare does, too, time and time again.

The Early Histories

IMAGINE in front of you there is a copy of John Baret's *Alvearie, A Quadruple Dictionarie*, published in London in 1580, and entered into this book is the annotation otherwhiles. You find the word positioned in the dictionary at O152–53, cramped immediately to the right of the printed entry, *Otherwhere vide Place*. You contemplate otherwhiles and wonder why a previous owner felt it necessary to add it to the page.

One of the first lexicographers to study archaic usages chiefly of Shakespeare and his contemporaries was Robert Nares. In his book on the words and phrases thought to require explication – first published in 1797 – we see the following entry for *Whiles*: "Long prevalent instead of *while*; it is so written generally in the old copies of Shakespeare, and has been, in the most instances, changed to *while*, by modern editors. Used also, as well as *while*, for *until*."[120]

For his example, Nares chooses the following lines from *Twelfth Night*:

☞ Olivia (4.3.28–29; FF Z4b)

    He shall conceal it,
    Whiles you are willing it shall come to note,

The Shakespeare concordance reveals no fewer than sixty-six usages of *whiles*. But what of our annotation, otherwhiles?

Otherwhiles does not appear in Nares, but it does appear in Shakespeare. Probably only the most seasoned, old-school Shakespeare scholar would quickly from memory pull the following speech in which it appears:

    Mars his true mouing, euen as in the Heauens,
    So in the Earth, to this day is not knowne.

> Late did he shine vpon the English side:
> Now we are Victors, vpon vs he smiles.
> What Townes of any moment, but we haue?
> At pleasure here we lye, neere Orleance:
> **Otherwhiles**, the famisht English, like pale Ghosts,
> Faintly besiege vs one houre in a moneth.

The speaker is Charles, King of France, in *1 Henry VI* (1.2.1–8; FF k3), a very early play in the chronology. The word *otherwhiles* continues to spark attention (as understandably do many of the unusual single-usage or "peculiar" words), and in most critical editions of the play there is a footnote. The eighteenth-century Shakespearean Edward Capell, in his edition of Shakespeare's collected works, actually changed the text to read "The whiles."[121] But the folio reading of *otherwhiles* stands and is generally accepted, if only for a lack of certainty. In modern English, one would translate *otherwhiles* to mean "at times."

Holinshed's *Chronicles* was Shakespeare's source behind the account of the meeting between Joan and Charles, which takes place in this scene where the English besiegers of Orleans are attacked by the French. Holinshed has long been acknowledged in Shakespeare studies and is probably the most celebrated of all sourcebooks. Many times in this process, we have stopped to speculate that if more scholars had written about the possibility of Shakespeare turning with great frequency to Baret, the likelihood of our eventually acquiring the copy we have studied in such detail would have been slim to none. One of our goals is to continue to highlight throughout this study the extent to which we believe our findings firmly demonstrate that Shakespeare must have used Baret – that T. W. Baldwin was right in that it must have been "oft" – and that much more attention is warranted irrespective of the question as to authorship of the annotations in our copy. In this regard, even a blank copy would prove revealing.

But, of course, our copy is not blank, and otherwhiles is not the only annotation.

Why begin our discussion of Shakespeare's early histories with such a relatively inconsequential example? There is no reason in particular. It is printed in Baret and underlined under the entry for *leave* – in keeping with the most consistent pattern the annotator has left behind, of forming his spoken annotations from an underlined word or sequence. It is not an instance, however, like so many we have located in Shakespeare, where the word is combined with a Baret *vide* alternative, or where a sample sentence provided under a key word seems to have been lifted off the page and into the mind of an impressionable Shakespeare. And it pales next to those occurrences where one sees parallels in the text vis-à-vis one annotation combining with another unrelated annotation, or, even better, when an annotation filters over into a neighboring printed text to combine into an echo cluster that one could argue provides new insight into Shakespeare's writing process.

It is none of that. Otherwhiles is simply a word adrift, standing alone just past the bulky text's midpoint, where at one moment, long ago, our annotator made a little entry because, presumably, he just happened to like the word. Certainly it is nothing in itself to go on in terms of identifying a possible annotator. But, for us, it was an absolute delight to find, and if it were the *only* annotation in the entire book, we would already have something interesting. A curious pebble, if you will.

This can be said to describe the early process by which we discovered annotations and sought to better understand them in the context of both the Baret and the verbal parallels found in Shakespeare, whether common or uncommon.

The *Three Parts of Henry VI*, along with *Richard III*, form a tetralogy covering the period in England's history marked by the Wars of the Roses. The number of marginal additions in Baret that are reflected in these works is so great that the effort to summarize the best examples is difficult, but a necessity – at least here in our printed study. The *Henry VI* cycle of plays were successful in their day, but today are rather maligned for no longer being stageable, and for seeming all-too-far removed in quality from the dramatist who would go on to write masterpieces such as *A Midsummer Night's Dream*, *Hamlet*, and *King Lear*. One can instead choose to view them as early efforts and marvel at the fantastic bits of poetic language that are harbingers of what was to come. Consider how a straightforward spoken annotation and an unrelated mute annotation combine into a magical little twist in *2 Henry VI*:

A753. /¶ an **Awle.** adds the awne or beard of corne

R443. /¶ **made rough,** or **Rugged,** . . .

☞ *2 Henry VI*. Warwick (3.2.175–76; FF n3b)

His well proportion'd **Beard, made ruffe** and **rugged,**
Like to the Summers **Corne** by Tempest lodged:

The locating of these lines allows us to see how a young man enamored with words – and talented at using them – would have been drawn to Baret's *Alvearie* as a favorite tool. Very briefly, let us look at how four additional annotations involving *corn* land within various Shakespeare texts. Each highlighted pairing, almost predictably, is used one or two times only; it is almost as if the author has decided to limit himself in terms of reaching down into the wellspring of wordplay available in relation to corn.

C726. /¶ **Cockle** among **corne**

☞ *Love's Labour's Lost*. Berowne (4.3.359; Q1598, F3b)

Alone alone sowed **Cockell**, reapt no **Corne,**

W273. /¶ to **Winnowe,** or fan **corne**: to make wind

🐾 *2 Henry IV*. Mowbray (4.1.192–93; FF gg2b)

Wee shall be **winnowed** with so rough a winde,
That euen our **Corne** shall seeme as light as Chaffe,

B788. Blasted
o The **blasting in corne**, trees or hearbes.

7 8 8 . | ✳ The blaſting in coꝛne, treẽs oꝛ hearbes.

🐾 *King Lear*. Edgar (3.6. 36–41; Q1608, scene 11, G4)

Let vs deale iustly sleepest or wakest thou iolly shepheard,
Thy sheepe bee in the **corne**, and for one **blast** of thy minikin
mouth, thy sheepe shall take no harme, Pur the cat is gray.

T188./ ¶ to **Thresh corne**

¶ to Thꝛeſh coꝛne.
perticis frumentum. Plin.

🐾 *Titus Andronicus*. Demetrius (2.3.122–3; Q1594, D3)

Stay Madame here is more belongs to her,
First **thrash** the **corne**, then after burne the straw:

Not even the corn on the foot is ignored by our annotator – or
by Shakespeare:

C1292. o A **corne** on the **toes**: an angnaile.

🐾 *Romeo and Juliet*. Capulet (1.5.16–17; FF cc5)

Welcome Gentlemen, Ladies that haue their **toes**
Vnplagu'd with **Cornes**, will walke about with you:

Returning to the *Henry VI* plays, notice how a variant on the
word *thrash*, previously seen combined with *corn* in *Titus Andronicus*, is also used in combination with the headword in the same
definition in *3 Henry VI*. This is the only use of *flail* in the entire
concordance, and the spelling *thresh* as opposed to *thrash* has in
this instance been preserved.

F640./ ¶ a **Flaile,** or other like thing to **thresh corne**

🖙 *3 Henry VI.* Warwick (2.1.130–2; FF p)

Our Souldiers like the Night-Owles lazie flight,
Or like a lazie **Thresher** with a **Flaile,**
Fell gently downe, as if they strucke their Friends.

The second instance in Baret for *thresh corn* (T188) that has
already been cited neighbors another word with the same root
beginning: *threshold* (T204). The annotator declares interest by
adding here and at a second position (H485) the two alternate
spellings for the word. Perhaps only by coincidence, later in the
same play in which *thresher* and *flail* combine, *threshold* appears.

T188. ╱ **Thresh** corne.
T204. **Threshold,** adds vel threshall
H485. to hit his toe against the threshall, adds vel threshold

🖙 *3 Henry VI.* Richard of Gloucester (4.8.10–12; FF q1b)

The Gates made fast?
Brother, I like not this.
For many men that stumble at the **Threshold,**
Are well fore-told, that danger lurkes within.

The sense of *mowing down corn* is identified by the annotator
with a slash designation, and further into *3 Henry VI* we see the
verbal affinity emerge:

M537. ╱ ¶ to **Mowe,** or cut **downe corne,** or grasse

🖙 *3 Henry VI.* King Edward (5.7.3–4; FF Q4b)

What valiant Foe-men, like to Autumnes **Corne,**
Haue we **mow'd downe** in tops of all their pride?

Not every marked usage of *corn* in Baret leads to a Shakespearean parallel:

G103. ¶ a **Gathering** together, an heape . . . .To gather about in heapes,
or plumpes. . . .To assemble, gather, or **leuie an armie.** . . .A gathering or
inning of corne.

"Inning of corn" does not appear in Shakespeare, although
gather and *corn* do appear close together on one occasion in the
first part of *Henry VI:*

🔖 *1 Henry VI*. Joan la Pucelle (3.2.4–5; FF l2)

> Talke like the vulgar sort of Market men,
> That come to **gather** Money for their **Corne**.

Of greater intrigue is the potential echo from this same bath of words under *gather* that we see in the underlining of *leuie an armie*. This leads to a spoken annotation under L352:

> L352. / ¶ a **Leuieng of monie**, adds leuie of armie

🔖 *1 Henry VI*. Mortimer (2.5. 87–89; FF l)

> Againe, in pitty of my hard distresse,
> **Leuied an Army**, weening to redeeme,
> And haue install'd me in the Diademe:

Money, as the definition states, can also be levied. The annotator marks it with a slash. Shakespeare is satisfied with a single such usage:

🔖 *2 Henry VI*. York (3.1.60–63; FF n1b)

> And did he not, in his Protectorship,
> **Leuie** great summes of **Money** through the Realme,
> For Souldiers pay in France, and neuer sent it?
> By meanes whereof, the Townes each day reuolted.

The annotator's continual cross-referencing of his own annotations with the printed Baret texts gives more substantial hope to the person desiring to improve the argument that Shakespeare was the annotator.

In the following example, the printed Baret text combines with a spoken annotation in French; *delay* is an example of a shared English/French word that goes back to both Middle English and Old French.

> R229. / ¶ to Reprie: to **deferre** vntill an other **time**, adds donner delay

🔖 *1 Henry VI*. Reignier (3.3.16–18; FF l2)

> **Deferre** no **time, delayes** haue dangerous ends,
> Enter and cry, the Dolphin, presently,
> And then doe execution on the Watch.

At C259, the annotator adds a cawdle vide felon. This is a cross-reference to the Baret definition of *fellon* (F382), which includes the figurative phrase on how to deal with felons: *with a* **cawdle** *of hempseede chopt halter wise, and so at the least to vomit them out, to cut them off from the quiet societie of Citizens, or honest Christians.*

The annotator cares enough to add this definition under *hempe* (H388), *an hempen halter, or rope*, but there is no room to do so immediately next to the key word, so he employs a mouse-foot, directing attention to the bottom margin, where he adds hemp-seed chopt halter vide felon.

The *OED* gives *cawdle* as a spelling variant of *caudle*, a warm drink consisting of thin gruel, mixed with wine or ale, sweetened and spiced, given chiefly to sick people, especially women in childbed. *Caudle* can also be used as a verb: to administer a caudle. Shakespeare uses *caudle* three times (in both senses), and *felon* five times, but never in conjunction. However, it may be significant that both words appear as uttered by Jack Cade in act 4 of *2 Henry VI* (note *cawdle of hempseede* from Baret).

☞ *2 Henry VI.* Jack Cade (4.2.66–72; FF n52)
Be braue then, for your Captaine is Braue, and
Vowes Reformation. There shall be in England, seuen
halfe peny Loaues sold for a peny: the three hoop'd pot,
shall haue ten hoopes, and I wil make it **Fellony** to drink
small Beere. All the Realme shall be in Common, and in
Cheapside shall my Palfrey go to grasse: and when I am
King, as King I will be.

☞ *2 Henry VI* (4.7.82–88; FF o1)
SAY: These cheekes are pale for watching for your good
CADE: Giue him a box o'th' eare, and that wil make 'em
       red againe.
SAY: Long sitting to determine poore mens causes,
       Hath made me full of sicknesse and diseases.
CADE: Ye shall haue a **hempen Candle** then, & the help
       of hatchet.

(Note: *caudle* is always misprinted *candle* in the First Folio.)

The plot thickens when we see that at C505, *to **Choppe***, the annotator adds chopt. Cade speaks of "the help of hatchet." Hatchet is a small axe used to chop; so that is another possible piece to the puzzle of Cade's line. Chopt, by itself, does not seem like much, but our annotator has not just underlined it, he's gone to the trouble of entering it as an additional marginal word. This same spelling is preserved in a Falstaff usage:

🖝 *2 Henry IV*. Falstaff (3.2.271–72; FF ggb)

> O, give me always a little, lean, old, **chopt**, bald shot.

We previously noted that in Sonnet 57, *chopt* appears in the 1609 quarto.

The spoken annotation at B196, bartring exchange, is an inversion from the printed text at E427 where the annotator has added an underlining (*exchange bartring*). *Exchange* is very commonly used in Shakespeare. *Barter*, however, only occurs once — echoed in combination with *exchange* in *1 Henry VI*.

🖝 *1 Henry VI*. Talbot (1.6.5–9; FF k4b)

> The Earle of Bedford had a Prisoner,
> Call'd the braue Lord *Ponton de Santrayle*,
> For him was I **exchang'd**, and ransom'd.
> But with a baser man of Armes by farre,
> Once in contempt they would haue **barter'd** me:

In this instance, two words are involved, and these examples by themselves may seem trivial, or not, depending on how the rest of the evidence registers with the scholar or curious layperson. We have seen regular examples where many more words are in play, and the ability to write off the confluence of occurrences as coincidental becomes increasingly arduous. Take the third marked sentence our annotator highlights under *laugh*:

> L138–39. o To slay his **laughing**, by putting a **napkin** to his mouth.

Shakespeare not only makes use of the words in this sentence but brings back *scorn*, not used here in the Baret sentence above but found within the same cluster, and, for good measure, adds *taunts*, which echoes the notion of being laughed at – also found marked at yet another position in the same cluster.

☞ *3 Henry VI.* Messenger (2.1.50–67; FF o6b)

Enuironed he was with many foes,
And stood against them, as the hope of Troy
Against the Greekes, that would haue entred Troy.
But *Hercules* himselfe must yeeld to oddes:
And many stroakes, though with a little Axe,
Hewes downe and fells the hardest-tymber'd Oake.
By many hands your Father was subdu'd,
But onely slaught'red by the irefull Arme
Of vn-relenting *Clifford*, and the Queene:
Who crown'd the gracious Duke in high despight,
Laugh'd in his face: and when with griefe he wept,
The ruthlesse Queene gaue him, to dry his Cheekes,
A **Napkin**, steeped in the harmelesse blood
Of sweet young *Rutland*, by rough *Clifford* **slaine**:
And after many **scornes**, many foule **taunts**,
They tooke his Head, and on the Gates of Yorke
They set the same, and there it doth remaine,
The saddest spectacle that ere I view'd.

At T10, a **Talie**, or **Score**. Vide **score**, the annotator adds the French une taille a marquer. *Tally* and *tallies* are each used once, each time with *score*. We previously considered the usage in Sonnet 122. Here it is in *2 Henry VI:*

☞ *2 Henry VI.* Jack Cade (4.7.30–35; FF o1)

Thou hast most traitorously corrupted the youth of
the Realme, in erecting a Grammar Schoole: and whereas, before, our Fore-fathers had no other Bookes but the
Score and the **Tally**, thou hast caused printing to be us'd,
and, contrary to the King, his Crowne and Dignity, thou
hast built a Paper-Mill.

But it does not end there. Just above T49, on the very next leaf, we find *A Tallage. Vide Taxe. and Custome.* It is followed immediately within the column by the spoken annotation subsidie.

A *tallage* is a form of tax going back to the late medieval period. Shakespeare does not use *tallage*, but we do have two *subsidy* uses – both from this very early *Henry VI* cycle of plays.

▶ *3 Henry VI.* Henry VI (4.10.6–15; FF q2)

> That's not my feare, my meed hath got me fame:
> I haue not stopt mine eares to their demands,
> Nor posted off their suites with slow delayes,
> My pittie hath beene balme to heale their wounds,
> My mildnesse hath allay'd their swelling griefes,
> My mercie dry'd their water-flowing teares.
> I haue not been desirous of their wealth,
> Nor much opprest them with great **Subsidies**,
> Nor forward of reuenge, though they much err'd.
> Then why should they loue *Edward* more then me?

The second instance immediately precedes the Jack Cade speech already cited where he uses *the Score and the Tally:*

▶ *2 Henry VI.* Messenger (4.7.18–21; FF n6b)

> My Lord, a prize, a prize! heeres the Lord Say,
> which sold the Townes in France. He that made vs pay
> one and twenty Fifteenes, and one shilling to the pound,
> the last **Subsidie**.

This is a fine illustration of the proximity usage of which we expect many more instances to be revealed as, collectively, scholars pay heed to Baret for the first time. These combinations of "proximity successes" may be especially encouraging to those interested in supporting our hypothesis, over many of the single-usage examples where Shakespeare's contemporaries may fare equally well.

Extracting and reducing individual examples is likely to be part of the critique from those wishing to eliminate the notion that they bear relevance. Isolated examples such as "light horse-men," "wedding torch," and "handicraftsmen" could fall into this category:

L445–46. o Light horsemen.

🖙 *1 Henry VI*. Talbot (4.2.42–43; FF l4)

He Fables not, I heare the enemie:
Out some **light Horsemen**, and peruse their Wings.

T243. a **Torch**. A <u>cresset</u> light.
T244. A torch: a <u>wedding</u>: a song at a wedding.

🖙 *1 Henry VI*. Joan la Pucelle (3.3.9–11; FF l2)

Behold, this is the happy **Wedding Torch**,
That ioyneth Roan vnto her Countreymen,
But burning fatall to the *Talbonites*.

C1536. o An **handie craftsman**, a man of an occupation.

🖙 *2 Henry VI*. Bevis (First Rebel) (4.2.11–12; FF n5b)

O miserable Age: Virtue is not regarded in **Handy-crafts men.**

Less common early modern words may be more compelling:

P67. The **braine pan.**

🖙 *2 Henry VI*. Jack Cade (4.9.11–12; FF o2)

my **braine-pan** had bene cleft with a brown Bill;

Or examples where three or four words are involved:

A693. / ¶ **Attaynted** seemeth to come from the french woorde *Teinct*
A694. o **Attaynture, or bloud stained** and **corrupted.**

🖙 *1 Henry VI*. Joan la Pucelle (5.6.36–53; FF m)

First let me tell you whom you haue condemn'd;
Not me, begotten of a Shepheard Swaine,
But issued from the Progeny of Kings.
Vertuous and Holy, chosen from aboue,
By inspiration of Celestiall Grace,
To worke exceeding myracles on earth.
I neuer had to do with wicked Spirits.
But you that are polluted with your lustes,

Stain'd with the guiltlesse **blood** of Innocents,
Corrupt and **tainted** with a thousand Vices:
Because you want the grace that others haue,
You iudge it straight a thing impossible
To compasse Wonders, but by helpe of diuels.
No misconceyued, *Ione* of *Aire* hath beene
A Virgin from her tender infancie,
Chaste, and immaculate in very thought,
Whose Maiden-blood thus rigorously effus'd,
Will cry for Vengeance, at the Gates of Heauen.

When it comes to word selection, sometimes it is a case of either/or:

W65. / ¶ **Warie, circumspect, wise**. Vide Circumspect, and **Heede**.

🖙 *2 Henry VI*. Cardinal Beaufort (1.1.154–55; FF m3)
Looke to it Lords, let not his smoothing words
Bewitch your hearts, be **wise** and **circumspect**.

🖙 *1 Henry VI*. Joan la Pucelle (3.2.1–3; FF l2)
These are the Citie Gates, the Gates of Roan,
Through which our Pollicy must make a breach.
Take **heed**, be **wary** how you place your words,

Often it is a case of both:

W298. / ¶ to **Wither**, to **corrupt**
W299. o **Corruption: withering**:

🖙 *3 Henry VI*. Richard Gloucester (3.2.155–58; FF p4b)
Shee did **corrupt** frayle Nature with some Bribe,
To shrinke mine Arme vp like a **wither'd** Shrub,
To make an enuious Mountaine on my Back,
Where sits Deformitie to mocke my Body;

I/J76. **Impudently**, without **shame**.
o An **impudent and shameless** face.

🖙 *3 Henry VI*. Queen Margaret (3.3.156; FF p5b)
Peace **impudent, and shamelesse** Warwicke,

I/J11. / ¶ to **Jarre**, or **discord**

🐟 *1 Henry VI.* Exeter (4.1.187–88; FF l4)

> But howsoere, no simple man that sees
> This **iarring discord** of Nobilitie,

Sometimes the sentence finds an altered expression directly in a speech:

G577. / ¶ I sleepe **Groueling, or upon my face**

🐟 *2 Henry VI.* Eleanor (1.2.7–10; FF m3b)

> What seest thou there? King *Henries* Diadem,
> Inchac'd with all the Honors of the world?
> If so, Gaze on, and **grouell on thy face,**
> Vntill thy head be circled with the same.

Other times, it is an archaic word used heavily by Shakespeare in a certain period of composition but less so elsewhere. Here is a suitable example:

B612. / ¶ to **Bewray:** to vtter: to disclose: to appeach: to destroy: to betray

This is an archaic word meaning "inadvertently revealing." Shakespeare loved it, using it three times in *Henry VI* plays and other early works, but also in *Coriolanus* – in the speech of Coriolanus's mother after which he *Holds her by the hand silent* in the stage direction.

We have observed that many of the words marked and manipulated by the annotator later resulted in *OED* citations for Shakespeare.

B844. o A worme that sucketh bludde, an horseleach, a bluddesucker.

Shakespeare uses *blood-sucker*, *blood-suckers*, and *blood-sucking*, each one time only and in three of the four earliest history plays. His use of *blood-sucking* is cited as the first usage in the *OED*.

🐟 *3 Henry VI.* Lady Gray (4. 5. 21–22; FF q)

> I, I, for this I draw in many a teare,
> And stop the rising of **blood-sucking** sighes,

➤ *2 Henry VI.* Warwick (3. 2.226; FF n4)

Pernicious **blood-sucker** of sleeping men.

➤ *Richard III.* Lord Grey (3.3.5; Q1597 G)

A knot you are of damned **bloodsuckers**

Shakespeare is also cited in the *OED* for a use, in Sonnet 66, of *disabled:* "to render incapable of action or use by physical injury or bodily infirmity." But it was more commonly used at the time in the broader sense of a disability to speak or express oneself, as in the usage in *1 Henry VI.*

➤ *1 Henry VI.* Suffolk (5.5.16–27; FF l6b)

Oh stay: I haue no power to let her passe,
My hand would free her, but my heart sayes no.
As playes the Sunne vpon the glassie streames,
Twinkling another counterfetted beame,
So seemes this gorgeous beauty to mine eyes.
Faine would I woe her, yet I dare not speake:
Ile call for Pen and Inke, and write my minde:
Fye *De la Pole*, **disable** not thy selfe:
Hast not a Tongue? Is she not heere?
Wilt thou be daunted at a Womans sight?
I: Beauties Princely Maiesty is such,
'Confounds the tongue, and makes the senses rough.

It is interesting that in both of the above usages of *disable*, *tongue* is involved, even in the case of the physical "limp" disability. We also have *tongue-tied* as a mute annotation – it is underlined in the introduction to the letter "E" section. It is especially important in the scene in *1 Henry VI* "when Plantagenet proposes that, since no one will speak out, any man who believes him to be right should pluck a white rose – and as he speaks he plucks a white rose."[122]

Given that we are of the opinion that the concatenation of all that we see in this copy of what would have been – and obviously was – a perfect book for Shakespeare – not to mention the

perfect title and the perfect copy of the title to go unnoticed –
we admit to proceeding into the public eye with a fair amount
of confidence. But we cannot emphasize enough how the beauty
of the usages has sustained us during the long hours of research
and discovery even when individual usages may or may not be
explained away as trivial. Who else, in thinking of *wings*, has so
perfectly used two words, each a single time, and each marked in
this copy of Baret?

F635. / ¶ **Flagging**, or hanging downward

☞ *1 Henry VI*. Captain (4.1.1–7; FF n5)

> The gaudy blabbing and remorsefull day,
> Is crept into the bosome of the Sea:
> And now loud houling Wolues arouse the Iades
> That dragge the Tragicke melancholy night:
> Who with their drowsie, slow, and **flagging** wings,
> Cleape dead-mens graues, and from their misty Iawes,
> Breath foule contagious darknesse in the ayre:

L515. / ¶ **Lithernesse**
o Most **lither** and slouthfull idlenesse.

☞ *1 Henry VI*. Talbot (4.7.20–22; FF i5)

> Coupled in bonds of perpetuitie,
> Two *Talbots*, winged through the **lither** Skie,
> In thy despight shall scape Mortalitie.

We have provided a selection of examples from the *Henry VI*
cycle that are spread out over three separate plays. In moving
from some of the least staged plays in our time to one of the most
staged (*Richard III*), let us look at the effects of a heavy concentration in a single act. The profusion of spoken and mute annotations is carried through the whole of the opening act of *Richard III*,
where the parallels are immediately evident in one of the most
famous starts in Shakespeare, Richard's own "Now is the winter
of our discontent."

Within the wide body of this speech, consider the following segment:

☞ *Richard III.* Richard Gloucester (1.1.10–23; Q1597, A2)

> And now in steed of mounting barbed steedes,
> To fright the soules of fearefull aduersaries.
> He capers nimbly in a **Ladies chamber**,
> To the **lasciuious pleasing** of a loue.
> But I that am not shapte for sportiue trickes,
> Nor made to court an amorous looking glasse,
> I that am rudely stampt and want loues maiesty,
> To strut before a **wanton** ambling Nymph:
> I that am curtaild of this faire **proportion**,
> Cheated of **feature** by dissembling nature,
> Deformd, vnfinisht, sent before my time
> Into this breathing world scarce halfe made vp,
> And that so **lamely** and **vnfashionable**,
> That dogs barke at me as I **halt** by them:

The highlighted words associated with spoken and mute annotations occur at various points throughout the printed text. For example, the annotator has underlined *give myselfe to lasciuious and wanton pleasure.*

A little circle is placed alongside The *feature and fashion*, or the *proportion and figure of the whole bodie.* There is no shortage of self-references made by Richard to the figure and proportion of his body and its wretched deformity. Embedded in the opening speech of the play is a combination that we see also on three other occasions in Shakespeare, the association of *halt* with *lame.* Several annotations, a mix of mute and spoken, attest to the annotator's interest:

> H256. Hauke & Hauche, adds hault or limpe **and** claudicare
> L63. ○ To hault, or be lame.
> L486. / ¶ to Limpe, or hault. Claudicare.

Halt and *limp* are not seen combined in *Richard III*, but do combine twice elsewhere (*Timon; Taming of the Shrew*).

Finally, one of our annotator's marginal biblical quotations is echoed in this opening speech. The spoken annotation chambering/couchis/rom. 13 is taken from *Romans 13*, and we find there, in the various translations of the period, *chambering wantonness*, a word pairing lifted from the memory of the biblical text and into the opening speech in question. *The Taming of the Shrew* contains the only other instance of these two words combined. Perhaps coincidentally, it is likewise at a beginning, falling in the prologue.

An additional profusion of echoes from annotations lands a few scenes later:

⤏ *Richard III*. Duke of Clarence (1.4.24–33; Q1597, C4b)

> Me thought, I sawe a thousand fearefull wracks,
> Ten thousand men, that fishes **gnaw'd** vpon,
> **Wedges of gold**, great anchors, heapes of pearle,
> Inestimable stones, vnualued Iewels,
> Some lay in **dead mens sculs**, and in those holes,
> Where eies did once inhabite, there were crept
> As twere in **scorne** of eies reflecting gems,
> Which woed the slimy bottome of the deepe,
> And **mockt** the dead **bones** that lay scattered by.

Twice the annotator's eye and pen have fallen on the link between *wedges* and *gold*, as is demonstrated in the underlined text: _wedges of gold_ – a precise recording of which we see in the extracted speech of the Duke of Clarence.

A parallel with the annotator's spoken French annotation, skulle tete l'homme mort, is also found, along with the underlined _gnawing bone_. *Gnaw* and *bone* are combined on only one other occasion (*Othello*). The much more frequently encountered combination of *scorn* and *mock* is treated in multiple mute annotations, including:

M432–33. o **To scorne or mocke.**

A few lines later the Duke of Clarence invokes the phrase "yield the ghost," printed in Baret with a simple slash and variant spelling addition provided by the annotator (*1 Henry VI* also contains "yield the ghost").

Y23. to die to **yeeld** vp the goast, adds vel ghost

☞ *Richard III.* Duke of Clarence (1.4.36–41; FF r2b)

Me thought I had, and often did I striue
To yeeld the Ghost: but still the enuious Flood
Stop'd in my soule, and would not let it forth
To find the empty, vast, and wand'ring ayre:
But smother'd it within my panting bulke,
Who almost burst, to belch it in the Sea.

But the character that dominates the opening act, and, of course, the entire play with his persona is the one in which we see the greatest number of echoes when combing the lines and considering the Baret. At their most convincing, they appear to be what Stanley Wells has distinguished as "mechanical" lifts.[123] Consider the remarkable likeness of this printed Baret text, which the annotator marks with a slash, with lines uttered by Richard in act 1, scene 2:

S748. / ¶ I will **Sporne, or strike thee with my foote.** Vide **Spurne.**

☞ *Richard III.* Richard (1.2.39–42; Q1597, A4b)

Vnmanerd dog, stand thou when I command,
Aduance thy halbert higher than my brest,
Or by Saint Paul Ile **strike thee to my foote,**
And **spurne** vpon thee begger for thy boldnes.

Notice how Shakespeare even retrieves the word following the *vide* to complete the thought. Not many lines later, the sense of *cheer* and *sun* that we see printed and marked in Baret is echoed.

S10. The **Sunne** cheereth and putteth away the sadnesse, or heauinesse of mans mind.

☞ *Richard III*. Richard (1.2. 127–30; Q1597, B1b–B2)

These eies could neuer indure sweet beauties wrack,
You should not blemish them if I stood by:
As all the world is **cheered** by the **sonne**,
So I by that, it is my day, my life.

A combination that seems more unusual, at least to the modern ear, is the pairing of *hate* with *dissembling*. In Shakespeare, we find them paired only in *Richard III*. Baret aligns the terms in the following sentence, marked by our annotator's slash:

G609. / ¶ privie **Grudge**, or **hatred** with **dissembling** of countenance

☞ *Richard III*. Richard (1.2.218–25; Q1597, B3)

What I that kild her husband and his father,
To take her in her hearts extreamest hate:
With curses in her mouth, teares in her eies,
The bleeding witnesse of her **hatred** by,
Hauing God, her conscience, and these bars against me:
And I nothing to backe my suite at all,
But the plaine Diuell and **dissembling** lookes,
And yet to win her all the world to nothing. Hah

Another instance of multiple annotations being echoed by the future King Richard III in act 1 comes at the start of scene 3.

C740. ¶ **Cognisance**, adds to cogge or foist a die
F654. o With **faire** and pleasant wordes, **flatteringly**.

☞ *Richard III*. Richard (1.3.47–49; Q1597, B4)

Because I cannot **flatter** and speake **faire**,
Smile in mens faces, smoothe, dcceiue and **cog**,
Ducke with french nods and apish courtesie,

The First Folio text substituted *looke* for *speake* in line 47, "Because I cannot **flatter**, and looke **faire**," and that change has been retained in modern editions. But the Baret mute little circle annotation is found to mark *With faire and pleasant wordes, flatteringly*, and so it would appear that Shakespeare intended Richard to declare himself incapable to "speak" flatteringly "with faire and pleasant wordes." And this is also another example of word order reversal from the Baret line (*fair, flatter*) into the actor's speech (*flatter, fair*).

R. W. Dent's book *Shakespeare's Proverbial Language* takes as its point of departure the "Shakespeare Index" in Morris Palmer Tilley's *Dictionary of the Proverbs in England in the Sixteenth and Seventeenth Centuries* (1950). It is essentially composed of appendixes of proverbs, arranged alphabetically. A number of the cited examples, either with precise wording or in the same spirit, are found printed and highlighted in our copy of Baret, providing us numerous means for comparison. One of the most interesting of these comparisons leads us to the opening act of *Richard III*.

The first entry in Dent's appendix A, under the letter "J":

JACK. "Jack would be a Gentleman."[124]

The proverb is said by Dent to date to circa 1500, and he cites its single use in Shakespeare, by the notorious Richard, in act 1, scene 3:

☞ *Richard III*. Gloucester (1.3.70–73; Q1597, B4b)
> I cannot tell, the world is growen so bad
> That wrens make pray, where Eagles dare not pearch,
> Since euery **Iacke became a Gentleman**:
> Theres many a gentle person made a Iacke.

In Baret's *Alvearie*, this proverb is printed, and notably closer to Shakespeare's wording than to the example cited by Dent. It reads, and is underlined in our copy:

> A530. A remo ad tribunal Plaut. A Prouerbe aptly to be applied to those which are aduanced from a base state vnto an high dignitie: and as our vulgare phrase is, <u>Jack is become a Gentleman.</u>

A previously mentioned spoken annotation, the archaic term ywis, appears in act 1, scene 3:

🖙 *Richard III*. Gloucester (1.3.100–3; Q1597, C)

> What mary may she, marry with a King,
> A batchelor, a handsome **stripling** too.
> **Iwis** your Grandam had a worser match.

Another word present in the same speech is *stripling*, found and marked in Baret under *lad:*

L34. / ¶ a Lad, or yong **stripling**

Although the soon-to-be Richard III (Duke of Gloucester in act 1) may have the lion's share of allusions between the realized play and the marked Baret, he receives throughout act 1 (and the whole play, for that matter) ample company. The following annotations are presented chronologically as they appear:

K87. Knappith, adds he knappeth the speare in sunder

"He breaketh the bow and knappeth the spear in sunder" is from Psalm 46.

🖙 *Richard III*. Mowbray (1.1.170–3; Q1597, A4b)

> I am disgraste, impeacht, and baffuld here
> Pierst to the soule with Slaunders venomd **speare**,
> The which no balme can cure but his heart bloud
> Which breathde this poyson.

F98. / ¶ a **Falchon**: a wood knife, or sword

🖙 *Richard III*. Lady Anne (1.2.93–95; Q1597, B1b)

> In thy foule throat thou liest, Queene Margaret saw
> Thy bloudy **faulchion** smoking in his bloud,
> The which thou once didst bend against her brest,
> But that thy brothers beat aside the point.

S305. o **shamefast**.

🖙 *Richard III*. Second Murderer (1.4.134–36; Q1597, D1b)

> It is a blushing **shamefast** spirit, that mutinies In a mans bosome:

N137. o **Taunting**, or nipping **scoffes: bitter taunts.**

☞ *Richard III*. Queen Elizabeth (1.3.103–10; Q1597, C)

> My Lo: of Glocester, I haue too long borne
> Your blunt vpbraidings and your **bitter scoffes,**
> By heauen I will acquaint his Maiesty
> With those grose **taunts** I often haue endured:
> I had rather be a countrey seruant maid,
> Then a great Queene with this condition,
> To be thus **taunted**, scorned, and baited at:
> *Enter Queen Margaret.*
> Small ioy haue I in being Englands Queene.

S835. / ¶ his **haire** Stareth, or **standeth on end**

☞ *Richard III*. Lord Hastings (1.3.302; Q1597, C3b)

> My **haire** doth **stand on end** to heare her curses.

There are many more, and the whole of the annotations found echoing throughout act 1 of *Richard III* fully suggests a familiarity with the language offered by Baret and made available in print. It is easy to see why T. W. Baldwin would have been so certain that Shakespeare could not have retained his Baret so well had he not "turned many a time and oft [to it] for his varied synonyms."

The vastly more problematic issue of authorship regarding the annotations in our copy cannot in short shrift be properly defended or rejected. All we can do here in this one instance is assert that the strength and number of the annotations echoed in the first act of *Richard III* seems categorically out of line with what one would imagine in a case of randomly selected texts.

The echoes, naturally, do not cease at the end of act 1. In fact, they are present in an exchange between King Edward IV and Lord Rivers at the very opening of act 2, calling up a mute annotation previously referenced in relation with act 1:

G609. / ¶ priuie **Grudge,** or **hatred** with **dissembling** of countenance

☞ *Richard III*. King Edward (2.1.8; Q1597, D3b)

> **Dissemble** not your **hatred,** sweare your loue.

❈ 192 ❈

☞ *Richard III*. Lord Rivers (2.1.9–10; Q1597, D3b)

> By heauen, my heart is purgd from **grudging hate**,
> And with my hand I seale my true hearts loue.

The beauty of this seemingly straightforward exchange, from our perspective, is how it demonstrates Shakespeare's love for twisting the language, and the joy he finds in dabbling with words. Much in the same way that Baret suggests in one of the introductory texts the importance of the *vide* in utilizing the *Alvearie*, so we see with Shakespeare the significance to him of bringing the *vide* technique into his characters, as he delights in changing the pace, altering the sounds, and striving to play the role of the master poet, always attempting to get it just right. This need to get it "just right" may in part explain the disproportionate number of single-word usages in Shakespeare. It never ceases to amaze both those who have spent the most amount of time with the works, and people who know them only very generally, that of the over 31,000 words to appear in the concordance, over 14,000 of these are used but a single time. Included in this mass is the word *nonage*.[125] It is found in the second act of *Richard III* and marked twice in Baret at two separate locations:

> N170. / ¶ the **Nonage**, or minoritie of a ward

> G417. o A **governour** of a kingdome in the **nonage** of a Prince.

☞ *Richard III*. Second Citizen (2.3.12–15; Q1597, E3)

> In him there is a hope of gouernement,
> That in his **nonage** counsell vnder him,
> And in his full and ripened yeres himselfe,
> No doubt shall then, and till then **gouerne** well.

Richard II is the first play in Shakespeare's second tetralogy of history plays that includes the two parts of *Henry IV* and concludes with *Henry V*. These plays are laden with proverbial language found underlined in our Baret, language that becomes more interesting still when we see additional verbal similarities between the text and further annotations.

A157. This Prouerbe is vsed when prowde men be beaten, and as we say, <u>pride will haue a fall</u>.

The only Shakespearean use of this well-known proverb takes place in the final scene of *Richard II*, and with numerous mute annotations to boot, including the doubling up of a sense of falling, and lots of horse imagery, headlined by a "stumbling jade."

☞ *Richard II*. Richard (5.5.84–94; Q1597, I4b)

So proud that Bullingbroke was on his backe:
That **Iade** hath eate bread from my royall hand,
This hand hath made him proud with clapping him:
Would he not **stumble**, would he not fall downe
Since pride must haue a fal; and breake the necke,
Of that **prond man**, that did vsurpe his backe?
Forgiuenes **horse** why do I raile on thee?
Since thou created to be awed by man,
Wast borne to beare; I was not made a **horse**,
And yet I **beare a burthen** like an asse,
Spurrde, galld, and tirde by iauncing Bullingbrooke.

I/J4. / ¶ **Iade**, or naughty **horse**
o A **stumbling iade**.

S782. ¶ a Spurre. To spurre an horse
o To **spurregall**.

B282. ¶ To **Beare**: to carrie a weight or **burden**
B297. o A porter, a carier or **bearer of burdens**.

Two lesser-known proverbs appear in a bath of words at T101 under *to tell*:

T101. ¶ to **Tell**, to shewe, or declare

T111. An apt and fitte Prouerbe for those <u>vnprofitable Drones</u>, which neither haue a will nor disposition, in endeuoring to seeke <u>anie comoditie, or profite for their countrie</u>. *Ovid* calleth such **Catterpillers of a Commonwealth,** ... **An vnprofitable lumpe of claie**.

The latter underlining we find in *1 Henry VI:* "Vnable to support this **Lumpe of Clay**" (Mortimer, 2.5.14; FF K6b). The middle underlining is in *Richard II*, alongside the wording found in an unrelated mute annotation:

W139. / ¶ to **Weede**, or **plucke** out <u>weedes</u>

☞ *Richard II*. Bolingbroke (2.3.165–66; Q1597, E3b)

The **caterpillers of the commonwealth**,
Which I haue sworne to **weede** and **plucke** away.

One of Shakespeare's favorite words is *pluck*. He uses it an as-
tounding 109 times — counting variations, 170 times.

F1213. o Old **age** maketh **furrowes** in the forehead.

☞ *Richard II*. Gaunt (1.3.219–25; Q1597, C)

But not a minute King that thou canst giue,
Shorten my daies thou canst with sullen sorrowe,
And **plucke** nights from me, but not lend a morrow:
Thou canst helpe time to **furrow** me with **age**,
But stoppe no wrinckle in his pilgrimage:
Thy word is currant with him for my death,
But dead, thy kingdome cannot buy my breath.

An example of a period spelling occurring in a quarto appears
under *violet*:

U/V89. Violet, adds a violl

☞ *Richard II*. Mowbray (1.3.154–59; Q1597, B4)

My natiue English, now I must forgo,
And now my tongues vse is to me, no more
Than an vnstringed **violl** or a harpe,
Or like a cunning instrument casde vp,
Or, being open, put into his hands
That knowes no touch to tune the harmonie:

Violl as the stringed instrument is used once, but *Richard II* also
has the same spelling *Violl* for the modern *vial* (see *Richard II*, act 1,
scene 2, in U/V89 above). *Vial* is also used in *Hamlet* (once), *Romeo
and Juliet* (twice), and Sonnet 6 (once). In *Hamlet* and Sonnet 6 it is
spelled *viall*, and in *Romeo and Juliet*, spelled *violl* both times.

At T327 we find the following:

/ ¶ to **Trample**. Vide **Tread**, adds conculcare

¶ to **Trample**. vide **Tread.** *Conculare*

The method for using the *Dictionarie* as suggested in Baret at the beginning stresses the importance of not just the core word, but the *vide*, and that is precisely how our annotator has gone about making his marks. The annotator adds a slash to the head-word and adds the Latin conculare, "to tread with force." *Trample* and *tread* combine in a speech one time only, and it is a famous speech indeed, and one that contains additional verbal affinities with Baret annotations.

☞ *Richard II*. King Richard (3.3.142–74; Q1597, G1b–G2)

> What must the King do now? must he submit?
> The King shall do it: must he be deposde?
> The king shall be contented: must he loose
> The name of King? a Gods name let it go:
> Ile giue my iewels for a set of Beades:
> My gorgeous pallace for a hermitage:
> My gay apparel for an **almesmans** gowne:
> My figurde goblets for a dish of wood:
> My scepter for a Palmers walking staffe:
> My subiects for a paire of carued Saintes,
> And my large kingdome for a little graue,
> A little little graue, an obscure graue,
> Or Ile be buried in the **Kings hie way**,
> Some way of common trade, where subiects feete
> May hourely **trample** on their soueraignes head;
> For on my heart they **treade** now whilst I liue:
> And buried once, why not vpon my head?
> Aumerle thou weepst (my tender-hearted coosin)
> Weele make fowle weather with despised teares;
> Our sighs and they shall lodge the summer corne,
> And make a dearth in this reuolting land:
> Or shall we play the **wantons** with our woes,
> And make some pretty match with sheading teares,
> As thus to drop them still vpon one place,
> Till they haue fretted vs a paire of graues

Within the earth, and therein laide; there lies
Two kinsmen digd their graues with weeping eies:
Would not this ill do well? well well I see,
I talke but idlely, and you laugh at me.
Most mightie Prince my Lord Northumberland,
What saies king Bullingbroke, will his maiestie
Giue Richard leaue to liue till Richard dye,
You make a leg and Bullingbroke saies I.

The whole notion of Shakespeare utilizing associated word pairings and clusters together, sometimes in a single speech, other times as a course of pattern throughout a scene or act, never ceases to delight us in the ongoing process of exploring and comparing the language of Baret, and specifically the selected language of Baret with personal additions on the part of our annotator, with what is found in Shakespeare. In Richard II's speech above, we note also the phrase "the king's high way" printed and marked in Baret under *incroach*.

I110. / ¶ to **Incroch** the **kinges high way**

Also present is the combination of *wanton* with *almsman*, as found in these neighboring little circles:

A306. o **Wantonly**: with wanton intisings and alluring.
A317. o **An almoner** or giuer of almesse.

If we are correct in having identified the annotator, we wonder if the proximity of these two little circles could be responsible for some seedling in Shakespeare's mind that had him also using a variant on *almoner* and *wanton* in this same speech. The argument would be that he studied this book so carefully that such incidents may have occurred simply as a result of the way the information in Baret was stored in his one-of-a-kind mind.

Abraham Fleming's lovely final paragraph in Baret, a paragraph that precedes the index, reads as follows: "These observations being most beneficiall, let none thinke it a **tedious travell** to transverse from leafe to leafe, or from number to number, though multiplied by millians to find out the certaintie of that which is doubtful. For if the gathering of this whole booke, being of a reasonable bigness, was comberous, the writing **wearisome**, the examining painful, and yet all by diligence conquered: why should the reading, which requireth less labour, be carelessly neglected."

Fleming is bringing Baret's lexical philosophy to a close, and we are swayed by how closely our annotator, whatever annotator one wishes to imagine – be he to be declared nameless or otherwise – has with diligence conquered, overcoming what must have been, even for a great lover of language, tedious travel. We imagine it as no accident that the first marking in the book is an underlining of the word *lightsome* on the title page, and one of the last markings in the book is the word *wearisome*. From first page to last, from *lightsome* to *wearisome*, then, there is perhaps a subtle, but conscious, looking back by the annotator himself at his extended effort.

The words *tedious travel* that appear in this ending paragraph with *wearisome* are echoed in act 2, scene 3, of *Richard II* – and contained in the same speech is one of only three instances of *wearisome*.

☞ *Richard II.* Northumberland (2.3.2–18; Q1597, E1–E1b)

Beleeue me noble Lord,
I am a stranger here in Glocestershire,
These high wild hils and rough vneuen waies,
Drawes out our miles and makes them **wearisome**,
And yet your faire discourse hath beene as sugar,
Making the hard way sweete and delectable,
But I bethinke me what a weary way
From Rauenspurgh to Cotshall will be found,
In Rosse and Willoughby wanting your company,
Which I protest hath very much beguild,
The **tediousnesse** and processe of my **trauell**:
But theirs is sweetned with the hope to haue

The present benefit which I possesse,
And hope to ioy is little lesse in ioye,
Then hope enioyed: by this the weary Lords
Shall make their way seeme short as mine hath done,
By sight of what I haue, your noble company.

There are numerous occasions in the works when *travel* combines with a form of either *weary* or *tedious*, but *tedious* and *travel* merge only in this speech, and it so happens that we find *wearisome* there as well – perhaps coincidence, perhaps part of a pattern of echoes that reveals something more profound.

Falstaff

IT IS generally recognized that Shakespeare's depiction of Falstaff stands apart on the Elizabethan stage. We have come to realize that our two primary annotation types, often working together, can help contribute to an understanding of how Shakespeare assembled Falstaff's rich vocabulary of insult, exaggeration, desperation, and drink, in the service of wit. Baret's dictionary specializes in archaic word usages as well as uncommon combinations of common English words, and we encounter many instances that illustrate how a Baret usage may have helped to define Falstaff's character, either with a Falstaffian phrase itself or through the adversarial or descriptive speech of his companions. From these examples, we have selected a sampling to highlight this section on Falstaff.

In act 4, scene 3, of *2 Henry IV*, Falstaff delivers what Stephen Greenblatt has called an "ecstatic rhapsody to the virtues of sherry-sack."[126] Thomas North's translation of Plutarch is herein cited as a potential source for this passionate speech on Falstaff's beloved Spanish wine, "a mock-scientific analysis of its power to inflame both wit and courage."[127]

North's Plutarch first appeared in 1579, a year prior to the publication of the second edition of Baret's *Alvearie*. The printer was Thomas Vautrollier. Richard Field assumed the rights to the book following Vautrollier's death, and reprinted a second edition in 1595. It has long been recognized as one of the most important Shakespeare sourcebooks, and the following passage has been noted in relation to the Falstaff speech in question: "Alcibiades being **puffed vp with vanitie** and opinion of himselfe, as oft as Socrates tooke him in hande, was made fast and firme againe by his good perswasions."

The pervasive influence of North's Plutarch[128] on Shakespeare is not in dispute, but it is clear that when he wrote *this* particular Falstaff speech, Shakespeare's memory had turned not to his Plutarch but to his Baret. Look at how much more closely a marked text in our copy mimics the wording in Falstaff's speech:

P831. / ¶ a **Puffe**
o **Puffed vp with great** hope **and courage.**

☞ *2 Henry IV.* Falstaff (4.2.107–9; FF gg3b)
    . . . the Heart; who **great**, and **pufft**
vp with his Retinue, doth any Deed of **Courage**: and this
Valour comes of Sherris.

To reinforce the relevance here of Baret's language over North's, consider a further portion of Falstaff's same speech and the amazing verbal parallel – this time, a triple word usage from another single little circle the annotator has marked:

H756. o An **husbandman**: he that **tilleth** and **manureth** the ground.

☞ *2 Henry IV.* Falstaff (4.2.113–17; FF gg3b)
                    . . . Hereof
comes it, that Prince *Harry* is valiant: for the cold blood
hee did naturally inherite of his Father, hee hath, like
leane, stirrill, and bare Land, **manured, husbanded, and
tyll'd**, with excellent endeauour of drinking good, and
good store of fertile Sherris,

A small group of spoken annotations in a lower margin relating to the word *faine* yields an opportunity to do more than simply compare contemporary source texts. Here we are able to follow the annotator's thought process from one section of his dictionary to another, and, on this particular path, discover a fabulous little bit of Falstaff.

> F28. To faine in singing: to speake in a small faining voice, also to speake, or sing, as one could hardly vtter his voice.

The annotator's mouse-foot directs attention from the examples provided in the printed text to five separate spoken annotations that are written in the bottom margin:

> We are faine to use
> nous sommes....(?)
> prefat in letteratum A.
> I was faine to seeke
> My lips will be faine when I sing unto thee Ps. 71.21

The first thing that the mouse-foot tells us is that the annotator wishes to say more on the matter. It is a classic example of following the instructions suggested by the preface. The third annotation, prefat in letteratum A, is telling us "aforementioned in letter 'A,'" i.e., directing us to turn back to the paragraph of preliminary remarks for the letter "A" section. It is there that we see two mute underlinings with great separation: _shuffled togither by ignorance_ and _are faine to_. (Shuffled, if we recall, ends up being added in the margin under the letter "S" – one of three distinct instances where the annotator imitates the capital calligraphic "S" as it is printed in Baret.)

The first of these paragraphs under the letter "A" begins:

> **A.** Is the name of the fyrst letter on the crosrowe among the Hebrues, Greekes and Latines. But whether this common vsuall order in our Alphabet or crosrowe, was so placed and appoynted by counsell and learning from the beginning, or was <u>shuffled</u> togither by ignorance: neyther am I able, nor at this time haue I sufficient leysure to determine.

The paragraph finishes (some 200 words later):

> . . . So likewise of I. and V. which shapes for lacke of letters wee <u>are faine</u> to vse both for Uowels and Consonants. But for this you shall finde more in the letter C.

This returns us to the question of the preambles. Baret is credited with pioneering the study of comparative alphabet development in various languages, based on the phonetics, as shown in his essays prefacing each letter of the alphabet.[129] As we have previously identified, our annotator is enamored with these prefaces, and, in going through them carefully, notes many of the words and phrases with his mute underlinings that frequently will then turn into alphabetically inserted spoken annotations. In the preface to letter "A," the underlined elements, _shuffled_ and _are faine_, combine to suggest Falstaff:

☞ *Merry Wives of Windsor*. Falstaff (2.2.23–29; FF D5)

I, I, I my selfe sometimes, leauing the feare of heauen on
the left hand, and hiding mine honor in my necessity, **am
faine to shufflle**: to hedge, and to lurch, and yet, you
Rogue, will en-sconce your raggs; your Cat-a-Moun-
taine-lookes, your red-lattice phrases, and your bold-
beating-oathes, vnder the shelter of your honor? you
will not doe it? you?

To have the seemingly unrelated and far removed underlined elements of *faine* and *shuffle*, extracted from a lengthy profusion of words in the prefatory bath that precedes the entries in letter "A," combine to form a bit of Shakespeare may not seem so exceptional, as Shakespeare wrote many words. But that they combine to form a phrase that is singular to Shakespeare – and uttered by Falstaff – raises the question of whether this is to be argued as another mere coincidence, or whether we are observing a subliminal memory echo that took place for Shakespeare when in the midst of composition.

The Falstaff plays, as we will call them (not traditionally grouped in this sense), contain some of the best examples of proximity usages that suggest challenges for future efforts to explain them away as coincidental.

Let us now look at two of these, one from *1 Henry IV* and another from *2 Henry IV*.

Beginning with the later play, at C438, the definition of *che-sill*, we note a mute slash mark annotation. The spoken annotation arbor in Affrica is squeezed into the column space above this definition, and we also have here a seldom used mute marking that creates a connecting line between a *manuscript* word or phrase written into the text with a *printed* word or phrase.

The connective line clearly goes from the last letter of *celtis* to the first letter of *arbor*. In Pliny's *Natural History*, a book Shakespeare is known to have consulted, the African lotus tree is also called by the Latin *celtis* in Libya, hence arbor in Affrica.

In the Baret definition *celtis* also is Latin for *chesill* (chisel) or tool. Shakespeare makes extraordinary use of both of these meanings of *celtis*. *Chesill* has only one Shakespeare usage, in the last climactic scene of *The Winter's Tale* (act 5, scene 3), where Paulina gradually discloses to Leontes that the wife he had been told had died was actually still alive. She first appears to Leontes in the form of a statue, but he soon has reason to suspect that she is not:

🐾 *The Winter's Tale*. Leontes (5.3.75–79; FF Cc1b)

Doe, Paulina:
For this Affliction has a taste as sweet
As any Cordiall comfort. Still, me thinkes,
There is an ayre comes from her. What fine **Chizzell**
Could euer yet cut breath? Let no man mock me,
For I will kisse her.

The *OED* cites Shakespeare for this first usage of *chisel* as a sculptor's tool. But, referring to Pliny's mention of *celtis*, which he noted here as a spoken annotation, arbor in Affrica, he had already used both **arbor** and **Africa** in the same scene in *2 Henry IV* (act 5, scene 3). It is the only usage of **Africa** in his works. (*Afric* is used four times, once adjectively, and three times for "Africa," but in each case the last syllable appears to have been dropped for the metric. *African* is also used once, as an inhabitant of Africa.)

SHALLOW: Nay, you shall see mine Orchard: where, in an
    Arbor we will eate a last yeares Pippin of my owne graf-
    fing, with a dish of Carrawayes, and so forth (Come Co-
    sin *Silence*, and then to bed.

FALSTAFF: Why now you haue done me right.

SILENCE: Do me right, and dub me Knight, *Samingo*. Is't
    not so?

FALSTAFF: 'Tis so.

SILENCE: Is't so? Why then say an old man can do somwhat.

DAUY: If it please your Worshippe, there's one *Pistoll*
    come from the Court with newes.

FALSTAFF: From the Court? Let him come in.
    Enter Pistoll
    How now Pistoll?

PISTOLL: Sir *Iohn*, 'saue you sir.

FALSTAFF: What winde blew you hither, Pistoll?

PISTOLL: Not the ill winde which blowes none to good,
    sweet Knight: Thou art now one of the greatest men in
    the Realme.

SILENCE: Indeed, I thinke he bee, but Goodman *Puffe* of
    Barson.

PISTOLL: Puffe? puffe in thy teeth, most recreant Coward
    base. Sir *Iohn*, I am thy Pistoll, and thy Friend: helter
    skelter haue I rode to thee, and tydings do I bring, and
    luckie ioyes, and golden Times, and happie Newes of
    price.

FALSTAFF: I prethee now deliuer them, like a man of this
    World.

PISTOLL: A footra for the World, and Worldlings base,
    I speake of **Affrica**, and Golden ioyes.

FALSTAFF: O base Assyrian Knight, what is thy newes?
    Let King *Couitha* know the truth thereof.

Whereas this scene is set in an arbor in Justice Shallow's orchard, the use of arbor, as written in our spoken annotation, is in
no way exceptional or even noteworthy. However, why Africa
in Pistol's reply to Falstaff? Were there no other places that could

evoke "golden joys"? Of course there were, and, though we cannot know how long before the composing of *2 Henry IV* this annotation was written into the *Alvearie*, his own annotation, arbor in Affrica, must have been brought up in the author's mind as soon as *arbor* entered the scene, and so *Africa* was already there when such a place needed to be named.

The example from *1 Henry IV* is no less involved. At P834, *puke*, our annotator adds the seemingly inconsequential spoken annotation in French, tanne.

Baret receives a citation, almost always referenced, for this peculiar Shakespearean usage of *puke*, equated with the Latin *pullus*, a color between russet and black. The French index printed at the back of the *Alvearie* notes that *tanne* is found at B1400. This falls under the heading *brown* (*brown: brown, tawny, swart, tanne*). Turning there, we see the familiar case of the annotator having cross-referenced a spoken annotation with the printed text, and adding a follow-up spoken annotation. A lack of available space requires that a mute annotation be placed there as a marker (in this case, a + sign), a marker that is then repeated in the lower margin to provide a unifying connector. It is there that we see the curious added phrase as fat as browne.

The first thing we can surmise is that our annotator has paid attention to *puke* as color, the same sense in which Hal uses it in act 2, scene 4 (*puking* as a verb, with an *OED* citation, in the "Seven Stages of Man" speech, is an altogether different usage). In Hal's very next line, he speaks the word *brown*.

🖛 *1 Henry IV* (2.4.68–75; FF c3b)

PRINCE: Wilt thou rob this Leatherne Ierkin, Christall
    button, Not-pated, Agat ring, **Puke stocking**, Caddice
    garter, Smooth tongue, Spanish pouch.
FRANCIS: O Lord sir, who do you meane?
PRINCE: Why then your **browne** Bastard is your onely
    drinke: for looke you Francis, your white Canuas doub-
    let will sulley. In Barbary sir, it cannot come to so much.

As inconsequential as this may appear, later in the very same
scene we find the more striking element, a single-line description
of Falstaff's fatness (2.4.517; FF c5):

CARRIER: **As fat as** Butter

The phrase *as fat as* is used twice only in Shakespeare (the second
occurrence in *The Winter's Tale* ("As fat as tame things"). We were
unable to locate as fat as browne anywhere in English literature,
and "as fat as butter" is unique to Shakespeare. Maintaining that
it is mere coincidence to find the phrase *as fat as* here in the same
scene as the word *puke*, when our annotator has clearly linked the
word to the added marginal phrase, would, at the very least, seem
improbable were it not for the enormousness of the stakes.

As an added bonus, two additional spoken annotations involving fatness also land in this act, one from the same scene and one
from an earlier scene:

T421. Adds a tunbelly or gorbellie

🖛 *1 Henry IV* (2.2.84–89; FF c2b)

TRAVELERS: O, we are vndone, both we and oures for euer.
FALSTAFF: Hang ye **gorbellied** knaues, are you vndone? No
    ye Fat Chuffes, I would your store were heere. On Ba-
    cons, on, what ye knaues? Yong men must liue, you are
    Grand Iurors, are ye? Wee'l jure ye i'faith.

🖛 *1 Henry IV*. Prince Hal (2.5.453; FF c5)

…a **Tunne** of Man is thy Companion:

(This is the same scene that includes *puke-stocking / brown bastard / as fat as butter.*)

The compulsive need that the annotator has to express the same thing in multiple ways is exposed time and time again — and, at minimum, he shares this need with Shakespeare, if they are argued to not be one and the same. *Gorebellied* is equated with "having an extended stomach," and *tunbelly*, very obscure, is not found in Shakespeare, although *tun* can certainly be thought of as an able substitute.

Poking fun at Falstaff's fatness is a sport in which Hal engages with great enthusiasm, followed by even greater irritability. The annotator plays around with clothes and the like, demonstrating his own appreciation for girth.

M348. / ¶ the **Midriffe**, which divideth the heart and lightes of man, or beastes, from the other bowels

☞ *1 Henry IV* (3.3.150–56; FF f2)

FALSTAFF: The King himselfe is to bee feared as the Lyon:
Do'st thou thinke Ile feare thee, as I feare thy Father? nay
if I do, let my **Girdle** breake.
PRINCE: O, if it should. how would thy guttes fall about
thy knees. But sirra: There's no roome for Faith, Truth,
nor Honesty, in this bosome of thine: it is all fill'd vppe
with Guttes and **Midriffe**.

This usage of *midriff* also has an *OED* citation.

G223. ¶ to **Gird**, or compasse about
G225. o   The girdlestead.
G226. o   A girding, or girdle.
G227. o   A girdler.
G229. o   A sword girdle: also a trusse.

☞ *2 Henry IV*. Falstaff (1.2.6; FF g1b)

Men of all sorts take a pride to **gird** at mee:

The annotator has numerous cross-pollinating spoken and mute annotations relating to the hose or stocks that were part of traditional costume in Elizabethan theater: aprons, breeches, doublets, overstocks, galligaskins, gird, girdlestead, trusse, etc. The interest demonstrates a fascination, even an obsession, with all the possibilities of variation, and the annotator seems especially tuned in to oversized forms of the garments.

D1105. ¶ a **Doublet**, or a breast plate. Vide Dublet

Here the annotator adds a seldom used straight slash to mark the definition for emphasis, but abandons the thought: " ----- " as it appears in the margin. The printed text reads: *would you haue your lined doublet, or your trusse and wast doublet?* Note the annotator's mute attention to *trusse*. The underlining and attention lead to a spoken annotation:

T402. ¶ **Trusse**, adds trusse doublet pourpoint doublet

(Note: *Mon pourpoint est trop large* is printed in Baret under *doublet*.)

☞ *1 Henry IV*. Falstaff (2.5.164–68; FF c4)

I am a Rogue, if I were not at halfe Sword with
a dozen of them two houres together. I haue scaped by
miracle. I am eight times thrust through the **Doublet**,
foure through the Hose, my Buckler cut through and
through, my Sword hackt like a Hand-saw, *ecce signum*.

The jokes follow Falstaff around, with a bounty appearing in act 1, scene 2, of *2 Henry IV*. The scene opens with a stage direction:

Enter sir Iohn alone, with his page bearing his sword and buckler. (Q1600, B)

This contains a verbal parallel with Baret:

P16. a **Page**, or <u>custrell bearing</u> his maisters **shield**, or **buckler**.

This mute annotation paves the way for the later insertion of custrell bearing vide page at C1813.

Could this cross-examination of the Baret text have resulted in the simple little stage direction? Much of the scene is a riot, as

Falstaff, who wishes his means greater and his waist slenderer, famously recognizes not only that he is witty by himself, "but the cause that wit is in other men."

When it comes to the food that helped make him so, there are echoes in Baret to support the habit. You can imagine the sense of visual excitement suggested by the following set of spoken annotations when peeking into the following exchange in *Merry Wives*:

> F1137. ¶ a **Fritter,** or pancake, adds vide froize
> F1140. / ¶ a **Froize,** or, pancake, adds vide fritter
> P61. Adds pancake
> P548. Adds pol garmentes, vide frize

☞ *Merry Wives of Windsor* (5.5.134–44; FF E6b)

> FALSTAFF: Haue I laid my braine in the Sun, and dri'de it,
> that it wants matter to preuent so grosse ore-reaching as
> this? Am I ridden with a Welch Goate too? Shal I haue
> a Coxcombe of **Frize**? Tis time I were choak'd with a
> peece of toasted Cheese.
> EUANS: Seese is not good to giue putter; your belly is al
> putter.
> FALSTAFF: Seese, and Putter? Haue I liu'd to stand at the
> taunt of one that makes **Fritters** of English? This is e-
> nough to be the decay of lust and late-walking through
> the Realme.

Immediately preceding the spoken annotations relating to a pancake, froize and fritter, we can see how the annotator has massaged the text around *frize*, the coarse cloth referred to by Falstaff.

> F1132. ¶ a **Frize,** or rough garment, that souldiers used, a mantle to cast on a bed, a carpet to laie on a table, a dagswaine

> F1133. ¶ Pol garmentes **frized** onely on the one side: it is sometime taken for veluet

The proximity of the spoken annotations froize and fritter with *frize*, followed by Falstaff's peculiar usage of *fritter*, and his one of only two Shakespearean usages of *frize* (the other is found in *Othello*), strikes us as unlikely to be coincidental, given the totality of what is found in this copy of Baret, and especially as one Falstaff usage *immediately* follows the other. On the subject of *frize*, itself, we account for no fewer than five instances where the annotator provides a spoken annotation:

P548. Adds pol garments vide frize and friz et d'ung roste
B1099. Adds braide crispans frize
C1472. ¶ Courled, adds frize
D5. Adds a dagswaine vide frize…papys mante

The annotation frize alongside *courled* is especially intriguing when it is observed that a subsidiary definition has been marked by the annotator that includes a reference to *belly* —

o The **bellie** crouleth, or courleth.

— and that *belly* is used by Evans between Falstaff's lines wherein we find both *fritters* and *frize*.

Returning to froize, which were traditionally bacon pancakes, we note that all usages of *bacon* are in Falstaff plays. Two of the four Shakespeare usages of *bacon* belong to Falstaff himself, and one of the carriers speaks precisely of "a gammon of bacon," also marked in Baret:

G47. / ¶ a **Gammon**, or flich of **bacon**

☞ *1 Henry IV*. Second Carrier (2.1.24–25; FF e2)
I haue **a Gammon of Bacon**, and two razes of
Ginger, to be deliuered as farre as Charing-crosse.

The temptation for both our annotator and Shakespeare, whether they are one and the same or not, is all about choice. Why choose one when you can have more than one?

B1365. / ¶ a **Brooch**, or, **ouch**

☞ *2 Henry IV*. Falstaff (2.4.47; FF g4b)
Your **Brooches**, Pearles, and **Owches**:

Of course we would like it better if the annotator had inserted *pearl* in between the two printed words, but you can't have everything. Our contention is not that Shakespeare would have had this book open while writing Falstaff speeches, or that he annotated the book with Falstaff in mind. The greater likelihood, as we imagine it, is that over the youthful course of vigorously annotating this book, he found it the perfect enabler to further his innate appreciation for words and to allow them to filter into a memory bank unlike any other.

There are a significant number of words that the annotator marks or applies to his Baret for which there is but a singular usage in Shakespeare and that happens to be either by Falstaff or directed at Falstaff, typically at his expense. These words include *bowcase, quilt, bigness, currie, barrow, pick-thanks*, and *shot-free (scotfree)*, and where there are multiple senses of the word, the usage almost always takes the form of what is printed and marked in Baret. Among non-Falstaff usages, but in this set of plays, we find *pismire, wain*, and *bavin*. Then there are numerous "rare words" used between three and seven times; these include *bootie, bombast*, and *baboon*. *Baboon* is especially interesting because the marginal addition is a babion – archaic for "baboon," which equated to "dimwit" in Elizabethan slang.

There are disputed lines in Falstaff that may eventually be considered less disputable as a result of what is found in this copy of Baret. Consider the reading of "…your red-lattice phrases, and your bold-beating-oathes" in *Merry Wives* (Falstaff, 2.2.28–29; FF D5). Scholars have often been puzzled by the word *bold-beating*, even going so far as to call it nonsensical. Sir Thomas Hanmer altered this to read "your **bull-baiting** oaths."[130]

B1478. / ¶ **Bulbaitinges**

Halliwell brings attention to a later surviving manuscript that reads "blunderbust oaths."[131] In his *Notes to Shakespeare*, Samuel Johnson thought the phrase should be "a beating oath," meaning "a thwacking or swinging thing."[132] Finally, a Mr. Barron Field suggests in his paper, "Conjectures on some Obscure and Corrupt Passages of Shakspeare," that *bull-baiting* is correct.[133] The *OED* cites the first appearance as the 1580 Baret. Then it is cited as used in 1583, 1652, 1711, and as late as 1802. For Shakespeare's *bold-beating*, the *OED* cites only that Shakespeare usage but adds: "Apparently a confusion of *bold-faced* and *brow-beating*." Time will tell whether the simple mute slash helps to sway future editors. It may be worth noting that this same speech contains *faine to shuffle*.

Other verbal similarities crossing over from Baret into Falstaff include the little circle under *weep*:

W145. o **Weeping**, or **teares trickling** downe.

🖝 *1 Henry IV*. Falstaff (2.5.395; FF c4b)

Weepe not, sweet Queene, for **trickling teares** are vaine.

And there is the added phrase like an aspen leafe at A607, which is first echoed in *Titus Andronicus* and later in *2 Henry IV*:

🖝 *2 Henry IV*. Hostess Quickly (2.4.105–6; FF g5)

Doe I? yea, in very truth doe I, if it were **an Aspen
Leafe**: I cannot abide Swaggerers.

The following lines from Hotspur contain the spoken annotation axletree, added after A757, the last Baret entry under "A," as well as a twist on the underlined segment from Baret at C1571: *to **grinde the teeth***.

🖝 *1 Henry IV*. Hotspur (3.1.125–31; FF e6)

I had rather be a Kitten, and cry mew,
Then one of these same Meeter Ballad-mongers:
I had rather heare a Brazen Candlestick turn'd,
Or a **dry Wheele grate** on the **Axle-tree**,
And that would set my **teeth** nothing an edge,
Nothing so much, as mincing Poetrie;
'Tis like the forc't gate of a shuffling Nagge.

We also have *cartwheele* as a spoken annotation:

C152. A cart with two wheeles, adds a cartwheele

Although this word does not appear in the speech, it can be argued to be instrumental in tying the elements together. An old proverb states, "A dry cart-wheel cries the loudest"[134] – meaning it makes a lot of noise or, to put it another way, is the source of excruciating sound. May it have been from personal memory that Shakespeare recalled such a sound that would set his teeth on edge?

At I/J152, the annotator adds inholder hoste – a seemingly banal example, in that *host* is used widely. But there is one time when it is connected with *innkeeper*:

☞ *1 Henry IV*. Falstaff (4.2.45–47; FF f3)

and the Shirt, to say the truth,
stolne from my **Host** of S. Albones, or the Red-Nose
Inne-keeper of Dauintry.

Baret frequently receives multiple citations for the alphabetical neighbors *plight of bodie* and *plumme line*:

P503. / ¶ he **Plight** her his faith & trueth, adds plight of bodie v. like

☞ *1 Henry IV*. Falstaff (3.3.1–7; FF f1b)

Bardolph, am I not falne away vilely, since this
last action? doe I not bate? doe I not dwindle? Why
my skinne hangs about me like an like an olde Ladies loose
Gowne: I am withered like an olde Apple *John*. Well,
Ile repent, and that suddenly, while I am in some **liking**:
I shall be out of heart shortly, and then I shall have no
strength to repent.

This is a cross-reference to the Baret definition L475, a set of subsidiary usages for *like*, one of which is: *If one be in better plight of bodie, or better liking*. *Plight of bodie* is also underlined in the text according to form.

Singer and Symmons cite this Baret definition to explain the Shakespeare usage: "*Liking* is *condition, plight of body*: 'If one be in better plight of bodie, or better *liking*.' *Baret*. L. 435."[135]

The second example is with *plum-line*.

P530. Plummet, adds plumme line

🖛 *Merry Wives of Windsor*. Falstaff (5.5.161–2; FF E6b)

Ignorance it selfe is a **plummet** ore me, use me as you will.

There continues to be much debate as to whether Falstaff here intended the use of plummet to imply a *plummet-line* or *plum-line*.[136]

One of the oddest words in all of Shakespeare has to be *chewet*, used by Hal when he pleads with Falstaff to "pipe down" during an address from his father in *1 Henry IV*: "Peace, **chewet**, peace."

Chewed and *chammed* are cross-referenced in the text, and our annotator writes chewet in the margin:

C310. Adds chammed vide chewet

Nares notes the odd single usage of *chewet*, and says: "Henry is reproving him for unseasonable chattering."[137] *Chattering* actually appears in Baret two pages further in from the *chewet* annotation, and receives by our annotator a little circle. Nares continues: "It is more likely that he alluded to the chattering bird, called in French chouette, by us chough, or jack-daw." Chough is a spoken annotation just beyond that. It seems as though Nares has nailed it.

Of chattering birds, the one that is most familiar to our contemporary minds is, of course, the parrot. The annotator of our Baret has also considered this bird:

P569–70. / ¶ a **Popiniaie** vide Parrat, adds papegay

The *popinjay* in medieval English was another word for *parrot*, and this is how Baret defines it. Later, the popinjay term would signify not a parrot but a woodpecker. Shakespeare is likely responsible, with his usage from *1 Henry IV*, of giving it its somewhat obscure, current meaning: a foppish person given to vain, pretentious displays and empty chatter. *Parrot* is used nine times in Shakespeare. The French *papagay* (found printed in the text under *parrot*) is additionally added by our annotator as a spoken annotation alongside a slash at the headword *popinjay*. The single appearance of *popinjay* in the works falls in *1 Henry IV*, where Hotspur uses it in a very long speech:

☞ *1 Henry IV*. Hotspur (1.3.27–51; Q1598, Biib)

> My liege, I did denie no prisoners,
> But I remember when the fight was done,
> When I was drie with rage, and extreame toile,
> Breathles and faint, leaning vpon my sword,
> Came there a certaine Lord, neat and trimly drest,
> Fresh as a bridegroome, and his chin new rept,
> Shewd like a stubble land at haruest home,
> He was perfumed like a Milliner,
> And twixt his finger and his thumbe he helde
> A pouncet boxe, which euer and anon
> He gaue his nose, and tookt away againe,
> Who therewith angry, when it next came there
> Tooke it in snuffe, and still hee smild and talkt:
> And as the souldiours bore dead bodies by,
> He cald them vntaught knaues, vnmanerlie,
> To bring a slouenly vnhandsome coarse
> Betwixt the winde and his nobilitie:
> With many holly-day and ladie termes
> He questioned me, amongst the rest demanded
> My prisoners in your Maiesties behalfe.
> I then, all **smarting** with my **wounds** being cold,
> To be so **pestred** with a **Popingay**,
> Out of my griefe and my impacience
> Answerd neglectingly,

S531. / ¶ the **Smarting** paine of a sore, or bile

Shakespeare, no doubt, understood it to be a different word for parrot, a different-sounding term he could apply to represent this queer bird that annoyingly and inanely mimics human speech. But what is especially curious from the standpoint of our study of Baret is the appearance of the word *pester* in the same line. Some small number of pages earlier in the "P"s, alongside *pester*, we see the same slash-type annotation, and an underlining of the text *to cloie.*

P325. / ¶ to **Pester, to cloie**

Is it possible that the connection between these two words, the origin of this alliteration, has now been discovered within these two slashes close together in our Baret? While it may be impossible to prove such a thing, along with many other proximity coincidences, it represents a tantalizing dream.

Shakespeare relishes each word, *cloy* and *pester*, and the annotator thinks enough of them to add them as a spoken annotation, after marking the mute annotations:

C652–53. Adds to cloie to pester

The words *cloy* and *pester* receive a Baret citation in *Macbeth* ("to pester to cloie in the *Alvearie*"), and relates the meanings to an overloaded stomach. Other usages in Shakespeare bear this out:

☛ *Richard II.* Bolingbroke (1.3.259; FF c2)
Or **cloy** the **hungry** edge of **appetite**,

Both Shakespeare and the annotator seem obsessed with appetite, especially an overloaded appetite. The annotator adds hawtie stomach at H261. (Consider here a line from Ovid, Shakespeare's favorite poet: "In furious rage her **haughty stomach** burns.") Also from *Richard II* the phrasing *high-stomached* is understood to imply "haughty."[138]

Of course, when it comes to appetite and stuffing oneself, and fatness generally, no Shakespeare character is more celebrated than Falstaff, and we find in the epilogue to *2 Henry IV*:

☛ *2 Henry IV* (epilogue, 24–26; Q1600, Lb)
One word more I beseech you, if you bee not too much **cloyd** with fatte meate, our humble Author will continue the storie, with sir Iohn in it, and make you merry with faire Ka-

tharine of Fraunce, where (for any thing I knowe) Falstaffe
shall die of a sweat, vnlesse already a be killd with your harde
opinions; for Olde-castle died Martyre, and this is not the
man: my tongue is weary, when my legges are too, I wil bid
you, good night.

Of all the characters to be found chiming in through our margins and in the Baret text, none comes through as loudly as Falstaff (even irrespective of the extraordinary evidence found on
the soon-to-be-introduced trailing blank).[139] We started this
segment with a pair of classic Falstaff speeches, but little gems
throughout can be offered into the mix that coincide with the
previous emphasis on rare and peculiar words, proverbial language, and Baretisms flipped and reordered; all of these things
land in the Falstaff plays with great abandon.

When it comes to this annotated Baret, there is always more,
with almost all of it lying outside the realm of what one could
imagine a student of Shakespeare or contemporary theatergoer
marking if the argument were attempted that these marks were
an effort at a critical analysis.

Yes, there is always more, and no doubt significantly more
than we – even with great effort and diligence – have managed
to find. But there must be a stopping point, if only to introduce
more Falstaff. We console ourselves, and at the same time make
an effort not to lose you, by insisting that it is the most compelling evidence of all.

The Trailing Blank

Look, what thy memory can not contain
Commit to these waste blanks
                              —Sonnet 77

Transcription of Trailing Blank Annotations

Good fallot – An aglett *Esquilette*

Good morow

Bellefry. *Le befroy*

Book. *Bouquin*

Des bribes. To Bribbe.

Bucke-*bacquet* – a Brache *petite chienne Braque*

To Cramme *engraisser* Cramming. – Creme. A. *Creame*

Whurleburly. *Tumulte.*

Locke. *Un luquet*

A Knive. *un Canif*

Brailer. To Braule

a lopping v. to loppe of – *un lopin* lopper.

Chippes. Shippes.

To choke. *chocquer le choc*

To cramme cramming crammed. *Craimé.*

Encombride. To Combre. Combrous.

(?W me) Clenche. To clench.

Dawber. To Dawbe. *ou radouber.*

Wicket. *Guichet.* – Gare. Geer *Ung Jarre.*

Woodcock. (?Wocok)

Dounes. Dunes. – To Juggle a Juggler Juggling *Jongleur*

To Quaffe v. Quaffer. (?*cuiffor ch bemaine*) Quaffing.

Land. *Landes.*

To Ebbe. *L'Ebbe.*

Vide Mat fellow. *Compagne de la Matte.*

To hack. *bacher.* – hardes of henepe hardes *estoupe de chanure*

To hourde. (?+huarde) – To pant. panting. *pantoiser haleine*

Pewter. *Peautree.* – Beadle. *Bedeau*

a Bawdkin. un Bodkin. – Brache. *un Braque.*

un Befroy a bellfrey a Bell – Biche. *petite chienne. Biche femelle du cerf.*

A Brache. *un Braque.* – Brall. brailler (? *beairu*)

To clacke. *Clacquer ou Mains clacquet*

To dote. *radoter.* dotage. doter of.

The cantle. *Eshantillon.* (*Eschantiau?*)

Adoubber v radouber. Dub a knigth.

to hourde *amasser* – A lowse. *un pou. lou lou.*

a Pallecotte. *ung paletoc. habilliment des femmes.*

To lop. *coupper* of a lopping. *par loppine* (?)

A rewe of trees. tant. rewe.

Two lines in Latin at the bottom (see note 141):

deus producat vitam (^ dominus), conseruat honorem

regat et regnum (^ viribus)

One page of evidence stands apart from all the others, and that is a heavily annotated trailing blank. This binder's leaf – the last to appear in the book as it was initially bound – reveals a simple hunter's horn watermark, characteristic of similar horn watermarks going back as early as the first part of the sixteenth century. The paper is dotted with wormholes, and the pattern of the worming is in direct accordance with the original text block that precedes it. Following this profusely annotated page is an added blank from the eighteenth century, inserted when that binding took over and carried the book to the present day. This leaf is clean, free of writing, and entirely undotted by worming.

Our efforts to match precisely the watermark found on the annotated leaf [140] have thus far been unsuccessful; with the search likely to expand, perhaps someone will succeed, although that is far from a certainty. The notion of dating the watermark is an enticing one, but there are – in all probability – myriad permutations on similarly generic watermarks. Even on the chance that an exact match was found and contained a dated manuscript, this would, at best, supply us only with an approximate age for the watermark.

What the original binder's blank does contain is a veritable word salad of annotations, roughly forty distinct words – a few others are incomplete or indecipherable – and a small number of phrases. Several words appear on the page more than once. The majority of the words are translated into French alongside the English. Although much of it may have been written at one time, it does not appear to be the product of a single sitting, as one can assess from distinct fluctuations in the ink in several of the annotations. Most significantly, because the writing concentration is here so much greater than in any other single occurrence in the book, this page takes on the highest importance in terms of both the lexicology and the paleography. As a prism through which to examine the annotations as a whole, both the words and the penmanship on the trailing blank are telling in that they translate to complete harmony with the rest of the book.

Given the considerable size of the word sample on the trailing blank, there ought not emerge a relationship with the canon that is dramatically more impressive than is a comparison to other writers of the period (or any period, for that matter) unless there is some direct correlation to the works of Shakespeare. In spite of not having conducted a proper survey of other writers, we fully expect that this assessment will not just be upheld, but upheld rather generously in our favor, so overwhelming is the totality of the linguistic evidence. For it is not merely that the words we see on this once blank page carry over into Shakespeare, it is how they are used in Shakespeare in relation to the other words on this page, and the convincing concentration of the echoes within a tight, specific framework of plays – works that immediately precede the play that contains the greatest concentration of French words anywhere in the canon.

By any estimation, what we find on the trailing blank from a linguistic analysis is driven directly out of the plays that feature Falstaff and into *Henry V* where the audience learns of Falstaff's death. In spite of the palpable connections, there is absolutely no concerted allusion on the part of the annotator to these or any plays. The three Falstaff plays, *Henry IV*, *Parts 1 and 2*, and *Merry Wives of Windsor*, were likely written over the two or three years leading up to the composition of *Henry V*. Shakespeare uses substantially more French in *Henry V* than in any other play, and the trailing blank – if nothing else – was clearly being used as a French exercise of sorts. If our conclusion regarding authorship is correct, the trailing blank likely dates to around 1598 (the year prior to the composition of *Henry V*), with a margin of error of no more than one year.

In terms of the paleography, the annotations in the English and French word salad are in the same radically mixed hand as the individual responsible for the annotations throughout the book.[141] As with the paleography observed from the beginning of the book to the end, in moving from English to French, the annotator frequently incorporates more elements of Secretary script and a cursive hand, but there is no hard and fast rule about such a thing remaining consistent. What is consistent is the comparison between this page and the bulk, both in terms of the matching handwriting and the words themselves.

Whereas the possibility of multiple primary annotators could soberly be entertained by abstracting elements from different points throughout the text without regard to the overall picture, the English and French word salad on the trailing blank effectively puts the conversation to rest, because one would otherwise need to propose the absurdity of two or more annotators sitting together and passing the quill pen back and forth during composition, all the while having the words coalesce into Falstaff plays, and in the process matching the variable letter formations that appear in the margins throughout. As much fun as it might be to concoct a scenario whereby two or more people shared sack and took turns with a bilingual word game, this would seem to lead down a path even more absurd than the one we are likely to be accused of.

From a paleographic standpoint, the hand is undeniably a variable hand, a mix of Italic and Secretary scripts that matches the handwriting that is spread throughout the book. The style, while generally flourishing in harmony from one entry to the next, shows a marked tendency toward the formation of letters, not in perfect replication, but instead, in swift and often playful renderings, generating results that are marked by their unabashed inconsistency. Clearly this is an annotator that could care less about how consistently he forms his letters. We see, for example, no fewer than six distinct formations of both the letter "p" and the letter "w" – some of the variations present in a single line, or in one line directly above another. The overall picture is of an annotator who demonstrates, whimsically, frantically, and even passionately, a mixed hand. The variability emphasized by Leon Kellner[142] as a hallmark of Shakespeare's period is on almost exaggerated display across the annotated trailing blank.

The linguistic components of the word salad on the trailing blank are – almost without exception – additionally treated by the annotator at the point, or points, in the dictionary where they appear in print. This helps to reinforce a level of interest in these words beyond any random dabbling. If the argument is made that the selection is essentially random and can tell us nothing, that the words on this page are just words that one could never piece together or insist on culling any meaning from, the selection is, by any consensus, truly bizarre right from the start. Although for brief moments it can appear alphabetically driven, perhaps the most logical way to interpret the list is to imagine it as a subliminal channeling, words inside the annotator's mind for one reason or another as he jots them down and adds their French equivalents.

Near the bottom of the page we find an annotation combination that appears to connect to the opening scene in *The Merry Wives of Windsor*, a scene that some Shakespeare historians have argued makes reference to the deer-poaching incident involving Sir Thomas Lucy. The precise annotation reads: lowse...un pou...lou lou. Immediately below, almost squarely beneath that annotation, we find the annotation pallecotte along with the French equivalent.

Perhaps it is only by extraordinary coincidence that an 1827 French translation of *The Merry Wives of Windsor* (*Sur Les Joyeuses Bourgeoises de Windsor*) includes a textual note, aimed at clarifying a difficult point of translation, with the same sequence "lowse pou lou lou." The note reads: "Il a fallu changer le brochet en loup de mer, pour conserver quelque chose du jeu de mots que fait ensuite Evans entre luce (brochet), et lowse (pou). Lou lou est un mot populaire et enfantin pour designer cette espece de vermine."[142]

The translator explains the necessity of changing the French word for luce (*brochets*) to the French word for catfish (*loups de mer*), to preserve the game of words at play between *luce* and *louse*, and the comic misunderstanding that occurs as a result. *Lou Lou*, the note specifies, is a childish designation for this species of vermin, the louse.

In Baret, under *pike* (the full-grown pike is a luce; Latin, *lucius*, from the Greek *lukos*, wolf, meaning the wolf of fishes), the printed French mentions not only *un brochet* but also *un loup d'eau*. There are a number of annotations showing interest in the different usages of *pike*. Under *lowse* (louse) in Baret, we see another series of annotations marking clear interest, and we find there the printed French, *poulx*.

Let us take a look at the scene in question:

📖 *Merry Wives of Windsor* (1.1.1–20; FF D2)

SHALLOW: Sir *Hugh*, perswade me not: I will make a Star-
    Chamber matter of it, if hee were twenty Sir
    Iohn Falstoffs, he shall not abuse *Robert Shallow*
    Esquire.   (Coram.
SLENDER: In the County of *Glocester*, Iustice of Peace and
SHALLOW: I (Cosen *Slender*) and *Cust-alorum*.
SLENDER: I, and *Ratolorum* too; and a Gentleman borne
    (Master Parson) who writes himselfe *Armigero*, in any
    Bill, Warrant, Quittance, or Obligation, *Armigero*.
SHALLOW: I that I doe, and haue done any time these three
    hundred yeeres.
SLENDER: All his successors (gone before him) hath don't:
    and all his Ancestors (that come after him) may: they
    may giue the dozen white **Luces** in their **Coate**.
SHALLOW: It is an **olde Coate**.
EUANS: The dozen white **Lowses** doe become an **old**

> **Coat** well: it agrees well passant: It is a familiar beast to
> man, and signifies Loue.
> SHALLOW: The **Luse** is the fresh-fish, the salt-fish, is an **old**
> Coate.

Herein lies one of the most debated possible references to
Shakespeare's life to appear in the works.[144] Sir Thomas Lucy, the
story goes, is alleged to have been responsible for chasing Shakespeare from Stratford over an incident involving the poaching of
a deer, and, unforgotten, turns up here as Justice Shallow, sati-
rized over his coat-of-arms that bore three luces and not the doz-
en stated by Slender. The whole thing may sound like the stuff of
fable, but there were even later rumors of early never-published
poems mocking Lucy. Although the cited poems are reasoned to
be apocryphal, there are four independent accounts of the Lucy
story within the first century after Shakespeare's death, each formulated before the gossip hounds descended upon Stratford, so it
is difficult not to imagine some grain of truth to it all. When we
learn that Lucy was centrally involved in anti-Catholic dealings,
the suggestion becomes – given our entire body of annotations –
that much more intriguing.

Our success in turning up – through the use of Google – an
obscure note in a nineteenth-century French edition of Shakespeare's plays that seems to magically replicate the thought
process of an annotator, 250 or so years prior, fiddling with
English–French equivalents at the back of Baret's *Alvearie*, can
be viewed a variety of ways: blind luck, revealing, irritating, or
entirely inconsequential. But to attain this singular result (in
Google, for the extracted elements "lowse," "pou," and "lou
lou"), by any account, subsequent to multiple years (years!)
of wondering whether a convincing case can be made for Shakespeare as annotator from the evidence left behind in our book –
that would of and by itself qualify for cruel cosmic joke. Imagine
the near impossibility of writing down a sequence of words com-

bining English and French that did not constitute a unique line, or a portion of a line, from a poem or play belonging to Shakespeare, and achieving the same unique result of one strand only, and that strand being Shakespeare. If it is blind luck (or misfortune – countless hours have been logged), it certainly represents odds that are most exceptional. Perhaps a computer could begin to calculate them, but one imagines the chances of duplicating the feat to be astronomical. If lowse, un pou, lou lou were the only words to appear on that page, or if you found these words on a scrap of paper blowing along on the sidewalk, you would already have, louses aside, a serious head-scratcher.

What we do know, for sure, from the textual note in this French edition, is that the translator was attempting to extrapolate the meaning of the line and find the correct French translation. What we can be equally certain of is that we have an early English annotator, who, in messing around with French at the back of his *Alvearie*, happens to pick the same word sequence that a French translator would also choose in order to highlight the ignorant corruption of *luce* to *louse* used by Sir Evans. And to find any word relating, even tangentially, to the other half of the "joke," particularly an archaic term related to a short coat or cloak, immediately beneath these words?

Precise words be damned, the fact that *anything* to do with a coat or a cloak should appear under this annotation lowse, un pou, lou lou must be relevant, as it is the key ingredient in the very next line of the play. Shakespeare does not use the term *pallecotte*, but if we turn to P45 in our Baret, we find a revealing set of spoken annotation additions relating to the word, all culled from Baret: a pallecotte v. gowne; palletoc; habillement de femme. The *vide* in this sequence sends us to *gowne* (G425), where it is defined in the text: ***a womans gowne, a short cloke** with sleeves, called a pallecote* (underlined).

In *Merry Wives* there are laughs at Falstaff's expense on the possibility of fitting specifically into **a woman's gown** (or pallecotte):

☞ *Merry Wives of Windsor*. Mistress Page (4.2.62–64; FF E3b)

> Alas the day I know not, there is no **wo-**
> **mans gowne** bigge enough for him: otherwise he might
> put on a hat, a muffler, and a kerchiefe, and so escape.

And in *2 Henry IV*, Falstaff uses the other piece of the definition, phrased precisely as it appears in Baret's *Alvearie*.

☞ *2 Henry IV*. Falstaff (1.2.28–30; FF g1)

> What said M. *Dombledon*, about
> the Satten for my **short Cloake**, and Slops?

It is not surprising, of course, that in Shakespeare the words *coat*, *cloak*, and *gown* are common. But the only textual matches that we find in the works for *short cloak* and *woman's gown* are these two instances, and that is surely significant given the totality of what is found in these word association bits that are contained on this once-vacant blank.

The movement on the page is always toward finding more. Falstaff accounts for three usages of *cloak*, two in *2 Henry IV*, and the following in act 1, scene 3, from *Merry Wives*, where it is paired with *old* (think "old coat" in the opening scene and the connections with lowse annotation lying just above pallecotte).

☞ *Merry Wives of Windsor*. Falstaff (1.3.15–16; FF D3)

> *Bardolfe*, follow him: a *Tapster* is a good trade:
> an **old Coake**, makes a new Ierkin:

Similar to the multiple annotations around pallecotte in the main text of the Baret, we find a noteworthy concentration in dealing with the louse. The annotator inserts at L722 lowsie evill vide Aesope v. pag. preceed. The reference is not merely to Aesop, but to the preceding page where we see mute annotations:

> L703. / ¶ a Lowse
> L704. o the lowsie euill.
> L705. o Lowsie or full of lise.

Of the eight usages of *lousy* (lowsie), two are from *Merry Wives*, and four fall in *Henry V*. This is a heavy and noteworthy concentration, particularly in light of what we find elsewhere on the page.

The possible link between Shakespeare and Lucy and the poaching of a deer has long been written about extensively prior to this copy of Baret ever being studied, but it could easily prove a distraction, or even provoke hostility, so we strongly encourage those readers bothered by the inference to step away from conjecture and look simply at the annotations on this page alone beside the Shakespeare texts. The evidence is so compelling when examining the texts alone that one does not need to have formulated an opinion on Lucy and the poaching story, or allow it to become a distraction.

Almost all of the words that are added to this page – and it is truly a linguistic smorgasbord of tremendous variety – are found in at least one of the three plays where Falstaff appears, or in *Henry V*, where Falstaff's death is recorded. It is no exaggeration to say that the Falstaff character runs rampant over the page.

Consider some of the more obvious correlations between the word salad on the trailing blank and the texts. Included on the page, with French alongside, are the following: bribe, buck, basket, cram, and cream. The words are all grouped near the top of the page. Each word is situated no worse than in close proximity to the others, and yet there is no attempt to make a sentence. Most of the words appear to have been written swiftly without any real sense of importance, and as such are not always very easy to make out, but there should be no argument here among Shakespeareans when the name Falstaff is extended at the hearing of these words.

Bribe and *buck* are combined one time, by Falstaff in *Merry Wives*:

🖙 *Merry Wives of Windsor*. Falstaff (5.5.22–28; FF E6)

Diuide me like a **brib'd-Bucke**, each a Haunch:
I will keepe my sides to my selfe, my shoulders for the
fellow of this walke; and my hornes I bequeath your
husbands. Am I a Woodman, ha? Speake I like *Herne*
the Hunter? Why, now is Cupid a child of conscience,
he makes restitution. As I am a true spirit, welcome.

Shakespeare editor and linguist Harold Littledale has observed that "Harman, in his *Caveat*, seems to use bribery = theft, so perhaps it may mean poached."[145] This takes us back again to the opening scene in *Merry Wives* that depicts a pompous Justice Shallow complaining that Falstaff has killed his deer and threatening a Star Chamber suit.

There are no surviving copies of the first edition (1566) of Thomas Harman's *Caveat or Warning for Common Cursitors, vulgarly called vagabonds*. But we know that pirated copies soon followed a year later, as well as two editions from 1568 and a revised edition from 1573. It is frequently referenced as one of the central texts of Elizabethan rogue literature. Harman is one of the first writers to use the word *rogue*. A large part of his *Caveat* was included in William Harrison's "Description of England" as part of *Holinshed's Chronicle*, so more than likely Shakespeare would have been familiar with it.

As the word cream is another that is added to the trailing blank by our annotator, we cannot help but notice the parallel to Falstaff, and also in the sense of "stealing."

🖙 *1 Henry IV* (4.2.58–62; FF f3)

FALSTAFF: Tut, neuer feare me, I am as vigilant as a Cat, to
          steale Creame.
PRINCE: I thinke to **steale Creame** indeed, for thy theft
          hath alreadie made thee Butter: but tell me, *Iack*, whose
          fellowes are these that come after?

Bucke looks to have a hyphen mark at the end of the annotation, connecting it to bacquet (basket), turning it into buckebacquet. *Buck-basket* is used four times, all in *Merry Wives*, including a pair of usages by Falstaff:

☞ *Merry Wives of Windsor*. Falstaff (3.5.77–80; FF E2b)

You shall heare. As good lucke would haue it,
comes in one *Mist*. *Page*, giues intelligence of *Fords* approch: and in her inuention, and *Fords* wiues distraction,
they conuey'd me into a **bucke-basket**.

☞ *Merry Wives of Windsor*. Falstaff (3.5.82–86; FF E3)

Yes: a **Buck-basket**: ram'd mee in with foule
Shirts and Smockes, Socks, foule Stockings, greasie
Napkins, that (Master *Broome*) there was the rankest
compound of villanous smell, that euer offended nostrill.

At the top of the trailing blank, immediately after buckebacquet, we see the word crammed with French equivalent. Consider how in the second Falstaff example, the words *rammed me* follow *buck-basket*. And what is Falstaff's next line in the play? "**Crammed** into a **basket**."

As a case for how the trailing blank words are utilized throughout the Baret text, consider the mute annotations alongside *cram* all the way back at C1559:

C1559. / ¶ a **Cramming**, or **fatting**
C1560. o To cramme, or **feede fatte**.
C1563. o That is **franked**, or **crammed**.

☞ *2 Henry IV*. Prince Hal (2.2.137–38; FF g4)

Where suppes he? Doth the old Bore, **feede** in
the old **Franke**?

☞ *Merchant of Venice*. Shylock (1.3.45; FF O5b)

I will **feede fat** the ancient grudge I beare him.

☞ *Richard III*. Gloucester (1.3.312–13; Q1597, C3b)

He is **franckt** vp to **fatting** for his paines,
God pardon them that are the cause of it.

These archaic usages for *fat* are further examples of how our annotator has worked his way around the dictionary. Right under the little circle *that is franked or cramped*, we have the next following "C" headword *crampe* at C1564. Right underneath it, we have a little circle: *a kind of Crampe, <u>stiffnesse in the sinews</u>*. We previously noted the parallel usages by Hamlet and Claudius, and we find also a recalibration of this definition in act 3 of *Henry V* in one of the most famous speeches in all of Shakespeare, beginning:

🔖 *Henry V*. King Henry V (3.1.1–8; FF h5)

Once more vnto the Breach,
Deare friends, once more;
Or close the Wall vp with our English dead:
In Peace, there's nothing so becomes a man,
As modest stillnesse, and humilitie:
But when the blast of Warre blowes in our eares,
Then imitate the action of the Tyger:
Stiffen the sinewes, commune vp the blood,
Disguise faire Nature with hard-fauour'd Rage:

The continual massaging throughout the Baret of the usages and word combinations found on the trailing blank helps to strengthen the case already made for them by how decidedly entrenched they are within a given set of plays. The themes from these plays are also decidedly in tune with what we see on the trailing blank. The themes of hunting and poaching, for example, are apparent in the trailing blank's exploration of deer and dogs, and the reappearing figure of Falstaff, who, as Edward Berry recognizes in his book, *Shakespeare and the Hunt, A Cultural and Social Study*, is both poached and poacher at various moments.[146] Berry also highlights the climactic moment in the first part of *Henry IV*, where we find the metaphor of Falstaff as deer established through Hal's direct reference:

🔖 *1 Henry IV*. Prince Hal (5.4.106–9; FF f5b)

Death hath not strucke so fat a Deere to day,
Though many dearer in this bloody Fray:

Imbowell'd will I see thee by and by,
Till then, in blood, by Noble *Percie* lye.

The deer metaphor is carried over to Falstaff's last line in
Merry Wives: "When night-dogges run, all sorts of Deere are
chac'd" (5.5.260; FF E6b).

Brache and braque are added three separate times at various positions on the trailing blank (and presumably at multiple intervals if one examines closely the ink). Brach was an old English name for a dog that hunted by scent, used also to constitute a bitch. Shakespeare uses brach six times, including the stern protest by Henry Percy in *1 Henry IV*, when faced with the prospect of hearing the lady sing in Welsh: "I had rather heare (Lady) my **brach** howle in Irish" (3.1.232; FF c6b).

In addition to the word brach, the annotator plays with the word *bitch*, adding biche. petite chienne. biche femille du cerf.

It becomes apparent that the fiddling is being conducted not only with words and their French meanings, but also with sounds – and the meanings of words that sound the same or sound similar, or look the same but are different. *Biche* in French can represent a bitch or petite chienne, as the annotator observes, or, rather specifically femille du cerf, a female deer.

The seemingly banal English/French annotations vide mat fellowe and compaigne de la matte further our understanding of the annotator's playful engaging with sounds and meaning when we consider the textual possibilities.

Mate and *companion* are combined in lines twice only in Shakespeare, and one of these occurrences is in *2 Henry IV*:

☞ *2 Henry IV*. Doll Tearsheet (2.4.119–22; FF g5)

Charge me? I scorne you (scuruie **Companion**)
what? you poore, base, rascally, cheating, lacke-Linnen-
Mate: away you mouldie Rogue, away; I am meat for
your Master.

Along the lines of "sound play" we can hear how the annotation mat fellowe is reasonably close to "mad fellow" – another rare pairing in Shakespeare, used once by Hamlet and twice called upon by Falstaff in *1 Henry IV*:

☞ *1 Henry IV*. Falstaff (2.5.338–42; FF e4b)

That same **mad fellow** of the North, Percy; and hee of Wales,
that gaue *Amamon* the Bastinado, and made *Lucifer* Cuckold,
and swore the Deuill his true Liege-man vpon the Crosse of a
Welch-hooke; what a plague call you him?

☞ *1 Henry IV*. Falstaff (2.4.35–37; FF f3)

A **mad fellow** met me on the way, and told me, I had vnloaded
all the Gibbets, and prest the dead bodyes.

Book, bell, and cantle each appear, and, if the argument for sound play is here extended, allowing *candle* to also be in the annotator's ear when he writes cantle – in the same way that the annotation mat fellow gives way to "mad fellow" – this suggests a Catholic reference point. The clustering of book, bell, and *candle* equates to the Catholic Church pronouncement for one who has committed a grievous sin. Shakespeare makes reference to it in the seldom considered *King John*, also of this period, probably written (1595–96) just prior to the Falstaff plays:

☞ *King John*. Bastard (3.3.12–16; FF a6)

Bell, **Booke**, & **Candle**, shall not driue me back,
When gold and siluer becks me to come on.
I leaue your highnesse: Grandame, I will pray
(If euer I remember to be holy)
For your faire safety: so I kisse your hand.

There are other examples of sound play on the trailing blank, including ships and chips, but nowhere does the question of the exploration of sounds on the trailing blank waggle more enticingly than it does with one of the most difficult-to-decipher annotations – but one that, with the help of the alphabetically entered equivalents within the text block in letter "G," contains the words gar ... .jarre.

There are three instances of *jarre-tierre* (*iateer* in the First Folio). These occur when Dr. Caius refers to the Host of the Garter Inn, substituting a French word *jarre-tierre* for *garter*. The *OED* gives the English garter derivation from Old French as "gartier, jartier, jarretier, (also jartiere, F. jarretiere . . .)."

The Alexander Dyce 1857 edition of Shakespeare's works contains this editorial note: "The folio has 'mine host of de Iarteer.' The modern editors usually put 'mine host of de Jarterre.' We find in Cotgrave's Dict.: 'A garter, Jartier, Jarttiere, Jarreriere.' "[147]

The 1602 Quarto of *Merry Wives of Windsor* is a notoriously bad quarto. It omits the first scene of act 4 and the first four scenes of act 5. And the *jarre-tierre* instance from the First Folio (act 3, scene 1) that we first tried to compare with the same sentence using *garter* in the 1602 Quarto was so different because Q1602 was so mixed up that we could hardly make any connections.

Dr. Caius is French, and he is constantly using French words instead of English, like *garcon* for "boy," or mistaking English words for French words and mangling them. We are fairly certain that our annotator intended gare and jarre to correlate to Dr. Cauis's *by gar* and *jarre-teirre*. In the First Folio, an earlier sentence mentions that Caius is French, and then he says *Jarteer* for *garter*. But in the 1602 Quarto, that earlier sentence does not appear, and Caius says *garter* instead of *Jarteer*.

While looking into this, we came across a book by Georgio Melchiori called *Shakespeare's Garter Plays: Edward III to Merry Wives of Windsor*[148] that concerns itself with expanding the tetralogy of plays beginning with *Richard II* and ending with *Henry V*. By virtue of examining the texts and speculating upon "foul papers" and what "Shakespeare originally wrote," Melchiori extends the tetralogy to a sextet by including *Edward III*[149] and *Merry Wives of Windsor*. In addition to Falstaff or a Falstaff-like figure and the relevance paid to the theme of the order of the Garter, these plays share, among other qualities, "two basic principles that can be summarized in the words *Policy* and *Honor*."[150]

If our theory on authorship of the annotations is correct, then with the trailing blank and its wording intimately intertwined with Melchiori's Garter Plays, we effectively would have a Shakespeare manuscript that – even though it is largely a word salad – gives us another window into his early printed texts.

One might even begin to wonder if the selection of the name "Caius" cannot be traced to *Caius* being underlined in the preamble to letter "C" in this copy of Baret on the subject of pronunciation. As with *Gare–Jarre*, we see a further possible connection between the annotations on this page and Dr. Caius, in the sequence: To clacke, clacquet des mains, clacquet. The word clack does not appear in Shakespeare, but it does appear in Baret, and our annotator has paid earlier careful attention:

> C558. / ¶ to **Clack.** A **clacking** with the **tong**, to cheere a horse,
> adds clacquer clacqueter
> C559. o A mil **clack**

A mill clack is synonymous with the term *clapper*, "one that claps, one that applauds, the tongue of a bell."[151] Shakespeare does use *clapper* – six times – and in *Much Ado About Nothing* (also written at roughly the same time; 1598–99), it is paired with *tongue*.

☞ *Much Ado About Nothing*. Prince (Don Pedro) (3.2.11–12; FF K1b)
> . . . he hath a heart as sound as a bell.
> and his **tongue** is the **clapper**, for what his heart thinkes,
> his **tongue** speakes.

Three of the other five usages of *clapper* in Shakespeare occur in *Merry Wives* in a comical confrontation between the Host and Dr. Caius:

☞ *Merry Wives of Windsor* (2.2.59–63; FF D6b)

HOST: He will **Clapper-claw** thee tightly (Bully.)
CAIUS: **Clapper-de-claw**? vat is dat?
HOST: That is, he will make thee amends
CAIUS: By-gar, me doe looke hee shall **clapper-de-claw**
me, for by-gar, me vill haue it.

The term *clapper-claw* was a "low word" that implied scold-ing.[152] The other sense of *clap*, of course, pertains to what one can do with one's hands, and this returns us to the same sequence on the trailing blank: clacquet des mains.

Not only is the French *mains* used in *Henry V* –

☞ French Soldier (4.4.52–55; FF i4b)

Fre. Sur mes genoux se vous donnes milles remercious, et
*Ie me estime heurex que Ie intombe, entre les **main** d'vn Che-*
ualier Ie peuse le plus braue valiant et tres distinie signieur
d'Angleterre

– but the English *clap hands* is also found in the play, and this is the only time it appears phrased as such in the entire works of Shakespeare:

☞ King Henry (5.2.122–31; FF k1)

The Princesse is the better English-woman:
yfaith *Kate*, my wooing is fit for thy vnderstanding, I am
glad thou canst speake no better English, for if thou
could'st, thou would'st finde me such a plaine King, that
thou wouldst thinke, I had sold my Farme to buy my
Crowne. I know no wayes to mince it in loue, but directly to say, I loue you; then if you vrge me farther,
then to say, Doe you in faith? I weare out my suite: Giue
me your answer, yfaith doe, and so **clap hands**, and a bar-
gaine: how say you, Lady?

The *Henry V* French usages that are found on the trailing blank are not limited to simple words such as mains and chien.

Twice on the trailing blank the annotator takes an interest in the notion of *lopping off*. Near the top of the page we find: a lop-ping; to loppe off, loppor, un lopin. And at the bottom: to lop. coupper. a lopping

☞ *1 Henry IV*. Boy (4.4.33–35; FF k1)

*Il me commande a vous dire que vous faite vous prest, car ce soldat icy est disposee tout asture de **couppes** vostre gorge*

Variations on the English equivalent the annotator writes alongside coupper, lop, are twelve times used in the works, twice combined – *"limb lopped off"*:

☞ *1 Henry IV*. Hotspur (4.1.43; FF f2b)

A perilous Gash, a very **Limme lopt off:**

The annotator's interest is apparent under *loppe*, at L647.

L647. / ¶ to **Loppe trees**, to cut off **boughes**
L648. o A **lopping**, or shredding of boughs.
L649. o He that <u>pruneth</u>, picketh, or **dresseth trees**: he that cutteth off **superfluous boughes**: a **lopper.**

Notice how the texts used in Baret's examples that are marked by our annotator are essentially scrambled into lines from the Gardener's great speech in act 3, scene 4, of *Richard II*:

☞ Gardener (3.4.56–67; Q1597, G3)

Oh what pitie is it that he had not so trimde,
And **drest** his **land** as we this garden at time of yeare
Do wound the barke, the skinne of our **fruit trees**,
Lest being ouer prowd in sap and bloud,
With too much riches it confound it selfe
Had he done so to great and growing men,
They might haue liude to beare, and he to taste
Their fruits of duety: **superfluous** branches
We **loppe away,** that bearing **boughes** may liue:
Had he done so, himselfe had borne the crowne,
Which waste of idle houres hath quite throwne downe.

In his discussion of *Merry Wives*, Edward Berry turns our attention to the fact that "Like Falstaff's deer, the English language becomes a sacrificial victim, to be hacked and hewn in the interest of social peace."[153] Hacked also appears in the word salad – not far removed from lop – and it, too, is a trailing blank annotation that appears as a spoken annotation in the main text.

H4. / ¶ to **Hacke**, or cutte, adds hacked maimed

☞ *Merry Wives of Windsor*. Host (3.1.71–72; FF D6b)
Disarme them, and let them question: let them
keepe their **limbs** whole, and **hack** our English.

In these lines we hear again the earlier echo of *limbs*. Notice how the word *hacked* is described by Baret: ***hacked*** . . . *appropriate term for **chopping off** spurs of a **knight** when he was to be degraded.*

☞ *Merry Wives of Windsor*. Mistress Page (2.1.48–49; FF D4)
What? thou liest? Sir *Alice Ford*? these **knights** will **hacke**,

Perhaps it is no accident that knight is another among the cascading words in French and English on this trailing blank, and one that is made more interesting by its pairing on the page with dub. This leads us to expand the discussion to another piece in the long and ever-lengthening trail of source material drawn upon, or possibly drawn upon, by Shakespeare – material that was not exclusive of song. We see on the page an almost certain reference to one such ballad – a drinking song – *Monsieur Mingo*, that contains the additional enticement in that it relates directly to knights (cf.: knights of the garter). The annotation reads:

adoubber v. radouber – dub a knigth.

☞ *2 Henry IV*. Silence (5.3.74–76; FF gg6b)
Do me right, and **dub me Knight**, *Samingo*.

☞ *Henry V*. Henry V (4.8.86; FF i5b)
Fiue hundred were but yesterday **dubb'd Knights**.

Monsieur Mingo was set to music by Orlando di Lasso. A French version was first published in England by none other than Thomas Vautrollier in 1570 in a collection of di Lasso chansons.[154] From 1592 to 1604 several Elizabethan playwrights quote fragments of the English version, so it was evidently in wide circulation and popular to the point that the concluding phrase, *Dub me knight, Domingo*, became a common refrain. But the song opens with "Monsieur Mingo for *quaffing* doth pass," and the word quaffing is another of the forty or so English words added by our annotator on this trailing blank that continues our own refrain of raising doubts over theories that would prefer to label the ongoing linguistic parallels as purely coincidental, or something you could easily apply to a tight selection of the work by any number of other period writers.

The English on the trailing blank reads to quaffe, quaffer, quaffing, and the French equivalents are written alongside. This fragment appears only several lines above where adoubber v. radouber, dub a knigth has been written, only a slight separation. Annotations relating to quaffing appear earlier at Q1:

Q1. / to **Quaffe**, or drinke all vp, adds quaffing and a quaffer.

🖝 *Twelfth Night*. Maria (1.3.13–15; FF Y2b)

That **quaffing** and **drinking** will vndoe you: I
heard my Lady talke of it yesterday: and of a foolish
knight that you brought in one night here, to be hir woer

The mix of unusual words with ordinary ones is an intriguing aspect to what has been left behind on the trailing blank. The word cantle, an unusual word, is equated in Baret with a piece or segment, or a pattern or specimen. At two separate points the annotator has underlined the word, and at a third location he has added a spoken annotation:

L729. ¶ a **Lumpe**, or <u>wedge</u> of gold, or iron… A lump, or **cantell** of bread, xc

P188. ¶ a **Paterne**
P189. The shewe of some thing: the **cantle**: the exemplarie and paterne.
C58–59. Adds the cantle a paterne specimen

Only two usages exist for cantle in Shakespeare, including Hotspur's in *1 Henry IV*.

🔖 *1 Henry IV*. Hotspur (3.1.95–97; FF c6)

See how this river comes me cranking in,
And cuts me from the best of all my **land**
A huge half-moon, a monstrous **cantle** out.

This brings us to one of the trailing blank's most ordinary words: land. To see this very common word in Shakespeare combine with cantle may not raise eyebrows, but it is there; and it is also combined with the trailing blank words dubbed and knight in *King John*.

🔖 *King John*. Bastard (1.1.244–50; FF a2)

Knight, knight good mother, Basilisco-like:
What, I am **dub'd**, I haue it on my shoulder:
But mother, I am not Sir *Roberts* sonne,
I haue disclaim'd Sir *Robert* and my **land**,
Legitimation, name, and all is gone;
Then good my mother, let me know my father,
Some proper man I hope, who was it mother?

At the very top of the page, we find a most dramatic example of annotations balancing the unusual with the banal. For starters, these two annotations – the first annotations that were added to this page – stand out in that they are not translated into French (although the first does contain a French word): good fallot and good morrow. The question "what is *that* doing there?" could apply to any of the annotations on the page, but especially to these. Why start a laundry list of personal verbal interests with an obscure expression and follow it with a most common and ordinary greeting?

Perhaps a look at Rabelais holds the answer. In Rabelais, we find: "il est goud falot." Evidence that Shakespeare read Rabelais is "suggestive, if uncertain." But the parallels between *Henry IV Parts I and II* and *Gargantua and Pantagruel* are plainly clear. "In each work, a prince participates in a process of education in preparation to succeed his father. Each prince shares adventures with an unconventional, comic companion."[155]

It is possible, of course, that our annotator got good fallot from some source other than Rabelais. The expression is an archaic twist on "good fellow," which, not unsurprisingly, is used as a greeting in Shakespeare rather regularly. But *falot* was not just a word for *fellow*; it was also a word for "torch" or "lantern," and our annotator has understood this through his cross-referencing at the point at which the French, *falot*, appears in Baret:

F440. ¶ **Fired**, verie hoate
A fire brand: a **cresset light**: a linke, or other thing, which burning giueth light. *falot.*

The term *cresset light* is underlined in this definition, as it is under the entry for the word *torch*.

T443. a **Torch**, a cresset light….A tree, out of which issueth a liquor more thinne than pitch: vnproperly it is taken for all wood, which being dressed with rossen, or waxe, will burne like a torch: a torch: a wedding: a song at a wedding.

The annotator is sufficiently intrigued that he uses both of these texts to form spoken annotations where *cresset* would fall were it printed under the letter "C."

C1608. ¶ the herbe called **Cresses**, adds a cresset light torche and a cresset light vide fire

Shakespeare used the term only once:

☞ *1 Henry IV.* Glendower (3.1.12–16; FF c5b)
I cannot blame him: At my Natiuitie,
The front of Heauen was full of **fierie** shapes,

Of **burning Cressets**: and at my Birth,
The frame and foundation of the Earth
Shak'd like a Coward.

In Cotgrave, a French-English dictionary published in 1611, *fa-lot* is not only translated as "a cresset light" but the definition adds, "such as they use in playhouses."[156]

A few lines later after "goud fallot" appears in Rabelais, we see the line "Ainsi auras **falot et lanterns**" (in other words, *torch* or *lantern*).

That Shakespeare uses both *torch* and *lantern* many times is no surprise. An example of a usage of *torch* comes in these lines from Falstaff:

🖛 *1 Henry IV*. Falstaff (3.3.40–42; FF f1b)
　　　　　　. . . thou hast saued me a thousand
Markes in Linkes and **Torches**, walking with thee in the
Night betwixt Tauerne and Tauerne: . . .

Lantern occurs eight times, and four of the usages are in *1 Henry IV* (once in *Merry Wives*). The argument that our trailing blank's words can be seen as a sort of subliminal canvas where thoughts were transpiring that would bear themselves out over the course of those plays may seem less outrageous the further we go forward with the breakdown.

Which leads to possibly the least inspiring of all the words and brief phrases to appear on the page in question: good morrow.

It rests on its own, positioned just below good fallot with no added French equivalent. The greeting was very common, used 105 times in Shakespeare. Why it should be there at all is a question we may never know the answer to, but given everything else that we see on this page, the following simple exchange in act 2, scene 1, of *1 Henry IV* takes on potential interest beyond what may at first seem reasonable. The scene begins with a stage direction that sees a Carrier enter "with a **Lanterne** in his hand."

When a few moments later Gadshill enters, we find the following exchange:

🖙 *1 Henry IV* (2.1.32–40; FF c2)

GADSHILL: **Good-morrow** Carriers. What's a clocke?
CARRIER: I thinke it be two a clocke.
GADSHILL: I prethee lend me thy **Lanthorne** to see my Gelding in the stable.
FIRST CARRIER: Nay soft I pray ye, I know a trick worth two of that.
GADSHILL: I prethee lend me thine.
SECOND CARRIER: I, when, canst tell? Lend mee thy **Lanthorne** (quoth-a) marry Ile see thee hang'd first.

It is unlikely, even with the seemingly endless stream of Shakespearean criticism, that the mingling of good morrow and *lantern* in this scene has ever been looked at in isolation. But their pairing at the top of this page of annotations, annotations quirky and disparate by any measure, begins to give pause as more and more pieces fall into place.

Consider further that Falstaff's own use of *lantern* in *1 Henry IV* appears in combination with usages of *knight* and *burning lamp*, and this just precedes his already mentioned use of *torches*.

🖙 *1 Henry IV.* Falstaff (3.3.23–26; FF f1b)

Doe thou amend thy Face, and Ile amend thy
Life: Thou art our Admirall, thou bearest the **Lanterne**
in the Poope, but 'tis in the Nose of thee; thou art the
Knight of the **burning Lampe**.

The organic play between the Baret text and the trailing blank annotations and the Shakespeare texts rolls from top to bottom and covers everything in between.

Another of the commonalities added to the trailing blank is knive (knife). A French equivalent, un canif, is written parallel to it. But a *canif* is noted specifically in Baret to be a *penknife*. There are seventy-eight usages of *knife* in the canon, but the singular usage of *penknife* takes place in the second part of

Henry IV, and the linguistically accurate phrasing "short knife" occurs in *Merry Wives*. And in both cases the usages are Falstaff! The example of "penknife" becomes even more potent when we then stop alongside the trailing blank's annotation coupling: pewter – peautree.

☞ *2 Henry IV*. Falstaff (3.2.254–67; FF ggb)

> Will you tell me (Master *Shallow*) how to chuse
> a man? Care I for the Limbe, the Thewes, the stature,
> bulke, and bigge assemblance of a man? giue mee the
> spirit (Master *Shallow*.) Where's *Wart*? you see what
> a ragged appearance it is: hee shall charge you, and
> discharge you, with the motion of a **Pewterers** Ham-
> mer: come off, and on, swifter then hee that gibbets on
> the Brewers Bucket. And this same halfe-fac'd fellow,
> *Shadow*, giue me this man: hee presents no marke to the
> Enemie, the foe-man may with as great ayme leuell at
> the edge of a **Pen-knife**: and for a Retrait, how swiftly
> will this *Feeble*, the Womans Taylor, runne off. O, giue
> me the spare men, and spare me the great ones. Put me a
> Calyuer into *Warts* hand, *Bardolph*.

Only two other usages of pewter are held in the entire concordance, with one of these being Hal's in the first part of *Henry IV*.

The trailing blank is nothing if not an exotic mix of commonly used words found in the canon (e.g., knife, land, brawl) with less common (e.g., whurleburly, cantle, pewter). The Shakespeare intrigue behind the case for knife, a very common word, rises when we see that the following words added to the trailing blank are *all* combined in some form with speeches using the word knife: pant, daub, juggler, land, quaffe, choke, woodcock, trees, pewter. And three of these disparate words are utilized in the first half of King Henry IV's opening speech in *1 Henry IV*: pant, daub, and knife. A fourth trailing blank word, brawl, is in Middle English equated with *broil*, which is another word in that speech.

᠉ *1 Henry IV*. King Henry (1.1.1–33; FF d5b)

So shaken as we are, so wan with care,
Finde we a time for frighted Peace to **pant**,
And breath shortwinded accents of new **broils**
To be commenc'd in Stronds a-farre remote:
No more the thirsty entrance of this Soile,
Shall **daube** her lippes with her owne childrens blood:
No more shall trenching Warre channell her fields,
Nor bruise her Flowrets with the Armed hoofes
Of hostile paces. Those opposed eyes,
Which like the Meteors of a troubled Heauen,
All of one Nature, of one Substance bred,
Did lately meete in the intestine shocke,
And furious cloze of ciuill Butchery,
Shall now in mutuall well-beseeming rankes
March all one way, and be no more oppos'd
Against Acquaintance, Kindred, and Allies.
The edge of Warre, like an ill-sheathed **knife**,
No more shall cut his Master. Therefore Friends,
As farre as to the Sepulcher of Christ,
Whose Souldier now vnder whose blessed Crosse
We are impressed and ingag'd to fight,
Forthwith a power of English shall we leuie,
Whose armes were moulded in their Mothers wombe,
To chace these Pagans in those holy Fields,
Ouer whose Acres walk'd those blessed feete
Which fourteene hundred yeares ago were nail'd
For our aduantage on the bitter Crosse.
But this our purpose is a tweluemonth old,
And bootlesse 'tis to tell you we will go:
Therefore we meete not now. Then let me heare
Of you my gentle Cousin Westmerland,
What yesternight our Councell did decree,
In forwarding this deere expedience.

Detractors will need to contend with the fact that although daub and pant are in variations each used no less than half a dozen times, they are combined together just this one time, in a play that neatly fits into the pattern produced by the annotated page in question. The two French words pantoiser haleine added alongside the English to pant and panting reinforce the preciseness of the connections we see on the trailing blank to this cluster of plays, and here, in particular, with Henry's opening speech in *1 Henry IV*. Pantoiser is an old French equivalent of being *short winded*, and haleine means *breath*. (The annotator has marked *haleine* with a little circle where it falls in Baret under *breath*.) [156]

The very beginning of King Henry's speech is worth a second look:

>~ *1 Henry IV*. King Henry (1.1.1–3; FF d5b)
>   So shaken as we are, so wan with care,
>   Finde we a time for frighted Peace to **pant**,
>   And **breath shortwinded** accents of new broils

The annotation hardes of henepe (*hardes of hemp; henepe is old English*) with its French equivalent appears on the trailing blank just above the sequence in English and French beginning with to pant that was just referenced. The annotator has previously demonstrated interest where the phrase appears at H159 – ¶ / Hardes of hemp, xc. – and also adds a spoken annotation – hempseed chopt halter vide fellon – in coordination with the printed text at H388, *Hempe an hempen halter or rope*. The word hemp and its variations appear only six times in Shakespeare, with half of the usages in plays that are in harmony with the trailing blank:

>~ *2 Henry IV*. Hostess Quickly (2.1.59–60; FF g3)
>   Do, do thou Rogue: Do thou **Hempseed**.

>~ *Henry V*. Chorus (3.0.7–8; FF h5)
>   Play with your Fancies: and in them behold,
>   Vpon the **Hempen** Tackle, **Ship**-boyes climbing;

🖝 *Henry V*. Pistol (3.6.40–41; FF h6b)

> . . . let Gallowes gape for Dogge, let Man goe free,
> and let not **Hempe** his **Wind-pipe** suffocate: . . .

It is impossible to ignore that in the last of these examples, there is a struggle for breath, and this brings us back to the question of proximity as the annotator plays with variations on *panting* and *breath* on the trailing blank in the line directly below. The words choke and shippes added to the trailing blank are further echoes in these speeches.

There are other word combinations to be found in the Falstaff plays using the trailing blank annotations, and there is some temptation to bring all of the textual examples forward, even as we recognize the need to wind down the discussion. In a personal favorite, the words ebb and dote, each used multiple times in the Falstaff plays, appear once in combination, and what a lovely throwaway example it is of Shakespeare's gift, not to mention the only time that ebb and dote are combined in a speech.[157]

🖝 *2 Henry IV*. Duke of Clarence (4.3.125–28; FF gg4)

> The Riuer hath thrice flow'd, no **ebbe** betweene:
> And the old folke (Times **doting** Chronicles)
> Say it did so, a little time before
> That our great Grand-sire *Edward* sick'd, and dy'de.

But if we must conclude with one annotation combination from this page, let it be the combination book with bouquin.

The French annotation bouquin is an archaic usage referring to an old book. That Shakespeare considers old books at all in his works is granted to be trivial, but we feel as though we have earned the right to amplify the romantic quality of this chapter's conclusion by bringing up the following lines of poetry from Shakespeare on the subject of old books:

Show me your image in some antique **booke,**
–Sonnet 59

To blot old **bookes,** and alter their contents,
–*Rape of Lucrece*

The question is, have we found – to borrow again from *Luc-rece* – "subtle-shining secrecies writ in the glassy margents" that will prove convincing enough to sustain our theory? Will the trailing blank have people seeing his image in this antique book? Moving from Sonnet 59 to Sonnet 77:

> Thy glasse will shew thee how thy beauties were,
> Thy dyall how thy pretious mynuits waste,
> *The vacant leaues thy mindes imprint will beare,*
> And of this booke, this learning maist thou taste.
> The wrinckles which thy glasse will truly show,
> Of mouthed graues will giue thee memorie,
> Thou by thy dyals shady stealth maist know,
> Times theeuish progresse to eternitie.
> *Looke what thy memorie cannot containe,*
> *Commit to these waste blacks, and thou shalt finde*
> *Those children nurst, deliuerd from thy braine,*
> *To take a new acquaintance of thy minde.*
> These offices, so oft as thou wilt looke,
> Shall profit thee, and much inrich thy booke.

Does this once-vacant leaf bear an imprint of Shakespeare's mind or of another mind? That must be one of the critical debates going forward. The question is, does another hand make more sense than what we are suggesting – given that the evidence on the trailing blank ties to the evidence found throughout the book? Would a theory of "any number of language lovers" actually be considered *more* plausible in regard to this trailing blank?

We have long recognized that if there is a single aspect of our conclusion that is likely to be regarded as most unthinkable, most outlandish, it is that an entire page of disparate words in English – the majority translated into French on the same page – has survived for over four centuries with nary a glint of suspicion at having been penned there by the most celebrated author of all time. Our own conclusion is that the trailing blank is precisely that: this once-vacant leaf bears an imprint of Shakespeare's mind and not that of another.

Regardless of the conclusions that others will have – whether present and future scholars or intrigued persons generally – the basic questions should not be in dispute: *Dare we to ask what exactly is going on here? What is the significance to the words clustered over this page from top to bottom? And, finally, is there an actual function to them being there and, if yes, how does this function inform us?*

An annotator could add an infinite number of variations to a blank page at the back of a book. Over our many years in books, we have encountered myriad examples. Often, one is left with mere scribbles, great and small, sparse or plentiful, that do not equate to a picture of any real or unusual significance. Sometimes, there is a direction that one can follow and it is straightforward – a recipe, for example. On other occasions, there is a puzzle, and that puzzle may or may not be solvable or worth trying to solve. In the final analysis, the annotations we see on this page in this copy of Baret's *Alvearie* leave behind the most stirring puzzle imaginable, and one that we feel – for the most part – has been solved.

Surely, by any estimation, it is a baffling word assortment. Perhaps in the case of Shakespeare's prodigious memory, these words could have been contained, but the efforts at fiddling with the French required some additional practice nonetheless. Among the alternate explanations for this page could be a scenario that involved someone else with an interest in the plays – after seeing them performed or reading them – making these notes, but this seems to us a rather highly unlikely theory, for no reason greater than it would have to bear the additional weight of the entire annotated book to gain traction. Others may argue for computer-aided linguistic analysis relative to other period authors before committing any opinion. We are nothing if not eager to see honest attempts at correlating the results on the page with other writers: from premodern, straight on through the present day – as well as further efforts toward understanding the page from any number of additional points of departure.

If we are correct, how poignant, how truly splendid is it, that among the many wormholes that dot the leaf, none have touched a single word?

Baret as Shakespeare's Beehive

OW DOES one constantly go about finding language that offers fresh ways of depicting characters constrained by the same basic human motivations, circling similar dramatic situations, while playing out their various impulses and desires? No writer ever concerned himself less with the strain of having to do so, nor delighted in the conceit of challenging himself to accomplish more under that principle, than did Shakespeare. As such, Baret's *Alvearie* was for him the perfect tool, a honey-combed beehive of possibilities that may not have formed his way of thinking, but certainly fed his appetite and nourished his selection.

In act 2, scene 3, of *Coriolanus*, shortly after Coriolanus exits the stage under the impression that all has gone well, the citizens reconvene to discuss his merits regarding whether or not he ought to be confirmed.

🖙 *Coriolanus* (2.3.155–65; FF bb1)

Enter the Plebeians.

SICINIUS VELUTUS: How now, my Masters, haue you chose this man?
FIRST CITIZEN: He ha's our Voyces, Sir.
BRUTUS: We pray the Gods, he may deserue your loues.
SECOND CITIZEN: Amen, Sir: to my poore vnworthy notice,
He mock'd vs, when he begg'd our Voyces.
THIRD CITIZEN: Certainely, **he flowted vs** downe-right.
FIRST CITIZEN: No, 'tis his kind of speech, **he did not mock vs**.
SECOND CITIZEN: Not one amongst vs, saue your selfe, but sayes
He vs'd vs scornefully: he should haue shew'd vs
His Marks of Merit, Wounds receiu'd for's Countrey.
SICINIUS VELUTUS: Why so he did, I am sure.

This playful back-and-forth banter between the citizens, wherein Coriolanus's ascent to the top is swiftly undone, highlights Shakespeare's love of alternatives, a love that must have been greatly enriched through the use of his Baret.

Of *flout*, *mock*, and *scorn*, the annotator's expressions include the following:

M432. o To **scorne** or **mocke.**

F772. /¶ to **Flout,** or **mocke,** adds to flowt or mocke

S100. /¶ a saucie **Scoffer,** or flattring jester. Vide **Mocke,** Bourd, Jest, Laugh, and Flout

In this one small word salad alone, one can see how the annotator's mingling of spoken and mute annotations is formed around a cluster of interest that takes place at various positions in the dictionary.

In addition to providing a tool for exploring linguistic alternatives, Baret gave our annotator the opportunity to see things that he would not have seen anywhere else. John Jamieson, in his 1825 book *An Etymological Dictionary of the Scottish Language*, cites Baret alone for the term *flamefew:* "I have met with Flamefew nowhere else."[158]

The annotator marks this word:

F642. /¶ a **Flamefew** vide Toy, adds flambard

We could find no record of this word having been used by any writer of the period, but looking more closely, we see that Baret defines *flamefew* as "The Moonshine in the Water." This is an ordinary enough phrase, and that it is found in *Love's Labour's Lost* is not so exceptional: "Thou now request'st but moonshine in the water."

It gets more interesting, however, as we follow Jamieson's note, where he adds that Baret "seems to explain it [*flamefew*] as synonymous with Toy, for he adds, vide toy, which he gives in pl. toies, referring to trifle."

The annotator, paying close attention, as always, seeks out

the *vide* word after making his slash, and then (presumably, in this order) adds his little circles, many pages removed, under the entries for *laugh* and *trifle*. This action is one that is repeated and repeated and repeated: the annotator relishes Baret's dictum that it be noted in as many ways as it can be noted. Shakespeare, even if he is to be argued as a separate entity, shares the same appreciation. Here, the annotator dabbles in what is suggested for *toy*, synonymous with the obscure *flamefew*.

T336. ¶ **Trifles**, toies
o a **toie** or **trifling** thing.

L129. ¶ to **Laugh**
o A thing to be **laughed** at, **a foolish toie.**

D24. / ¶ to **Dallie**, to **trifle** and **toy** with **trifling** wordes

Look at what Shakespeare manages to do with the assortment:

🖙 *Hamlet.* Laertes (1.3.5–6; FF nn6)

For *Hamlet*, and the **trifling** of his fauours,
Hold it a fashion and a **toy** in Bloud;

🖙 *Antony and Cleopatra.* Cleopatra (5.2.160–4: FF zz1b)

Say (good *Cæsar*)
That I some Lady **trifles** haue reseru'd,
Immoment **toyes**, things of such Dignitie
As we greet moderne Friends withall,

🖙 *Love's Labour's Lost.* Biron (4.3.168; FF M1b)

laugh at idle **toyes**

🖙 *Twelfth Night.* Feste (5.1.387; FF Z6)

A foolish thing was but a **toy**,

🖙 *Venus and Adonis* (st. 18, 123–28)

To **toy**, to wanton, **dallie**, smile, and iest,

Observe now these annotation recordings around *patch* and *botch*, and how Shakespeare finds use for the words in a great clown speech from *Twelfth Night*:

P184. / ¶ to **Patch,** or make whole again…to botch: to make amends for, adds **a patch**

B974. / ¶ to **Botche** or amende garmentes

B975. o A **botcher** that amendeth garments.

☞ *Twelfth Night.* Feste (1.5.43–49; FF Y3)

Two faults Madona, that drinke & good counsell
wil **amend**: for giue the dry foole drink, then is the foole
not dry: bid the dishonest man **mend** himself, if he **mend,**
he is no longer dishonest; if hee cannot, let the **Botcher**
mend him: any thing that's **mended,** is but **patch'd**: vertu
that transgresses, is but **patcht** with sinne, and sin that **a-**
mends, is but **patcht** with vertue. If that this simple
Sillogisme will serue, so: if it will not, vvhat remedy?
As there is no true Cuckold but calamity, so beauties a
flower; The Lady bad take away the foole, therefore I
say againe, take her away.

In attempting to put together a cogent summation that allows our readers to feel the essence of how our annotator has used his Baret – and to demonstrate how much of Baret can be found in the canon – we have had no choice but to eliminate a great mass of what we feel are fine additional examples. There are, no doubt, many more still left to be discovered (particularly as relating to the proximity question), and having a website with a digitization of our Baret should allow for these to trickle in as others are able to locate them. Our organization of the annotations alongside the works has been structured to highlight the areas of the canon where we see the greatest concentration of echoes and curiosities. As we have already noted, there does seem to be a trailing off in the late middle works and the very late works, but this does not mean that there are not gems to be found from all periods.

Among the earlier works that did not receive prolonged attention are the tragedies *Romeo and Juliet* and *Titus Andronicus*. These plays contain important echoes of Baret, including one of the very first that caught our eye.

D1321. **Due,** adds drought in sommer

☞ *Titus Andronicus.* Titus (3.1.16–22; Q1594, E3–E3b)

> O earth I will befriend thee more with raine,
> That shall distill from these two auntient ruines,
> Then youthfull Aprill shall with all his showres
> **In summers drought,** Ile drop vpon thee still,
> In winter with warme teares Ile melt the snow,
> And keepe eternall spring time on thy face,
> So thou refuse to drinke my deare sonnes blood.

The words are twisted, and we see the spoken annotation come to life in this early play. *Summer* is, of course, a common word, but this is the only time that Shakespeare uses *drought;* thus it is one of Alfred Hart's "peculiar" words, those words with only a single usage.

When the annotator adds peale vide sing or ring a peale he is again using the *Vide* to direct attention to the other Baret definition, this time of *sing,* which includes, at S432, the phrase *to sing or ring a peale.* The only usage close to the spoken annotation is found in *Titus Andronicus.*

☞ *Titus Andronicus.* Titus (2.2.1–6; Q1594, D)

> *Enter Titus Andronicus, and his three sonnes.*
> *Making a noise with hounds & hornes*
> The hunt is vp, the Moone is bright and gray,
> The fields are fragrant, and the woods are greene,
> Vncouple here and let vs make a bay
> And wake the Emperour, and his louelie Bride,
> And rowze the Prince, and **ring a** Hunters **peale,**
> That all the Court may eccho with the noise.

In studying *Romeo and Juliet* alongside our annotator's Baret, we find a surplus of examples, examples wherein we witness the bending of language, including legal language, and the flair for turning idiom into poetry, proverb into plot.

A358. / ¶ to **Amerce:** to punishe by the purse: to put to a **fine**

☞ *Romeo and Juliet*. Prince (3.1.189–90; FF ff3)

> I haue an interest in your hearts proceeding:
> My bloud for your rude brawles doth lie a bleeding.
> But Ile **Amerce** you with so strong a **fine**,
> That you shall all repent the losse of mine.

F435. Adds ficklenesse of fortune

☞ *Romeo and Juliet*. Juliet (3.5.60–64; FF ff5)

> O **Fortune, Fortune,** all men call thee **fickle**,
> If thou art **fickle,** what dost thou with him
> That is renown'd for faith? be **fickle Fortune**:
> For then I hope thou wilt not keepe him long,
> But send him backe.

But perhaps the most remarkable annotation in our copy of Baret, relatable to *Romeo and Juliet,* is the added word vagina at the definition of *Scabberd,* which itself was given a mute slash.

S79–80. / ¶ a **Scabberd** Vide Sheath, adds vagina

Vagina is Latin for both *scabberd* and for *sheath,* as holders for a sword. The *Vide* is a cross-reference to the Baret definition of *sheath* where *vagina* is given in the printed text as the Latin equivalent.

The words are found in Shakespeare, as follows: *scabbard* (four times), *sheath* (four), *sheathed* (nine). *Sheath* and *sheathed* generally refer to a covering or case for a sword, except for two important instances where they are meant to be taken in the sexual context implied by *vagina.* The first is in Juliet's last speech as she stabs herself in her breast with Romeo's dagger and dies.

☞ *Romeo and Juliet*. Juliet (5.3.169–71; Q2 1599, L4)

> Yea noise? then ile be briefe. O happy dagger
> This is thy **sheath,** there rust and let me dye.

This is echoed by Capulet, later in the same scene, upon the discovery of Juliet's body:

☞ *Romeo and Juliet.* Capulet (5.3.201–4; Q2 1599, L4b)

> O heauens! O wife looke how our daughter
> This dagger hath mistane, for loe his house (bleeds!
> Is emptie on the back of *Mountague*,
> And it **missheathd** in my daughters bosome.

A. D. Nuttall, in *Shakespeare the Thinker*, specifically links *sheath* with the common anatomical meaning of *vagina* in Juliet's last words: "Her language is sexual. The Latin for 'sheath' is vagina."[159]

Sheath is also included in this sense as part of Falstaff's torrent of scurrilous invective directed at Prince Hal in the famous meeting in the Eastcheap Tavern in *1 Henry IV*. The word that follows, *bowcase*, is also found among our spoken annotations.

☞ *1 Henry IV.* Falstaff (2.5.248–51; FF c4)

> Away you Starueling, you Elfe-skin, you dried
> Neats tongue, Bulles-pissell, you **stocke-fish**: O for breth
> to vtter. What is like thee? You Tailors yard, you **sheath**
> you **Bow-case**, you vile standing tucke.

Two usages of *sheathed* occur each in *Venus and Adonis* and *Rape of Lucrece*:

☞ *Venus and Adonis* (st. 186, 1111–16)

> Tis true, tis true, thus was Adonis slaine,
> He ran vpon the Boare with his sharpe speare,
> Who did not whet his teeth at him againe,
> But by a kisse thought to persuade him there.
>   And nousling in his flanke the louing swine,
>   **Sheath'd** vnaware the tuske in his soft groine.

☞ *Rape of Lucrece* (st. 247, 1723–29)

> Euen here she **sheathed** in her harmlesse breast
> A harmfull knife, that thence her soule **vnsheathed**,
> That blow did baile it from the deepe vnrest
> Of that polluted prison, where it breathed:
> Her contrite sighes vnto the clouds bequeathed
>   Her winged sprite, & through her wo ds doth flie
>   Liues lasting date, from cancel'd destinie.

Interestingly, the *OED* does not find the first use of *vagina* in print as an English anatomical word until 1682, in Gibson's *Anatomy*. So our question was, did our annotator have the anatomical meaning of *vagina* in mind when he wrote his spoken annotation at S79–80, or was he just referring to the Latin translation of *sheath* as an ordinary functional object, as given in Baret? Could *vagina* have entered the Latin anatomical nomenclature during Shakespeare's lifetime and then gradually made its way into the English nomenclature, while on the way becoming known to students of Latin for its sexual meaning, as well? As we were pondering this, we learned of a much more likely, but unexpected, channel.

Lewis and Short[160] cite Plautus's play *Pseudolus*, act 4, scene 7, line 85, as the first usage of the Latin word *vagina* in the anatomical sense. Our great interest is in the third sub-definition for **vagina** occurring under "covering sheath, holder of anything." It is as follows, with the reference:

-3. The female vagina, Plaut. Ps. 4, 7, 85.

The twenty surviving Roman comedies of Plautus (c. 254–84 BC) are the earliest extant complete Latin literary works. One of Shakespeare's early comedies, *The Comedy of Errors*, is clearly based on Plautus's *Menaechmi*, and T. W. Baldwin, as well as other scholars who have researched the Latin instructional syllabus during the Elizabethan period, have shown that students were given Plautus's comedies to translate and perform, so it is likely that Shakespeare knew of *Pseudolus*, one of the best known of Plautus's plays.

🖙 Plautus, *Pseudolus* (4.7.85)
Ballio: . . . . conveniebat ne in *vaginam* tuam machaera militis?

(Translates: Not fitting into thy **sheath** soldier?)
Given the Plautus association, together with Shakespeare's known familiarity and use of Plautus as the source of *The Comedy of Errors*, we feel certain that the spoken annotation at S79–80,

vagina, definitely alludes to the female anatomy in addition to being the Latin translation of *scabbard* and *sheath*.

Thus it is fairly clear that A. D. Nuttall was correct in making the sexual connection for *sheath*, although by not himself citing Plautus (if he had realized that that was the source – he most likely did not) he left himself open to a line of questioning by the reviewer of his book in the *TLS*: "But then the late Professor Nuttall seems almost never to have read historians . . . ; he thinks Shakespeare punned on the word vagina, which tells us that he has not read Thomas Laqueur, from whom we learn that classical and Renaissance medical scholars spoke a very different Latin since they used the same words for the male and the female sexual organs."[161]

We are prepared and expect to face critical approaches of this kind. In fact, had we first come upon the *TLS* review of Nuttall's book, with its Thomas Laqueur reference, before we had discovered the citation from Plautus's *Pseudolus*, we too would have come to the reviewer's conclusion. But, at least in this instance, it seems certain that our annotation establishes that Plautus was considerably ahead of his time and that Shakespeare and Nuttall were right after all.

Dodging one problem is no sure proof of being able to sidestep another. It is not impossible to imagine the whole of our efforts being described by lines from *Rape of Lucrece* (st. 157, 1098–99):

> Like an vnpractiz'd swimmer **plunging** still,
> With too much labour drowns for want of skill.

But we will quickly point out that *plunging* is a "peculiar" usage and is also found marked in our Baret with a mute slash:

P531./ ¶ a **Plunging** horse that casteth the rider

A subsidiary definition to this entry mentions water:

o To **plunge**, or dip in **water**.

There are sure to be textual points of interest to scholars regardless of how the debate involving authorship of the annotations unfolds. These may include – but will certainly not be limited to – question marks over authorship in poems such as *A Lover's Complaint* and the sequence that makes up *The Passionate Pilgrime*.

The annotation a maunde or baskette contains a word, *maund*, found in *A Lover's Complaint* but nowhere else in Shakespeare.

☞ *Lover's Complaint* (st. 6, 36–42; Q1609, K1b)

A thousand fauours from a **maund** she drew,
Of amber christall and of bedded Iet,
Which one by one she in a riuer threw,
Vpon whose weeping margent she was set,
Like vsery applying wet to wet,
Or Monarches hands that lets not bounty fall,
Where want cries some; but where excesse begs all.

One of the more poetic of the thousand-plus spoken annotations is peepe of daye vide – breake. *Vide* indicates a cross-reference to B1201, ¶ *the* **Breake** *of the daie*. The first sentence underneath, *before daie breaking,* has a little circle mute annotation. It is followed by *: I will get me away to morowe at daie breake, or at peep of daie.*

Peep day and *tomorrow* occur on the last two lines of the last of three stanzas of section xv of *The Passionate Pilgrime*. Although each six-line stanza has the same format as the stanzas of *Venus and Adonis*, they fall within the portion of *The Passionate Pilgrime* that is considered doubtful to be of Shakespearean authorship. According to E. K. Chambers: "Of the rest, xvi cannot be his, and those who think that vii, x, xiii, xiv–xv, and xix may be do not express themselves with much confidence."[162]

☞ *The Passionate Pilgrime* (st. 14, 25–30; octavo 1599)

Were I with her, the night would post too soone,
But now are minutes added to the houres:
To spite me now, ech minute seemes an houre,
Yet not for me, shine sun to succour flowers.

Pack night, **peep day**, good day of night now borrow
Short night to night, and length thy selfe **to morrow**

Chambers has earned his magisterial tone as no one else, but perhaps some will soon beg to differ here. The expression *break of day* is commonly used throughout, but *peep day* only here.

The interest over textual confusion in works where exclusive authorship is less subject to debate should be equally strong. Consider this annotation and a line from *Henry V* that appears in the First Folio and has subsequently been changed.

W28–29. to laie **Wait,** adds waiting servant lacquay

We find in Baret at L33: **Lackies or waiting servant**s.
In *Henry V:*

🖝 Dolphin (4.2.2; FF i3b)
Monte Cheua: My Horse, ***Verlot Lacquay:*** Ha.

This line has subsequently been changed to **"Varlet, laquais,"** but this alteration is still debated in some critical editions, such as *The Arden* edited by T. W. Craik,[163] which offers extensive notes. The annotation *lacquay* is an example where the issue of spelling – understood to be tricky in terms of establishing credibility in the promotion of any argument – is unusually intriguing.

This brings us back to the question of the French, which may still be bothersome to some. The annotator is demonstrably in-terested in French words and meanings throughout the process of annotating. What many may fail to realize is the extent to which many of the English words in Baret are said to be of French origin. The massaging of the French would help provide greater possi-bilities in utilizing language as a whole, and most certainly that is a quality Shakespeare would have been dedicated to, apart even from his straightforward use of French in *Henry V* and elsewhere.

Here is a fairly typical example of how the annotator uses the Baret text to pick up on an English word and add a French one:

B1453. / ¶ a **Bugge**

The slash by the word *bugge* (bug) will not raise the eyebrows of most modern readers, but in the *Alvearie* the word has nothing to do with an insect – it's an object of terror, such as an apparition.

Shakespeare has two usages:

☞ *3 Henry VI*. King Edward (5.2.2; FF q3)
For *Warwicke* was a **bugge** that fear'd vs all.

☞ *The Winter's Tale*. Hermione (3.2.91; FF Aa6)
The **Bugge** which you would fright me with, I seeke:

There is a spoken annotation in French at the end of the definition, and that is where it really begins to get interesting:

B1453. Adds fantosme

Shakespeare, unsurprisingly, does not use this archaic French word, but he does, one time, use *phantasma*:

☞ *Julius Caesar*. Brutus (2.1.60–69; FF kk3b)
'Tis good. Go to the Gate, some body knocks:
Since *Cassius* first did whet me against *Cæsar*,
I haue not slept.
Betweene the acting of a dreadfull thing,
And the first motion, all the *Interim* is
Like a *Phantasma*, or a hideous Dreame:
The *Genius*, and the mortall Instruments
Are then in councell; and the state of a man,
Like to a little Kingdome, suffers then
The nature of an Insurrection.

In Shakespeare's *Select Plays* (1879), edited by William Aldis Wright, the following textual note is supplied: "The modern word 'phantom,' which is derived from '**phantasma**,' comes to us through the French fantome, originally **fantosme**."[164]

As an example of how our own thought process evolved while studying the Baret, consider the annotator's simple addition of vide returne under the text at H485, *Hit: not to hit the truth, Vide Amisse and Deceived.* The annotation was recorded, as all of the annotations were, but only long after the adjoining text from Baret was realized to be of utmost significance did we go back to the annotator's contribution at H485, vide returne. Much as the opening text from *Coriolanus* brought to mind the notion of characters playing their own game of *vide*, the exchange between Isabella and Duke Vincenzo in act 3, scene 1, of *Measure for Measure* seems to us now as anything but coincidental.

☞ *Measure for Measure* (3.1.191–209; FF F6b)

ISABELLA: I am now going to resolue him: I had rather
my brother die by the Law, then my sonne should be vn-
lawfullie borne. But (oh) how much is the good Duke
deceiu'd in *Angelo:* if euer he **returne**, and I can speake
to him, I will open my lips in vaine, or discouer his go-
uernment.

DUKE: That shall not be much **amisse**: yet, as the matter now stands, he will auoid your accusation: he made
triall of you onelie. Therefore fasten your eare on my
aduisings, to the loue I haue in doing good; a remedie
presents it selfe. I doe make my selfe beleeue that you
may most vprighteously do a poor wronged Lady a me-
rited benefit; redeem your brother from the angry Law;
doe no staine to your owne gracious person, and much
please the absent Duke, if peraduenture he shall euer **returne** to haue hearing of this businesse.

ISABELLA: Let me heare you speake farther; I haue spirit to
do any thing that appeares not fowle in the **truth** of my
spirit.

The common nature of the words could initially lead one to argue that this is a foolish reach, but consider that the texts link the word *return* and the word *deceive* in a speech three times only, and the words *amiss* and *return* only twice. This establishes them as uncommon combinations, and both exchanges occur here, in a single scene, with conversation moving from one character to the next. Shakespeare may not have had his Baret open when he wrote this scene. But our argument – not exclusively based on the simple added word returne cramped within the text column, but rather all the evidence in our book – is that Shakespeare had in his brain that *return* could be a *vide* word for either *deceive* or *amiss* because of his intimate familiarity with Baret generally, and this copy of Baret specifically.

The printed Baret, we remind our readers, is not in question at all, nor are the existence of the works, nor are the existence of our annotations. As such, the comparative nature of these three sources should remain the primary focus *before* the difficult questions of paleography are asked, and previous assumptions modified.

Regrettably, we have condensed many of our favorite finds, including those from the classic tragedies *Othello*, *King Lear*, and *Macbeth*.

The obsolete word *grise* is in *Othello*, perhaps plucked from a Baret memory.

G559–60. / ¶ **Grises, or steps** were made to go vp vnto the entrie

☞ *Othello*. Duke (1.3.198–200; Q1622, C4)

Let me speake like your selfe, and lay a sentence
Which, as a **greese or step** may helpe these louers
Into your favour.

Minikin gets an *OED* citation for the second use of the meaning: diminutive or shrill voice. However, the sense of Baret seems to be the main sense of *minikin*, "a playful, or endearing, term for a female." The word is underlined in our copy beside the key word, *elegant*, which has a slash. *Minikin* is used one time only, in *King Lear*.

E147. / ¶ Elegant. <u>minikin</u>, tricke, or trimme - - - -

☞ *King Lear*. Edgar (3.6.36–41; Q1608, scene 11, G4)

Let vs deale iustly sleepest or wakest thou iolly shepheard,
Thy sheepe bee in the corne, and for one blast of thy **minikin**
mouth, thy sheepe shall take no harme, Pur the cat is gray.

Also underlined at W238 is <u>Maugre his head.</u>

☞ *King Lear*. Edgar (5.3.128–33; Q1608, scene 24, L1b)
Maugure thy strength, youth, place and eminence,
Despight thy victor, sword and fire new fortun'd,
Thy valor and thy heart thou art a traytor.
False to thy Gods thy brother and thy Father,
Conspicuate gainst this high illustrious prince,
And from the 'xtreamest vpward of thy **head,**

A third speech from the mouth of Edgar, this time in the midst of an exchange with the Fool, contains a small sampling of spoken annotations around the key words to describe the areas:

G624. A swallowe, gulfe, or **whirlepoole**, a <u>**quagge**</u> mire, that sucketh up, or swalloweth.

M391. <u>**A quagge**</u> mire.

Q1–2. Adds a quagge and gulfe

W191. / ¶ a **Whirlepoole**, or a turning round of the water: a **whirlewind**

S299. / ¶ water Shallower and deeper. Vide Foord, adds vel fourd

☞ *King Lear*. Edgar (3.5.45–55; Q1608, scene 11, G1b)
Who giues any thing to poore *Tom*, whome the foule
Fiende hath led, through fire, and through **foord,** and
whirli-poole, ore bog and **quagmire**, that has layd kniues vnder his pillow, and halters in his pue, set ratsbane by his <u>pottage</u>,
made him proud of heart, to ride on a bay trotting horse ouer
foure incht bridges, to course his owne shadow for a traytor.
blesse thy fiue wits, *Tom*s a cold, blesse thee from **whirle-winds,**
starre-blusting, and taking, doe poore *Tom* some charitie, whom
the foule fiend vexes, there could I haue him now, and there, and
and there againe.

From *Macbeth*, a simple but unusual little coupling, one of many in our book, is seemingly lifted straight out of Baret and into the closing lines of Macbeth's first soliloquy:

U/V18. / ¶ a **Vaulter** that **leapeth** vp and downe from a horse. Vide **Leape** and Light, adds vaulting

🐎 *Macbeth*. Macbeth (1.7.25–28; FF mm2)

> I have no Spurre
> To pricke the sides of my intent, but onely
> **Vaulting** Ambition, which **ore-leapes** it selfe,
> And falles on **th'other**.

Inspecting the *vide* reference in the Baret text further, at L431, under *light*, we see a slash, and *leap* is there as a spoken annotation. At another subsidiary example at L440, marked with a little circle, we find *vaulting* listed in print along with *horse* and *another*, further clarifying Shakespeare's figurative usage above, cited in the *OED* as the first usage of *vaulting* as "that vaults or leaps."

> L431. / ¶ to **Light**, or sitte downe as birds do after flight, to settle, adds
> vide leap
> L440. o Lighting downe, **vaulting** from one **horse** to **another**.

Vault and *horse* are combined three times, once also with *leap*, in *Henry V*:

🐎 *Henry V*. Henry V (5.2.137–43; FF k)

> If I could winne a Lady at Leape-frogge, or by
> **vawting** into my Saddle, with my Armour on my backe;
> vnder the correction of bragging be it spoken. I should
> quickly **leape** into a Wife: Or if I might buffet for my
> Loue, or bound my **Horse** for her fauours, I could lay on
> like a Butcher, and sit like a Iack an Apes, neuer off.

N. F. Blake in *Shakespeare's Non-Standard English: A Dictionary of his Informal Language* interprets this for sex, "vault. to leap onto a horse. hence, to have sexual intercourse."[165]

Moments such as these took some time for us to discover in relation to our annotations sets. But there were other instances where lines leapt right off the page, as with Hamlet and the examples of *posset* with *curd* and *thaw* with *resolve*. Such was also the experience when we heard the witches' brew:

> B1416. / ¶ to **Bubble**, or **boyle** out in great plentie

This became more invigorating when we took the trip from the spoken annotation at C1734: culleis vide potage.

Culleis is a type of broth or gravy, beef or fowl, and is not found in Shakespeare. *Potage* is used only in the first two quartos of *King Lear* that were printed in 1608 and 1619, both preceding the First Folio, which substituted *porredge* instead. Many modern editions, including widely used concordances, have adopted the First Folio's choice. But the annotator has been so kind as to direct us to the Baret definition of *potage*. At P601, we see it defined by Baret with *gruel* and *slabber*, each underlined by our annotator:

P601. ¶ **Potage**: **gruell**
    To **slabber** vp potage halfe cold.

This appears to validate Shakespeare's intended "peculiar" usage of *potage* in *King Lear*, since he marks Baret's placement with his two mute underlinings to note *gruel* and *slab*, which are also each used only once, in the same line of the second brew of the Weird Sisters following the one with *boil* and *bubble*:

☞ *Macbeth* (4.1.12–34; FF mm6–mm6b)

SECOND WITCH: Fillet of a Fenny Snake,
    In the Cauldron **boyle** and bake:
    Eye of Newt and Toe of Frogge,
    Wooll of Bat and Tongue of Dogge:
    Adders Forke and Blind-wormes Sting,
    Lizards legge and Howlets wing:
    For a Charme of powrefull trouble,
    Like a Hell-broth **boyle** and **bubble**.
ALL: Double, double toyle and trouble,
    Fire burne and Cauldron **bubble**.
THIRD WITCH: Scale of Dragon, Tooth of Wolfe,
    Witches Mummey, Maw and Gulfe
    Of the rauin'd salt Sea sharke:
    Roote of Hemlocke, digg'd i'th'darke:
    Liuer of Blaspheming Iew,
    Gall of Goate, and Slippes of Yew,
    Sliuer'd in the Moones Ecclipse:

Nose of Turke, and Tartars lips:
Finger of Birth-strangled Babe,
Ditch-deliuer'd by a Drab,
Make the **Grewell** thicke, and **slab**.
Adde thereto a Tigers Chawdron,
For th' Ingredience of our Cawdron.

Discoveries such as these were moments of great satisfaction, and it is difficult to convey the level of emotional victory that we admittedly felt when falling into annotations such as *gruel* and *slab*. Consider for our final examples in this chapter the massaging that takes place around less colorful verbiage, but nonetheless the vitally important Shakespearean themes of deception contained in the words – and the variations on the Baret entries for – *visor* and *visard, mask* and *masker*.

The *OED* notes that *vizard* comes from the same place as the word *visor* and means "mask." C. T. Onions expands by declaring it as the "mask to conceal the face, often kept in place by a tongue or interior projection, held in the mouth."[166] The usages in Shakespeare are as abundant – *vizard* (six times), *vizards* (seven), *vizarded* (two), *vizard-like* (one), *visor* (ten), *maskers* (three), *masker* (one), *masquers* (four) – as the annotator's interest is explicit:

M178. /¶ a **Masker**, one **disguised**, one wearing a **visard**
V92. /¶ a **Visor**. Vide **Masker**, adds visiere masquer and visour visard

In act 5, scene 2, of *Love's Labour's Lost*, seven usages of *vizard* or a variation of occur following this entrance of the concealed:

☞ *Love's Labour's Lost.* Boyet (5.2.156; Q1598, G3b)

     Sound Trom.
The Trompet soundes, be maskt, the maskers come.
*Enter Black-moores with musicke, the Boy with a
speach, and the rest of the Lordes disguysed.*

Speeches as disparate and as wide apart as those in *Macbeth, 3 Henry VI, Troilus and Cressida,* and *Merry Wives* combine usages involving *vizard* with the notions of being "masked" and "disguised."

☞ *Macbeth*. Macbeth (3.2.30–36; FF mm4b)

So shall I Loue, and so I pray be you:
Let your remembrance apply to *Banquo*,
Present him Eminence, both with Eye and Tongue:
Vnsafe the while, that wee must laue
Our Honors in these flattering streames,
And make our Faces **Vizards** to our Hearts,
Disguising what they are.

☞ *Troilus and Cressida*. Ulysses (1.3.80–83; FF yy1b)

When that the Generall is not like the Hiue,
To whom the Forragers shall all repaire,
What Hony is expected? Degree being **vizarded**,
The vnworthiest shewes as fairely in the **Maske**.

☞ *The Merry Wiues of Windsor*. Fenton (4.6.38–39; FF E5)

(The better to deuote her to the *Doctor*,
For they must all be **mask'd** and **vizarded**)

☞ *3 Henry VI*. King Lewis XI (3.3.222–26; FF p5b)

Then Englands Messenger, returne in Poste,
And tell false Edward, thy supposed King,
That *Lewis* of France, is sending ouer **Maskers**
To reuell it with him, and his new Bride.
Thou seest what's past, go feare thy King withall.

In *Romeo and Juliet*, twice – in back-to-back scenes in act 1 –
the *maskers* enter and *visors* are revealed.

☞ *Romeo and Juliet*. Mercutio (1.4.27–32; FF ee4b)

Enter Romeo, Mercutio, Benuolio, with fiue or sixe
other **Maskers***, Torch-bearers.*
If loue be rough with you, be rough with loue,
Pricke loue for pricking, and you beat loue downe,
Giue me a Case to put my visage in,
A **Visor** for a **Visor**, what care I
What curious eye doth quote deformities:
Here are the Beetle-browes shall blush for me.

(Midway between these two speeches, Mercutio gives his *Queen Mab* speech.)

☞ *Romeo and Juliet*. Capulet (1.5.16–33; FF ee5)

Enter all the Guests and Gentlewomen to the
Maskers.

Welcome Gentlemen,
Ladies that haue their toes
Vnplagu'd with Cornes, will walke about with you:
Ah my Mistresses, which of you all
Will now deny to dance? She that makes dainty,
She Ile sweare hath Cornes: am I come neare ye now?
Welcome Gentlemen, I haue seene the day
That I haue worne a **Visor**, and could tell
A whispering tale in a faire Ladies eare:
Such as would please: 'tis gone, 'tis gone, 'tis gone,
You are welcome Gentlemen, come Musitians play:
  Musicke plaies: and the dance.
A Hall, Hall, giue roome, and foote it Girles,
More light you knaues, and turne the Tables vp:
And quench the fire, the Roome is growne too hot.
Ah sirrah, this vnlookt for sport comes well:
Nay sit, nay sit, good Cozin *Capulet*,
For you and I are past our dauncing daies:
How long 'ist now since last your selfe and I
Were in a **Maske**?

The further we delved into our copy of Baret's *Alvearie*, the more real the idea of Shakespeare and Baret became. Shakespeare's understanding and his utilization of Baret was intricate, more so than T. W. Baldwin could have imagined when he glorified the book by heralding it as "the dictionary of Shakespeare's youth." Without this particular copy of Baret in his grasp, Baldwin can readily be excused for glossing over it, almost in passing, in a two-volume set spanning over 1400 pages. Through the studying of our copy of Baret, we began to see the *dictionarie* as Shakespeare's Beehive – how he used it and why it was the perfect book for him. As the annotator's contact inevitably also left behind personal traces, one candidate emerged from the enormous heap of those known and those unknown.

What's in a Name?

OR SHAKESPEARE, whether by observation or the studying of texts, language was a tool, an elastic cosmos without boundaries or limits. For the annotator of our *Alvearie*, a similar engaging in the vicissitudes of words is on display. We have tried to bridge the gap between the awe of Shakespeare and the seemingly ordinary annotator of our Baret.

It we could only find links that led us to names of plays, or the names of characters from the plays. There seemed to be nothing in this regard, but as the pursuit of familiarizing ourselves with the book lengthened and lengthened and lengthened, we begin to see a pattern of finding names in the margins. In the chapter on the trailing blank, we noted that not only is <u>*Caius*</u> underlined in the preamble of letter "C," but that the underlining takes place in the midst of a discussion on the misunderstanding of letters.

This led us to seek out a few other instances where annotations seemed to be oddly aligned with names from the plays. Beginning with one that may not resonate all that dramatically, we find the following cluster of mute annotations relating to *crab* and *sour*:

C1523.　/　¶ **Crabbedly**, **sowrely**, grimly, lowringly
C1526.　/　¶ a **Crabbe** tree
C1528.　o **Sowrenesse**, lowring, **crabbed** looking: crooked: frowning.
G551.　/　¶ Grimmely, **sowrely**: lowringly: **crabbedly**

🔈 *Two Gentlemen of Verona*. Launce (2.3.5–6; FF C)

I think **Crab**, my dog, be the **sowrest** natured dogge that liues:

Having a character in *Two Gentlemen of Verona* name his dog *Crab*, and liken him to being *sour* is not going to rattle anyone's bones. A stronger example between the names and the annotations – again, strangely enough, using dogs – is found in *King Lear:*

The annotator twice links *blanch* and *bark* as *vides*:

B175. Barked, pilled, adds vide blanche
B779. to Blanche, adds vide barche

This association actually has to do with the rind of a tree as these mute annotations attest:

R334. ╱ a **Rinde**. Vide **Barke**.
B779. ╱ to **Blanche**, or pull of the **rinde** or pille.

When the annotator adds at R333–34 after *Rinde vide Barke* the word *nothing* (one of several words used in such instances of a mistake, *frustra* being another) he is noting that a certain *vide* has been omitted where it ought to be printed. All in all, it's a quite detailed look at *blanch*, *bark*, and *rind*, that our annotator demonstrates. Look now at Lear:

☞ *King Lear.* Lear (3.6.57–59; Q1608, G4)

The little dogs and all,
Tray, **Blanch**, and Sweetheart, see, they **bark** at me.

Perhaps the linguistic echoes from Baret helped to shape Shakespeare's name selections, after all, at least when it came to dogs.

Some characters in Shakespeare have no names; they are simply given identities. Have you ever used the *fruiterer* in a sentence? Well, minimally we know that our guy marked a sentence, and *the* guy wrote a sentence:

F1165. o The **frutterer**, or he that selleth apples.

☞ *2 Henry IV.* Shallow (3.2.28–32; FF g6b)

The same Sir *Iohn*, the very same: I saw him
breake *Scoggan's* Head at the Court-Gate, when hee was
a Crack, not thus high: and the very same day did I fight
with one **Sampson Stock-fish**, a **Fruiterer**, behinde Greyes-Inne.

In this instance, we imagine that Shakespeare was just flying through the scene, practically acting it in his head, speech by speech, almost as fast as it would take the actors to perform it, and so he comes up with the name "Sampson Stockfish" who has to have an occupation, certainly not a fishmonger or fisherman, and he either has the Baret in front of him (he has placed a lot of mute and spoken annotations on these "end of F" pages) or in his memory (more likely, we speculate), so when he comes upon, or remembers, *fruiterer*, that he has already marked with his "little circle," he doesn't hesitate.

A fruiterer is one thing, so he used fruiterer, you say. How about stockfish? *Sampson Stockfish?*

We do wonder if in our book somewhere we saw the spoken annotation "Sampson Stockfish" (or a Baret entry for "Stockfish," with the name, "Sampson" written above it), would those who will be in a position to argue our annotations as trivial, and in no way more connected to the work of Shakespeare than to other plausible writers, throw in the towel, and admit that the annotations must have *something* to do with Shakespeare? Alas, there is no such annotation combination, but we do have a spoken annotation: at S918, Stockes, where the annotator adds stockdove, after previously marking the printed word as a mute annotation:

D1085. a Dove, or Pigeon....Of a <u>ringdove, woodculver, or stockdove</u>.

Each of these underlined examples ends up as its own spoken annotation, with *woodculver* receiving one of the special "W" formations. Perhaps Shakespeare simply altered "Stockdove" into "Stockfish" — after all, what kind of a name is "Sampson Stockdove"! Besides, Falstaff himself had already made use of "stockfish" in *1 Henry IV*, in the Eastcheap Tavern scene that we have already cited for *sheath* and *bowcase*, so we know that Shakespeare favored it and thought of it as a form of insult:

🖝 *1 Henry IV*. Falstaff (2.5.248–51; FF c4)

> Away you Starueling, you Elfe-skin, you dried
> Neats tongue, Bulles-pissell, you **stocke-fish**: O for breth
> to vtter. What is like thee? You Tailors yard, you **sheath**
> you **Bow-case**, you vile standing tucke.

To use another example from a Falstaff play, consider the thought process that may have taken place during the composition of *The Merry Wives of Windsor*. In *Merry Wives*, Shakespeare needed to name both a Country Justice and a Gentlemen Living at Windsor. We know, for sure, that the annotator enjoyed the words Shallow and Ford together, as we have three mute and one spoken annotation to attest to that:

> F1049. ∕ a Fourd, a <u>shallowe</u> place, where men may go over.
> S299. ∕ Shallower vide foorde, adds vel fourd

Shakespeare likes the words enough to pair them in verse:

🖝 *Rape of Lucrece* (st. 190, 1324–30)

> To see sad sights, moues more then heare them told,
> For then the eye interpretes to the eare
> The heauie motion that it doth behold,
> VVhen euerie part, a part of woe doth beare.
> Tis but a part of sorrow that we heare,
>   Deep sounds make lesser noise th **shallow foords**,
>   And sorrow ebs, being blown with wind of words.

So, why not, he thinks to himself; *Shallow* and *Ford* it shall be.

These words can be written off as ordinary words that anyone could have used for names, and Shakespeare would not have required a copy of Baret's *Alvearie* to find them. Enter Susan Grindstone.

Our annotator liked the word *grindstones* enough to underline it when he saw it under the entry for *water*. He follows this thought by inserting it as a spoken annotation: G557, "to grind," where he adds a grindstonne.

Grindstone itself is a peculiar word, used only as a servant's name for this one First Servant's speech in act 1 of *Romeo and Juliet* shown below and simply to introduce the hectic preparations for the Capulet feast where Romeo makes his appearance a few lines later. But, here is where it gets interesting. The speech of the Second Servant just above mentions the foulness of "unwashed hands."

☞ *Romeo and Juliet* (1.5.1–9; FF ee5)

FIRST SERVANT: Where's *Potpan*, that he helpes not to take away?
   He shift a Trencher? he scrape a Trencher?
SECOND SERVANT: When good manners shall lie in one or two mens
   Hands, and they **vnwasht** too, 'tis a foule thing.
FIRST SERVANT: Away with the Ioynstooles, remoue the Court-
   cubbord, looke to the Plate: good thou, saue mee a piece
   of Marchpane, and as thou louest me, let the Porter let in
   Susan Grindstone, and *Nell, Anthonie* and *Potpan.*

Looking directly across the gutter to the previous page from where grindstonne is added, we can see the entries for *wash*. One of the subsidiary definitions toward the bottom of the page has "wash my hands."

This whole *Romeo and Juliet* First Servant–Second Servant scene with Susan Grindstone is much too vibrant relative to its importance in the play, and there is yet another verbal connection in it via Baret and our mute annotations. The whole Baret line containing *wash my hands* is: *"fetch, or geue me some water to wash my hands."* And…we also have a little circle mute at *fetch:*

o Go fetch **trenchers**.

When we go back one speech further, to the First Servant's opening sally, what do we see? "Where's Potpan, that he helps not to take away? He shift a **trencher**? he scrape a **trencher**!"

Fetch, trencher, unwashed hands are all in there with Susan Grindstone!

For kickers, we have a second mute annotation under *plate*:

o *A saucer, a* **plate** *occupied at the table for a* **trencher**.

Why is this relevant? Consider the First Servant's next line after he uses *trencher*: "Away with the joint-stools, remove the court-cupboard, look to the **plate**."

To complete the discussion, *wash* and *hands*, are not surprisingly used frequently together, sometimes figuratively. But *unwash* and *hands*? Only once, by our old friend:

🖛 *1 Henry IV*. Falstaff (3.3.184–85; FF f2)

Rob me the Exchequer the first thing thou do'est,
and do it with **vnwash'd hands** too.

We feel we are unable to make a better case for the name *Grindstone* coming from this particular copy of Baret's *Alvearie*.

Requiring less in the way of dictionary gymnastics, the name of another seldom considered Shakespeare character may be indeed be locatable vis-à-vis the interplay between Baret text and annotation in this copy. That character is Apemantus from *Timon of Athens*.

Beside M441, where we see the Baret text *to make a Moe like an ape*, the annotator adds many moe.

To help make the example more compelling, consider that the word *moe* is used on three occasions in *Timon of Athens*, and each time Apemantus is in the scene.

🖛 *Timon of Athens* (4.3.398–400; FF hh3b)

APEMANTUS: Liue, and loue thy misery.
TIMON: Long liue so, and so dye. I am quit.
APEMANTUS: **Mo** things like men,
                    Eate *Timon*, and abhorre then.
                         Exit Apemantus

The three Benditti then enter and engage with Timon. As part of his reply:

🖛 Timon (4.3.433–35; FF hh3b)

      Trust not the Physitian,
His Antidotes are poyson, and he slayes
Moe then you Rob:

There may well be Shakespeare character names that we were unable to detect from working through the annotations and the printed text. Our own efforts have led to those mentioned and the following two additional discoveries.

In the margin at the top of the column where we see the head-word definitions of *scrone* (S105) and *scotfree* (S109) we find the spoken annotation scotches v. scarre with a mouse-foot placed in the column directing the eye to the position just above "Scot-free" where the spoken annotation is meant to be placed alphabetically. Shakespeare likes this word, *scotch*.

☞ *Macbeth* (3.2.15; FF mm4b)
We haue **scotch'd** the Snake, not kill'd it:

☞ *Coriolanus* (4.5.191–92; FF bb6)
"he **scotcht** him, and notcht him"

Beatrice refers to the measures of music twice in *Much Ado About Nothing* "like a Scotch jig" and "as a Scotch jig" (2.1.65–67; FF I4b).

But "scotches," as a noun plural, is used only once:

☞ *Antony and Cleopatra* (4.8.6–7; FF y4b)
Wee'l beat 'em into Bench-holes, I have yet
Roome for six **scotches** more.

What is the name of the character in the play who happens to have the room for six more scotches? **Scarus!** Annotator: scotches v. scarre.

Scarus is another very minor character, appearing in only two scenes and hardly features in the plot. In the Arden Shakespeare Edition of *Antony and Cleopatra*, there is an editorial note on the name Scarus: "As Capell notes, the name is not from Plutarch, the hero of this sally being merely 'one of his [Antony's] men of armes.'" The character, as he further says, was a necessity, in order to fill up the place about Antony left vacant by Enobarbus."[167]

For the last of our "obscure name" examples, possibly originating with this copy of Baret, we turn to S177. The annotator adds sedges vide flagges and glayeul puant. Here are two usages:

🖝 *Two Gentlemen of Verona*. Julia (2.7.25–32; FF C2b)

> The Current that with gentle murmure glides
> (Thou know'st) being stop'd, impatiently doth rage:
> But when his faire course is not hindered,
> He makes sweet musicke with th' enameld stones,
> Giuing a gentle kisse to euery **sedge**
> He ouer-taketh in his pilgrimage.
> And so by many winding nookes he straies
> With willing sport to the wilde Ocean.

🖝 *Antony and Cleopatra*. Octavius (1.4.44–47; FF x2–x2b)

> This common bodie,
> Like to a Vagabond **Flagge** vpon the Streame,
> Goes too, and backe, lacking the varrying tyde
> To rot it selfe with motion.

Sedge is commonly used as a water plant that bends to the wind and current, and *flag* – used many times as a banner – is used in this one instance as a water plant, as well. Shakespeare uses it multiple times in variation in the same speech or verse. *Sedge* is from the Anglo-Saxon *Secg*, and stood for almost any waterside plant. So far it seems as though not much is there. But if we turn to *flagges* (F638), we find a slash and a little circle beside *flagges or sedges*. Underneath the printed French reads *glayeul puant*. This translates to a specific plant: the *Iris*. Perhaps it is just a coincidence, you will say, but we think it nice that the *Tempest* usage of *sedges* is by the character *Iris*:

🖝 *Tempest*. Iris (4.1.128–29; FF B2)

> You Nimphs cald *Nayades* of ye windring brooks,
> With your **sedg'd** crownes, and euer-harmelesse lookes,

Then again, perhaps it is no mere coincidence. Our annotator's prodigious memory has, once again, returned to his *Alvearie*.

"My Darling"

D141–42. A deanerie. Adds dearling – and my dearling Ps. 22

| 1 4 1 | ✶ A deanerie. Decanatus,tus,pen.prod.ma.gen. Bud. *Doyenne.* :‐*Dearling.* my do~~ling~~ *pf.* |
| 1 4 2 | ¶ Dearth, or scarsitie of corne and victu= |

M y dearling Ps. 22, this two-word quotation identified as being from the 22nd Psalm, has come to be, in our minds, the most interesting and most important spoken annotation in the entire text portion of our *Alvearie*. As one of our twelve biblical quotations, it already had a significance common to all of these quotations written into the text, as we have described earlier. But, having verified its source as indeed Psalm 22, we were soon led along a very promising pathway bounded by Shakespeare's biography and with excerpts from his published works. For this reason we have made the choice to expand our description and indulge in a practice that we have hereto carefully tried to avoid, but that we feel is sanctioned in this singular case, at least in part, by the final sentences in Stephen Greenblatt's preface to his biography, *Will in the World: How Shakespeare Became Shakespeare:* "To understand who Shakespeare was, it is important to follow the verbal traces he left behind back into the life he lived and into the world to which he was so open."[168]

Of course, the verbal traces in this copy of Baret that we have concluded are Shakespeare's may not ever be accepted as such. But for the sake of the exercise, and because we are certainly left with *someone's* "verbal traces," we will use Greenblatt's suggested guideline of using one's imagination to follow this verbal trace, the my dearling annotation, "back into the life he lived."

Notice what has happened here in this double annotation. It appears that the annotator had first written just the word dearling in the column between the definitions of *deanerie* at D141 and *dearth* at D142, and then remembered the short phrase *my dearling* from Psalm 22, writing it into the space remaining in the same column, but necessarily with smaller lettering because of the now reduced space. But what is most significant about writing dearling this second time; what is different? Only the addition of the two-letter pronoun my, and the naming of the biblical source, Ps. 22, in which it originated. It is precisely these two distinguishing points that will enable us to trace it back into the life he lived.

Let us first consider Psalm 22, the biblical source of the quotation. These are the five early modern English translations of the Hebrew Bible for the line of Psalm 22 that contains "my dearling."

Coverdale Bible (1535)	Delyuer my soule from the swearde, **my dearlinge** from the power of the dogge.
Great Bible (1540)	Delyuer my soule from the swearde, **my dearlynge** frō the power of the dogge.
Bishops' Bible (1568)	Delyuer my soule from the sworde: and **my dearlyng** from the dogges pawes.
Geneva Bible (1587)	Deliuer my soule from the sword: **my desolate soule** from the power of the dogge.
King James Bible (1611)	Deliuer my soule from the sword: **my darling** from the power of the dogge.

For those who are not familiar with it, as well as for those who are, the question naturally arises as to why extract just these two words, this short phrase, as representative of the entire text of the psalm? In our note on the Great Bible and the Bishops' Bible, we mention the findings of Peter Milward and Jonathan Bate, as well as others, that, through the period of the early plays, Shakespeare was more likely to remember the language of the Great Bible or the Bishops' Bible from hearing it read in church as a child. Let us then take ourselves back to the Church of the Holy Trinity in Stratford-upon-Avon, circa 1570, and try to absorb the language of Psalm 22 from the Great Bible while also imagining what William Shakespeare, as a young boy, sitting with his mother and father in church, would have heard as it was read aloud:

PSALM 22

My God, my God: (loke vpō me) why hast thou forsakē me: and art so farre fro my health, and frō the wordes of my complaynte? O my God, I crye in the daye tyme, but thou hearest not: and in the nyght season also I take no rest. And thou continuest holy, O thou worshyppe of Israel. Oure fathers hoped in the: they trusted in the, and thou dyddest delyuer them.

They called vpon the, and were helped: they put theyr trust in the, and were not confounded. But as for me, I am a worme & noām : a very scorne of men & the outcast of the people. All they þᵗ se me, laugh me to scorne: they shote out theyr lyppes, & shake þᵉ heade sayinge.

He trusted in God that he wolde delyuer him: let him delyuer him, yf he wyll haue him. But þᵘ art he þᵗ toke me out of my mothers wombe: thou wast my hope, when I hanged yet vpō my mothers brestes.

I haue bene left vnto þᵉ euer sence I was borne: thou art my God, euē fro my mothers wombe.

O go not fro me, for trouble is harde at hande, and ther is none to helpe me.

Greate oxen are come aboute me, fatt bulles of Basan close me in on euery syde.

They gape vpon me with theyr mouthes as it were a rampynge and roarynge lyon.

I am powred out lyke water, & all my bones are out of ioynt: my hert also in the myddest of my bodye is euen lyke meltynge waxe.

My strength is dryed vp lyke a potsherde, & my tonge cleueth to my gūmes: and thou shalt brynge me into the dust of death.

For (many) dogges are come aboute me, & the coūcell of the wycked laye seage agaynst me. They pearsed my handes and my fete, I maye tell all my bones, they stonde starynge and lokynge vpon me.

They parte my garmētes amonge thē and cast lottes vpon my vesture. But be not þᵘ farre fro me, O Lord: thou art my succoure, haste the to helpe me. Delyuer my soule from the swearde, **my dearlynge** frō the power of the dogge. Saue me from the lyons mouth: thou hast hearde me also from amonge the hornes of the vnicornes.

I wyll declare thy name vnto my brethren: in the myddest of the cōgregaciō wyll I prayse the.

O prayse the Lorde ye þᵗ feare hī: Magnifye hym all ye of the sede of Iacob, & feare hī all ye sede of Israel. For he hath not despysed ner abhorred the lowe estate of þᵉ poore he hath not hyd hys face frō hym, but whē he called vnto him, he harde him. My prayse is of the in the great cōgregacion, my vowes wyll I perfourme in the syght of them that feare hym. The poore shall eate, & be satisfyed: they that seke after þᵉ Lorde, shall prayse hym. youre herte shall lyue for euer. All the endes of the worlde shall remēbre thē selues, & be turned vnto the Lorde, & all þᵉ kynreds of the nacions,

shall worshyppe before him. For the kyngdom is the Lordes, and he is the gouernoure amonge the people.

All soche as be fat vpon earth haue eatē & worshypped. All they þᵗ go downe into the dust, shall knele before him & no man hath quyckened hys awne soule. My. Sede shall serue him: they shalbe counted vnto þᵉ Lorde for a generacyon. They shall come, and the heauens shall declare hys ryghteousnes: vnto a people that shall be borne, whom the Lorde hath made.

If we may repeat and expand the question: why settle on just these two words, this short phrase, *my dearlynge*, to represent the text of the entire 22ⁿᵈ Psalm? What was so memorable about just these two words given the context of the entire psalm? We believe it is possible that this could have been, for Shakespeare, one of the earliest of memories.

First to backtrack, and review an important finding about the serious outbreak of plague that had struck Stratford just at the time of Shakespeare's birth, in April 1564. This is from Chapter 2, "Mother of the Child," of Park Honan's biography *Shakespeare, A Life* [169]: "In the last six months of 1564, Mary's infant was the object of more than a mother's usual care and vigilance, if only because the conditions of a severe plague were unusual. . . . A pattern of Mary's special care for her son is also likely to have been set in these months. . . . In early life he must have been the focus of Mary's very urgently watchful, intense love."

Although Edmund Malone had known of the plague outbreak in Stratford at that time, Honan is the first biographer we are aware of to stress the special bond of Mary Shakespeare's intense love for William, her first son and oldest surviving child. We believe that the my dearling annotation relates to this close intense relationship of Shakespeare to his mother, which lies at the core of his memory.

We imagine William Shakespeare sitting in church beside his mother at about the age of six, when his precocious awareness of the English language would have been able to register the stark imagery and terror of the biblical language but without giving him the accompanying understanding of the literary and religious conventions that it embodied. By the time the reader had come to the lines just preceding line 21, with *my dearling*, William would have heard:

> Great oxen are come about me, . . . They gape upon me with their mouths as it were a ramping and roaring lion. . . . my heart also in the midst of my body is even like melting waxe. . . . and thou shalt bring me into the dust of death.

This would be followed by the crucifixion imagery:

> the wicked lay siege against me. They pierced my hands and my feet, I may tell all my bones, they stand staring and looking upon me.

Most assuredly, he would have become disturbed and visibly upset, which, in turn, would have greatly disturbed Mary Shakespeare who, upon hearing the words *my dearling* in the next line –

> Deliver my soul from the sward, my darling from the power of the dog.

– could have taken this chance to reach out to comfort him, perhaps clasping his hand, and whispering, "you are my dearling." William Shakespeare would have then experienced a compelling and deeply emotional physical and verbal assurance.

An imagined scene, to be sure, but one that accounts for our spoken annotation and that may also account, in a surprising way, for the crucial climactic scene in *Coriolanus*, a play that William Shakespeare would write almost forty years later, close to the time of Mary Shakespeare's death.

The importance of this moment in Shakespeare's life, or of a moment very similar to this, cannot be overestimated. This was a time before there were media of any kind, when, aside from occasional visits by traveling players, seasonal rural festivals, and weekly market days in the town's center, the Sunday church service was basically the only regular public event where the townspeople formally composed themselves as an audience. Attendance allowed the precocious boy to gradually experience his awakening to language as part of such an audience, while also in the midst of his close family. Could this vivid moment, almost imperceptible except for mother and son, have created an unforgettable memory as an emotional resolution to an event that demonstrated to a young boy, although perhaps not as expressly, a dual ability of language both to alarm and traumatize, but also to comfort and assuage?

The word *dearling*, in the sixteenth century, took on a particular premodern meaning of "preciousness" and not the full range of meanings of *darling* in today's English. N. F. Blake, in *Shakespeare's Non-Standard English: A Dictionary of His Informal Language*, defines it as "precious little one,"[170] so young William would have heard his mother saying to him "you are my precious little one." *Dearling* appears in Baret, as well, as part of the definition of *cockney*, which reinforces Blake's definition, and we have a mute annotation there:

C729. / ¶ A Cockney: a childe tenderly brought vp: a **dearling**

Shakespeare used a form of *darling* eight times — *darling* five times, *darlings* twice, and *darling's* once — in *2 Henry VI, 3 Henry*

VI, Sonnet 18, *Othello* (two mentions), *All's Well That Ends Well*, *Pericles*, and *Tempest*. The *OED* cites him for it twice, once for its early figurative use as "of things" in *Othello* —

☛ *Othello*. Othello (3.4.55–68; FF tt6)

That's a fault: That Handkerchiefe
Did an AEgyptian to my Mother giue:
She was a Charmer, and could almost read
The thoughts of people. She told her, while she kept it,
'T would make her Amiable, and subdue my Father
Intirely to her loue: But if she lost it,
Or made Guift of it, my Father's eye
Should hold her loathed, and his Spirits should hunt
After new Fancies. She, dying, gaue it me,
And bid me (when my Fate would haue me Wiu'd)
To giue it her. I did so; and take heede on't,
Make it a **Darling**, like your precious eye:
To loose't, or giue't away, were such perdition,
As nothing else could match.

— and again, for its first use as an adjective "of things," in the familiar Sonnet 18:

☛ *Shake-speares Sonnets*. Sonnet 18 (1–4)

Shall I compare thee to a Summers day?
Thou art more louely and more temperate:
Rough windes do shake the **darling** buds of Maie,
And Sommers lease hath all too short a date:

The first use of *darling* in *Othello* (act 1, scene 2), as printed in the First Folio, has the spelling *Deareling*, which is closer to the spelling in Shakespeare's spoken annotation, whereas it is printed in the first *Othello* quarto of 1622 as *Darling*. Every other use of *darling* and its variants in the early printed texts is also spelled *darling*.

☛ *Othello*. Brabantio (1.2.63–72; FF ff4b)

O thou foule Theefe,
Where hast thou stow'd my Daughter?
Damn'd as thou art, thou hast enchaunted her

For Ile referre me to all things of sense,
(If she in Chaines of Magick were not bound)
Whether a Maid so tender, Faire, and Happie,
So opposite to Marriage that she shunn'd
The wealthy curled **Deareling** of our Nation,
Would euer haue (t'encurre a generall mocke)
Run from her Guardage to the sootie bosome,
Of such a thing as thou: to feare, not to delight?

Interestingly, the appearance of *my dearling* in the Great Bible and Bishops' Bible translation of Psalm 22 was not a precisely accurate translation of the Hebrew word יְחִידָתִי which is archaic and appears only one other time in the Hebrew Bible. As a result, its meaning is still open to interpretation.[171] Currently the English translation is usually given as *mine only one* or *my singular one*. The Geneva Bible translated it as *my desolate soule*, which has not been repeated in any later translation, although Talmudic studies also relate it to the soul because a person is said to have his one and only soul. The King James Bible restored it to *my darling* but with a note indicating "Heb. my only one." It appears that many Protestant denominations now translate this as *my life*, although there are still current translations using *my darling*.

Shakespeare was forty-four years old when his mother died in the late summer of 1608. The son she had carefully nurtured through the first months and years of his life had already written almost all of his plays, including *Richard III*, *Richard II*, *Romeo and Juliet*, *Midsummer Night's Dream*, the *Henry IV* plays, *Julius Caesar*, *Hamlet*, *Twelfth Night*, the sonnets, *Othello*, *King Lear*, and *Macbeth*, and had just completed *Coriolanus*. To what extent Mary Shakespeare may have fully understood the enormous scope that her son had achieved as a poet, playwright, and man of the theater is not known. Nor is it known how their relationship had evolved as they both grew older. She had given birth to five more children, three sons and two daughters, and there is no record of her ever having traveled far from Stratford.

But one of the main themes of *Coriolanus* concerns a willful and dedicated Roman mother, Volumnia, who, from her son Caius Martius's birth, was determined to construct and mold him into an ideal Roman soldier who could exult in battle, and then emerge scarred and victorious to reap its honors. Because this play must have been written as his mother's health was failing (the latest play chronologies have its first performance in 1608), some critics have felt that Volumnia and her intense relationship to her son was meant to correlate in some sense, even if in a directly opposite mode, to Shakespeare's relationship with his own mother. However, E. K. Chambers wrote that "there is no reason to suppose that Volumnia was inspired by Shakespeare's mother, who was buried on 9 September 1608."[172] But perhaps we can show that the spoken annotation in our *Alvearie* suggests otherwise.

A. D. Nuttall, in *Shakespeare the Thinker*,[173] looks at *Coriolanus* primarily through the lens of Volumnia's deliberate "construction" of her son, from his birth, into a great Roman warrior. This is the climactic scene (5.3.95–190; FF cc2):

VOLUMNIA
Should we be silent & not speak, our Raiment
And state of Bodies would bewray what life
We haue led since thy Exile. Thinke with thy selfe,
How more vnfortunate then all liuing women
Are we come hither; since that thy sight, which should
Make our eies flow with ioy, harts dance with comforts,
Constraines them weepe, and shake with feare & sorow,

CORIOLANUS'S WIFE VIRGILIA
I, and mine, that brought you forth this boy,
To keepe your name liuing to time.

CORIOLANUS'S SON YOUNG MARTIUS
A shall not tread on me: Ile run away
Till I am bigger, but then Ile fight.

CORIOLANUS
Not of a womans tendernesse to be,

Requires nor Childe, nor womans face to see:
I haue sate too long.

VOLUMNIA

. . . . There's no man in the world
More bound to's Mother; yet heere he lets me prate
Like one i'th 'Stockes. Thou hast neuer in thy life,
Shew'd thy deere Mother any curtesie,
When she (poore Hen) fond of no second brood,
Has clock'd thee to the Warres: and safelie home
Loden with Honor. Say my Request's vniust,
And spurne me backe: But, if it be not so
Thou art not honest, and the Gods will plague thee
That thou restrain'st from me the Duty, which
To a Mother's part belongs. He turnes away:
Down Ladies: let vs shame him with our knees
To his sur-name Coriolanus longs more pride
Then pitty to our Prayers. Downe: an end,
This is the last. So, we will home to Rome,
And dye among our Neighbours: Nay, behold's,
This Boy, that cannot tell what he would haue,
But kneeles; and holds up hands for fellowship,
Doe's reason our Petition with more strength
Than thou hast to deny't. Come, let vs go:
This Fellow had a Volscean to his Mother:
His Wife is in Corioles, and his Childe
Like him by chance: yet giue vs our dispatch:
I am husht vntill our City be afire, & then Ile speak a little.

[Holds her by the hand silent,]

CORIOLANUS

O Mother, Mother!
What haue you done? Behold, the Heauens do ope,
The Gods looke downe, and this vnnaturall Scene
They laugh at. Oh my Mother, Mother: Oh!
You haue wonne a happy Victory to Rome.
But for your Sonne, beleeue it: Oh beleeue it,
Most dangerously you haue with him preuail'd,
If not most mortall to him.

Nuttall emphasizes the importance of this stage direction: "In *Coriolanus* the crisis comes when Volumnia has broken her son, before the walls of Rome. The strongly formed soldier resists her plea for mercy but cannot hold out when hit by the word of simple, terrifying, conditioning power, 'mother.' It is here that we have the remarkable stage direction (surely Shakespeare's), 'Holds her by the hand, silent.'"[174]

Can the connection that we are drawing between the relationships of Mary Shakespeare and her son William (in our reconstruction of the creation of Shakespeare's core *my dearling* memory) and Volumnia and her son Martius Coriolanus be substantiated through similar hand gestures? This is perhaps not easy to recognize, since *both* involve imaginative reconstructions. As booksellers, and not Shakespearean scholars, we were not aware of the "Holds her by the hand, silent" stage direction in *Coriolanus* at the time that we envisioned the physical hand holding between William and his mother when they heard the words *my dearling* during the reading of the 22nd Psalm in church.

But we sensed that the similarity of a crucial hand gesture in each of these scenes, however derived, has an undeniable ring of truth that is truly remarkable. The first scene is an imaginative reconstruction drawn from what we know of Shakespeare's life and what we can surmise about the reason he chose to write my dearling Ps. 22 into the "margent" of his dictionary, an annotation that remained hidden for over 400 years and was surely never intended to be found and wondered at. The second is the actual scene, with the playwright's own stage direction, as it appeared in print for the first time in the 1623 First Folio, from a work of Shakespeare's imagination, intended to be played before an audience of thousands. Both scenes involve an intense moment of connection between mother and son, both having fateful consequences for the son, the first at the beginning of the son's life, the second at the end.

Could Mary Shakespeare's imagined clasping of her son's hand and whisper of "my dearling" have been the "Stratfordian moment," the beginning of it all, the signal event from Shakespeare's childhood that would have stayed in his memory as the seed of his supreme understanding of the power of language, and set the son of a glover in a small provincial sixteenth-century English town on his path to becoming the greatest writer the world has ever known?

To derive a "Stratfordian moment" by using two mother-and-son occasions, one based on biography and a two-word biblical notation hidden within the columns of a 1580 dictionary, and one taken from Shakespeare's late tragedy *Coriolanus*, may draw forth a note of caution that we would not want to reflect back on the carefully wrought calculus of the previous chapters. But our annotated Baret holds one more surprise:

Consider the interlude in Volumnia's long plea to her son to abandon his alliance with the Volces in which Virgilia, Coriolanus's wife, and his young son, Martius, speak:

☞ Coriolanus's wife Virgilia (5.3.126–28; FF cc2b)

> I, and mine, that brought you forth this boy,
> To keepe your name liuing to time.

☞ Coriolanus's son young Martius (5.3.128–130; FF cc2b)

> A shall not tread on me: Ile run away
> Till I am bigger, but then Ile fight.

To which Coriolanus replies:

☞ Coriolanus (5.3.130–2; FF cc2b)

> Not of a womans **tendernesse** to be,
> Requires nor **Childe**, nor womans face to see:
> I haue sate too long.

And then recall Baret's definition of *cockney* with its synonym, *dearling:*

C729. / ¶ A Cockney: a **childe tenderly** brought vp: a **dearling** and notice again the annotator's mute slash marking. Both *childe* and *tenderly* are used in the "Cockney" definition and are also used by Shakespeare in Coriolanus's rejection of their pleas. And there is *dearling* given in Baret as a synonym for "a child tenderly brought up," and, we must dare to say, undoubtedly in Shakespeare's mind as he wrote the scene. In effect, we have now circled back to our initial question: why single out "my dearling" in the 22nd Psalm? And achieved confirmation in a most astonishing way.

This became even clearer to us as we made yet a further discovery. We hadn't realized how closely Shakespeare had followed his source for all of his Roman plays, Thomas North's translation of Plutarch in the edition published by Richard Field in 1595, particularly in the case of Coriolanus where not only the major plot and characters, but even the settings of many of the important scenes, and within those scenes, much of North's actual narrative text as well. As an example, we can compare the opening lines of Volumnia's speech in act 5 with the same speech narrated by North:

☞ Volumnia. Thomas North translation, Plutarch's *Lives* (1595)

If we held **our** peace (my sonne) and determined **not** to **speake**, the **state of** our poore **bodies**, and present state of **our raiment, would** easily **bewray** to thee **what life we haue led** at home, **since thy exile** and abode abroad. But **thinke** now **with thy selfe, how** much **more vnfortunately, then all** the **women liuing we are come hither,** considering **that the sight which should** be most pleasant to all other to behold, spitefull fortune hath made most **fearefull** to vs :

☞ Volumnia. Shakespeare, *Coriolanus*

Should we be silent & **not speak, our Raiment**
And **state of Bodies would bewray what life**
We haue led since thy Exile. Thinke with thy selfe,
How more vnfortunate then all liuing women
Are we come hither; since **that thy sight, which should**
Make our eies flow with ioy, harts dance with comforts,
Constraines them weepe, and shake with **feare** & sorow,

And also, the similarities of Coriolanus's reply to his mother after "he holds her by the hand, silent" and realizes that she has broken him:

☞ Martius Coriolanus. Thomas North translation, Plutarch's *Lives* (1595)

Oh mother, what haue you done to me?

[And **holding her hard** by the right **hand,**]

oh mother said he **you haue wonne a happy victorie** for your countrie, but **mortall** and vnhappy **for your sonne**: for I see my selfe vanquished by you alone.

☞ Martius Coriolanus. Shakespeare, *Coriolanus*

[Holds her by the hand silent,]
        O Mother, Mother!
What haue you done? Behold, the Heauens do ope,
The Gods looke downe, and this vnnaturall Scene
They laugh at. **Oh** my **Mother**, Mother: Oh!
You haue wonne a happy Victory to Rome.
But for your Sonne, beleeue it: Oh beleeue it,
Most dangerously you haue with him preuail'd,
If not most **mortall** to him.

Of course, this has long been known, but it shows clearly that Shakespeare did not arrive at this critical scene through the logic of the developing drama alone. Instead, we can now see the signs of an attempt to register a definite memory. North's inclusion of the descriptive "holding her hard by the right hand" must have triggered that memory, the same youthful memory of *my dearling* from hearing Psalm 22 read in church that caused him to write the annotation in the column of his dictionary, and also brought to mind Baret's definition of *cockney*, a *dearling* denoted by the words *child* and *tenderly*.

But the real light bulb went on when we read this simple editorial comment in the Arden edition of *Coriolanus* edited by Philip Brockbank: "Virgilia and the young Martius do not intervene in

Plutarch's account."[175] So this intervention, too, was written as part of the author's response to North's narrative with the intent of embodying his "my dearling" memory. Mother and young son are each given two lines in the midst of a tense and dramatic confrontation and Coriolanus's reply to them, with the clear echo of Baret's definition of *cockney* as *a dearling*, was inserted by Shakespeare almost as a re-creation of the "Stratfordian moment" that we had imagined. In the same way that the pairing of Volumnia and Coriolanus mirrors the pairing of Mary Shakespeare and William Shakespeare, but in opposing modes, the intervention scene with Virgilia, young Martius, and Coriolanus uses *dearling* (or its synonym) in the opposing sense. Coriolanus, in his speech, is saying that he cannot risk any further exposure to the tenderness of a woman or a child – it will lead to his own destruction. We can now understand that our original sense of an "undeniable ring of truth" was, in fact, a sign that we had stumbled so unexpectedly upon a complex coincidence of memory and intent through the study of the annotations in our copy of Baret's *Alvearie*, and we are confident that it is capable of yielding a great deal more.

Afterword

WE ARE in the business of cataloguing old and rare books and manuscripts. We have fashioned *Shakespeare's Beehive* as a single-item catalogue, the content of which is our attempt at building a platform for someone who elects to argue that Shakespeare himself has authored the annotations in our copy of Baret's *Alvearie* 1580.

We have for some time been well aware that no matter how diplomatically we make the claim, we are still inevitably framing our discovery in terms of the authorship issue. Scholars, and Shakespeare scholars in particular, are so conditioned to be doubtful of any claims having to do with books, signatures, objects, etc., connected to Shakespeare himself that they cannot help but keep our work at arm's length, at least until it is all out in the open.

One of our goals all along was to present the material in measured and non-polemical ways, so that scholars and laypeople alike could extract from our study whatever linguistic elements they wished to focus on, should the strain of considering the authorship of the annotations be a distraction. What we have maintained will almost certainly be the case is that annotated books from alternative hands held in institutions or private collections worldwide will pale greatly should the search for Shakespearean echoes be sought elsewhere as a means for comparison.

We cannot get around the fact that we are approaching Shakespearean scholars as booksellers who are touting a discovery of the first definitive example of one of Shakespeare's own books, and not just a book, but a dictionary, and not just a dictionary with a few sporadic annotations, but one that is heavily and intricately annotated, with annotations ranging all the way down to the most nit-picky and mundane. Even the most open-minded scholar, who doesn't know us personally, is going to have a whole host of immediate instinctive reactions to this scenario: Is this all about authenticating a book to get the most money out of it? Is it a hoax? Are we over-enthusiastic amateurs? Will the financial implications of the book prevent a proper scholarly critique? And so on.

So we are aware that we are already starting with one strike against us in the minds of all of these scholars, at the very least on some subconscious level. But you can't very well deny who you are, and so we are left in the paradoxical position of trying to make a scholarly argument ourselves in order to convince a scholar to take enough of an interest to assume the burden of making a scholarly argument about the book. We recognize the unlikeliness of this scenario and so proceeded independently. We anticipate that many in the scholarly community will feel a greater sense of comfort once we release our study publicly, but this remains to be seen.

This brief summation of what brought us to this stage brings us to a question that we have asked all along, a subject of debate with no clear perfect answer: how to present our study?

A presentation of our book that contained essentially all the close analysis of the annotations that we have amassed, but without making any strong assertions about authorship of those annotations, would be received with enormous interest by many specialists in the field, and would likely give birth on its own to a debate about authorship. How quickly or how vigorously that debate would happen is harder to say, but it is in the very nature of scholarly inquiry that the more eyes are examining the evidence, the more things people will notice and the more textured the debate can become.

All of this was implicit in one of the most carefully constructed responses we received during the course of reaching out, when it was suggested that, at minimum, even if Shakespeare is eliminated as a possible annotator, our book is a very important discovery for how quickly Shakespeare was being integrated into the language during the early seventeenth century.

This carefully worded response was essentially highlighting the scholarly process itself over any kind of absolute pronouncements. Of course, we imagine this scholar would be as excited as anyone (just about anyone) if that process and debate demonstrated with strong probability that Shakespeare himself was the annotator, but in a sense we were being told that the scholar was not comfortable with the authorship claim being the driving force here, especially when it was expressed so strongly.

We have tried to balance our own authorship claim, even experimenting along the way with a plan that would allow it to emerge more gradually and gently. Would that have been a more persuasive means of exploring the possibility? Who knows?

There is a difference between a purely scholarly motivation and the more complex one we have. We are not merely gentlemen scholars; we admit to having a financial stake in the book, as well as an emotional one, and there is the desire to see some recognition for our discoveries and for the amount of time and energy and capital spent on this project. We have for some time been eager to see it unfold toward public release, but if satisfying the scholarly community means minimizing the claim that Shakespeare wrote the annotations, then what would a public release in that form actually yield? That is to say, why would the larger public be interested in this book if we weren't making a claim about Shakespeare? We are taking such a strong stance on the claim because we believe this to be true, but others may argue that we are doing so to make the biggest public splash possible; for that reason, we risk it being dismissed out of hand by the scholarly community.

We have attempted to satisfy both the need to express our own conclusions and to finally provide scholars with an open forum for discussion. A website has been built to contain a digitized copy of the Baret in its entirety, along with our own recording of every mark in the book, both spoken and mute. We expect to modify and update the website to allow for new discoveries, and also make note of either corrections to the recording of the spoken annotations, or alternative suggestions to the readings and interpretations that we have made here in *Shakespeare's Beehive*. We hope that this will allow scholars and other interested parties the freedom to explore this annotated copy of Baret from whatever perspective sparks an interest.

We gently remind our readers that what we have grappled with in these pages is based not on a new theory – as is frequently put forth concerning Shakespeare, even after all these years – but on an object containing hard evidence in the form of an extensive network of annotations. The recording of this extensive network of annotations, with its many layers and nuances, will offer a means of comparison when similar patterns are sought in other annotated books, and likewise when the work of other writers is applied and considered. The results will vary, but, overall, right down to the trailing blank, it may indeed be Shakespeare decisively over the others. If it does play out accordingly, the possibilities are relatively few.

The least likely scenario suggests that someone left a very strange set of notes and markers having been intimately familiar with the works of Shakespeare. Theoretically conceivable, but still at odds with statistical probability: someone left a very strange set of notes and markers with little or no familiarity with Shakespeare and just got really lucky. Possible, but to our minds, also highly questionable, the annotator had some exposure to Shakespeare, and the annotations in the book demonstrate how quickly the language found in Shakespeare was integrated into the language generally, and that we must accept the existence of certain annotations as either trivial or aberrational. The final possible conclusion, our own, is that Shakespeare and the annotator are one and the same.

However the search for alternative annotators unfolds, or the argument for a nameless annotator is insisted upon, the position that Baret's *Alvearie* was a vitally important sourcebook should never again be doubted. Objections to T. W. Baldwin's hitherto seldom accounted for assertion, that Shakespeare could not have "preserved the patterns so accurately if [he] had not himself turned many a time and oft to Baret for his varied synonyms," will be puzzling in light, especially, of the language unique to Baret wherein so many textual affinities are revealed. That so many of these affinities can be found in *any* copy of Baret speaks to the obscurity of a book never once reprinted since 1580.

Within the initial pages of the book's prefatory material is printed a delightful poem, by one Tho. M. It reads, in part:

> So Barret gone to God, in heauenlie seates,
> Hath left behind, a monument of praise,
> This Hiue of his, referst with honie meates,
> Which children feede, with sugred wordes and phrase:
> A booke for such, that can peruse it right,
> Of profite great when they their Vulgars write.

We have spent a good deal of time with "this hive of his," and still more time discussing it, over meals and on sidewalks, secretly while at book fairs, and through a deep burial ground of emails, mostly preserved. What we find in our Baret is evidence that is so much greater by being the sum of so many parts. We have often asked ourselves how this neglected copy could have survived so long without serious prior study. As a response to this, we urge our readers to consider that if our marginal note as fat as browne had instead read "as fat as butter," we might not have this book. If it had read "as fat as Falstaff" (or, even better, "as fat as Olde-castle") then we *certainly* would not have this book. But it reads as fat as browne, and, as is so often the case when pouring over the annotations in this Baret, what looks like nothing reveals everything.

The "vide" linguistic strategy, suggested by John Baret in his *Alvearie*, is a tool that Shakespeare obviously used throughout his life as a writer. No one, it can safely be said, approached the whole notion of linguistic alternatives – the whole idea of Baret's "vide" – as did Shakespeare. In that sense, the *Alvearie* was, for him, the perfect enabler. Once this is acknowledged, the miracle aspect of discovering this particular copy can safely be reduced, and perhaps we may even then conclude that Shakespeare used disconnected letters in a decidedly mixed hand when confined to small spaces – the narrow margents and the obscure interlineal crannies – as he proofread books such as Holinshed and Baret for Henry Denham. The more proficient we became at following the annotator's methods, and the more familiar we became with Shakespeare's works and with Baret's *Alvearie*, the more easily we could see that Shakespeare is everywhere throughout the book, and Baret is everywhere throughout Shakespeare. Baret's *Alvearie* was the perfect book for Shakespeare, and the evidence left behind in our copy demonstrates exactly how he would have used it. The works of Shakespeare prove that.

Acknowledgments

We would like to extend our deep thanks and gratitude to Lauren Avirom and Jessica Savage for the time and contributions they each made to this project, and for the emotional support they offered in regularly listening to the ongoing progress, the concerns, and the anxiety that accompanied such an undertaking as this one. Further gratitude and thanks are extended to editor Janice Fisher, who read each word carefully and offered great insight as she guided us toward the completion of this book.

Over the course of putting together this study, we also engaged with a number of prominent scholars, each of whom made valuable suggestions or offered encouragement. Occasionally the encouragement amounted to something along the lines of a friendly "good luck with that – curious to see where it goes"; other times, after sharing early selections from our work, we received specific criticism that enabled us to proceed advantageously. It would be difficult to overstate our gratitude to these individuals for their contributions, and we thank them all here as one, so as to respect both their confidentiality and their initial reactions to our early efforts, should interest in this copy of Baret accelerate following the release of our study and the unveiling of shakespearesbeehive.com.

Sources

Abbott, Edwin. *A Shakespearian Grammar: An Attempt to Illustrate Some of the Differences Between Elizabethan and Modern English*. London: Macmillan, 1869.

Acheson, Arthur. *Shakespeare's Lost Years in London 1586–1592, Giving New Light on the Pre-sonnet Period : Showing the Inception of Relations Between Shakespeare and the Earl of Southampton and Displaying John Florio as Sir John Falstaff*. New York: Brentano's , 1920.

Ackroyd, Peter. *Shakespeare: The Biography*. London: Chatto & Windus, 2005.

Alberge, Dalya. "Shakespeare's Fingerprints Found on Three Elizabethan Plays." *The Guardian*, October 12, 2013.

Allen, Michael J. B. and Kenneth Muir, eds. *Shakespeare's Plays in Quarto: A Facsimile Edition of Copies Primarily from the Henry E. Huntington Library*. Berkeley: University of California Press, 1981.

Andersen, Jennifer Lotte and Elizabeth Sauer, eds. *Books and Readers in Early Modern England: Material Studies*. Philadelphia: University of Pennsylvania Press, 2002.

Armstrong, Edward. *Shakespeare's Imagination: A Study of the Psychology of Association and Inspiration*. Lincoln: University of Nebraska Press, 1963.

Ash, John. *A New and Complete Dictionary of the English Language*. 2 vols. London: Edward & Charles Dilly, 1775.

Ayers, P. K. "Reading, Writing, and *Hamlet*." *Shakespeare Quarterly* 44 (1993), 423–39.

Baldwin, T. W. *On the Literary Genetics of Shakespere's Poems and Sonnets*. Urbana: University of Illinois Press, 1950.

————. *William Shakspere's Small Latine & Lesse Greeke*. 2 vols. Urbana: University of Illinois Press, 1944.

Bate, Jonathan. *Soul of the Age: A Biography of the Mind of William Shakespeare*. New York: Random House, 2009.

———— and Eric Rasmussen, eds. *The Sonnets and Other Poems*. Introduction by Jonathan Bate. The RSC Shakespeare. Basingstoke: Macmillan, 2009.

Beal, Peter. *A Dictionary of English Manuscript Terminology: 1450–2000.* Oxford: Oxford University Press, 2008.

[Bernard Quaritch.] *English Books.* Catalogue 1352. London: Bernard Quaritch, 2007.

Berry, Edward. *Shakespeare and the Hunt: A Cultural and Social Study.* Cambridge: Cambridge University Press, 2001.

Black, James. *Edified by the Margent: Shakespeare and the Bible.* Calgary: University of Calgary, Faculty of Humanities, 1979.

Blades, William. *Shakspere and Typography: Being an Attempt to Show Shakspeare's Personal Connection with and Technical Knowledge of the Art of Printing.* New York: Burt Franklin, 1969. First published 1872.

Blake, Norman. *Shakespeare's Non-Standard English: A Dictionary of His Informal Language.* London: Continuum, 2004.

Bloom, Harold. *Shakespeare: The Invention of the Human.* New York: Riverhead Books, 1998.

———, ed. *William Shakespeare's Sonnets.* New York: Chelsea House, 1987.

Booth, Stephen, ed. *Shakespeare's Sonnets.* New Haven, CT: Yale University Press, 1977.

Borges, Jorge Luis. *The Book of Sand and Shakespeare's Memory.* Translated by Andrew Hurley. New York: Penguin, 2007.

Brackmann, Rebecca. *The Elizabethan Invention of Anglo-Saxon England: Laurence Nowell, William Lambarde, and the Study of Old English.* Cambridge: D. S. Brewer, 2012.

Brockbank, Philip, ed. *Coriolanus.* The Arden Shakespeare. New York: Routledge, 1988. First published 1976.

Bucknill, John Charles. *The Medical Knowledge of Shakespeare.* London: Longman, 1860.

Bullough, Geoffrey, ed. *Narrative and Dramatic Sources of Shakespeare.* 8 vols. London: Routledge & Kegan Paul, 1966.

Burgess, Anthony. *Shakespeare.* New York: Knopf, 1970.

Case, R. H., ed. *The Tragedy of Antony & Cleopatra.* The Arden Shakespeare. London: Methuen, 1906.

Caldecott, Thomas, ed. *Hamlet, and As You Like It. A Specimen of a New Edition of Shakespeare.* London: John Murray, 1819.

Clark, W. G. and W. A. Wright, eds. *Richard II.* Oxford: Oxford University Press, 1884.

Chambers, E. K. *William Shakespeare: A Study of Facts and Problems.* 2 vols. Oxford: At the Clarendon Press, 1930.

Chesney, Elizabeth A., ed. *The Rabelais Encyclopedia*. Westport, CT: Greenwood, 2004.

Chomsky, William. *Hebrew: The Eternal Language*. Philadelphia: Jewish Publication Society of America, 1957.

Chute, Marchette. *Shakespeare of London*. New York: E. P. Dutton, 1949.

Clemen, W. H. *The Development of Shakespeare's Imagery*. Preface by J. Dover Wilson. Cambridge, MA: Harvard University Press, 1951.

Cooper, Tarnya, with essays by Marcia Pointon, James Shapiro, and Stanley Wells. *Searching for Shakespeare*. New Haven, CT: Yale University Press, 2006.

Cooper, Thomas. *Thesaurus Linguæ Romanæ & Britannicæ Tam Accurate Congestus, Vt Nihil Penè in Eo Desyderari Possit, Quod Vel Latinè Complectatur Amplissimus Stephani Thesaurus, Vel Anglicè, Toties Aucta Eliotæ Bibliotheca: Opera & Industria Thomæ Cooperi Magdalenensis... Accessit Dictionarium Historicum Et Poëticum Propria Vocabula Virorum, Mulierum, Sectarum, Populorum, Vrbium, Montium, & Cæterorum Locorum Complectens, & in His Iucundissimas & Omnium Cognitione Dignissimas Historias*. Impressum Londini: [By Henry Denham], 1578.

Coye, Dale. *Pronouncing Shakespeare's Words: A Guide from A to Zounds*. Westport, CT: Greenwood Press, 1998.

Craik, T. W., ed. *King Henry V*. The Arden Shakespeare, 3rd Series. London: Thomson Learning, 1995.

Craven, A. *Life of Lady Georgiana Fullerton*. London: R. Bentley & Son, 1888.

Crystal, David and Ben Crystal. *Shakespeare's Words: A Glossary and Language Companion*. Preface by Stanley Wells. London: Penguin, 2002.

Dawson, Giles E. and Laetitia Kennedy-Skipton. *Elizabethan Handwriting, 1500–1650: A Guide to the Reading of Documents and Manuscripts*. Foreword by T. J. Brown. Sussex: Phillimore, 1981. First published 1968 by Faber and Faber.

de Grazia, Margareta. *Shakespeare Verbatim: The Reproduction of Authenticity and the 1790 Apparatus*. Oxford: Clarendon Press, 1991.

———, Maureen Quilligan, and Peter Stallybrass, eds. *Subject and Object in Renaissance Culture*. Cambridge: Cambridge University Press, 1996.

de Grazia, Margareta, and Stanley Wells, eds. *The New Cambridge Companion to Shakespeare*. New York: Cambridge University Press, 2010.

Dent, R. W. *Shakespeare's Proverbial Language: An Index*. Berkeley: University of California Press, 1981.

Disraeli, Isaac. *Curiosities of Literature*. 3 vols. London: Edward Moxon, 1849.

Dobson, Michael and Stanley Wells, eds. *The Oxford Companion to Shakespeare*. Oxford: Oxford University Press, 2001.

Dossena, Marina and Ingrid Tieken-Boon van Ostade, eds. *Studies in Late Modern English Correspondence: Methodology and Data*. Berlin: Peter Lang, 2008.

Duffin, Ross W. *Shakespeare's Songbook*. Foreword by Stephen Orgel. New York: W. W. Norton, 2004.

Duncan-Jones, Katherine, ed. *Shakespeare's Sonnets*. The Arden Shakespeare. London: Thomas Nelson, 1997.

Duncan-Jones, Katherine. "Was the 1609 *Shake-speares Sonnets* Really Unauthorized?" *Review of English Studies*, n.s. 34:134 (May 1983), 151–71.

———. *Ungentle Shakespeare: Scenes from His Life*. London: Arden Shakespeare, 2001.

Dyce, Alexander. *The Works of William Shakespeare*, Vol. 1. London: Edward Moxon, 1857.

——— and Harold Littledale. *A Glossary to the Works of William Shakespeare*. London: S. Sonnenschein, 1902.

Efron, B. and R. Thisted. "Estimating the Number of Unknown Species: How Many Words Did Shakespeare Know?" *Biometrika* 63:3 (1975), 435–37.

Eliot, John. *Ortho-epia Gallica. Eliots fruits for the French: Enterlaced with a double new invention, which teacheth to speake truly, speedily and volubly the French-tongue*. London: John Wolfe, 1593.

Ellacombe, Henry N. *The Plant-Lore and Garden-Craft of Shakespeare*. London: Edward Moxon, 1896.

Ellrodt, Robert. "Self-Consciousness in Montaigne and Shakespeare." *Shakespeare Survey* 28 (1975), 37–50.

Elze, Karl. *William Shakespeare: A Literary Biography*. Translated by L. Dora Schmitz. London: George Bell, 1888.

Erne, Lukas. *Shakespeare and the Book Trade*. Cambridge: Cambridge University Press, 2013.

———. *Shakespeare as Literary Dramatist*. 2nd ed. Cambridge: Cambridge University Press, 2013.

Evans, Benjamin Ifor. *The Language of Shakespeare's Plays*. London: Methuen, 1952.

Fairbank, Alfred and Wolpe Berthold. *Renaissance Handwriting: An Anthology of Italic Scripts*. London: Faber and Faber, 1960.

Fairbank, Alfred and Bruce Dickins. *The Italic Hand in Tudor Cambridge: Forty-One Examples Introduced and Described*. Cambridge Bibliographical Society, Monograph No. 5. London: Bowes and Bowes, 1962.

Farmer, Richard. *An Essay on the Learning of Shakespeare: Addressed to Joseph Cradock, Esq*. Cambridge: Printed by J. Archdeacon, Printer to the University, for W. Thurlbourn and J. Woodfer, 1767.

Field, Barron, "Conjectures on some Obscure and Corrupt Passages of Shakspeare." *Shakspeare Society's Papers* 2 (1845).

Furness, H. H., ed. *A New Variorum Edition of Shakespeare: A Midsummer Night's Dreame*. Philadelphia: Lippincott, 1895.

Gervais, Francis P. *Shakespeare Not Bacon: Some Arguments from Shakespeare's Copy of Florio's Montaigne in the British Museum*. London: At the Unicorn, 1901.

Goldberg, Jonathan. "Hamlet's Hand." *Shakespeare Quarterly* 39:3 (Autumn 1988): 307–27.

————. *Shakespeare's Hand*. Minneapolis: University of Minnesota Press, 2003.

————. *Writing Matter: From the Hands of the English Renaissance*. Stanford, CA: Stanford University Press, 1990.

Gordon, George. *S. P. E. Tract No. XXIX: Shakespeare's English*. Oxford: Clarendon Press, 1928.

Graves, Thorton Shirley. "Notes on Elizabethan Theatres." *Studies in Philology* 13:2 (April 1916), 110–121.

Greenblatt, Stephen. *Shakespearean Negotiations: The Circulation of Social Energy in Renaissance England*. Berkeley: University of California Press, 1988.

————. *Shakespeare's Freedom*. Chicago: University of Chicago Press, 2010.

————. *Will in the World: How Shakespeare Became Shakespeare*. New York: W. W. Norton, 2004.

Greene, Robert. *Groats-Worth of Witte, Bought with a Million of Repentance. The Repentance of Robert Greene 1592*. London: John Lane, 1923.

Greenwood, Sir George. *Shakspere's Handwriting*. London: Bodley Head, 1920.

Greg, W. W. "Shakespeare's Hand Once More." In W. W. Greg, *Collected Papers*, ed. J. C. Maxwell. Oxford: At the Clarendon Press, 1966, 192–200.

Gurr, Andrew. *King Henry V.* Cambridge: Cambridge University Press, 1992.

Halliwell, James Orchard. *An account of the only known manuscript of Shakespeare's plays, comprising some important variations and corrections in the Merry wives of Windsor, obtained from a playhouse copy of that play recently discovered.* London: John Russell Smith, 1843.

Hamilton, Charles. *In Search of Shakespeare: A Reconnaissance into the Poet's Life and Handwriting.* San Diego, CA: Harcourt Brace Jovanovich, 1985.

Harman, Thomas. *A Caveat or Warening for Commen Cursetors vulgarely called Vagabones.* From the 3rd Edition of 1567, Belonging to Henry Huth, Esq., collated with the 2nd edition of 1567, in the Bodleian Library, Oxford, and with the reprint of the 4th Edition of 1573. *The Fraternitye of Vacabondes*, by John Awdeley. (Licensed in 1560-61, Imprinted Then, and in 1565) from the edition of 1575 in the Bodleian Library. *A Sermon in Praise of Thieves and Thievery*, by Parson Haben or Hyberdyne, from the Lansdowne Ms. 98, and Cotton Vesp. A. 25. Those parts of *The Groundworke of Conny-catching* (ed. 1592), that differ from *Harman's Caveat*. Edited by Edward Viles and F. J. Furnivall. London: Published for the Early English Text Society by N. Trübner & Company, 1869.

Hart, Alfred. "The Growth of Shakespeare's Vocabulary." *Review of English Studies* 19:75 (July 1943), 242–54.

Hart, John. *An Orthographie Conteyning the Due Order and Reason, Howe to Write or Paint Thimage of Mannes Voice, Most Like to the Life or Nature. Composed by I. H. Chester Heralt. The Contents Wherof are Next Folowing.* London: by Henry Denham for W. Seres, 1569.

Hartmann, R. R. K., ed. *The History of Lexicography: Papers from the Dictionary Research Centre Seminar at Exeter, March, 1986.* Amsterdam: John Benjamins, 1986.

Herrtage, Sidney J. H. *Catholicon Anglicum, an English-Latin Wordbook, Dated 1483. Edited from the Ms. No. 168 in the Library of Lord Monson, Collated with the Additional Ms. 15,562, British Museum, with Introduction and Notes . . . .* Preface by Henry B. Wheatley. London: Published for the Early English Text Society by N. Trübner & Company, 1881.

[Heywood, Thomas]. *An apology for actors Containing three briefe treatises. 1 Their antiquity. 2 Their ancient dignity. 3 The true vse of their quality. Written by Thomas Heywood.* EEBO facsimile reprint edition, 2010. First published 1612.

Hieatt, A. Kent, Charles W. Hieatt, and Anne Lake Prescott. "When Did Shakespeare Write 'Sonnets 1609?'" *Studies in Philology* 88:1 (Winter 1981), 69–109.

Higgins, John. *The Nomenclator, or Remembrancer of Adrianus Iunius Physician Divided in Two Tomes, Conteining Proper Names and Apt Terms for All Things Under Their Convenient Titles, Which Within a Few Leaves Doe Follow.* London: For Ralph Newberie and Henrie Denham, 1585.

Hinman, Charlton, ed. *The Norton Facsimile: The First Folio of Shakespeare.* New York: W. W. Norton, 1968.

Holinshed, Raphael. *The Chronicles of England, Scotlande and Irelande.* London: Printed by Henry Denham, at the expenses of Iohn Harison, George Bishop, Rafe Newberie, Henrie Denham, and Thomas Woodcocke, [1587].

Hollyband, Cl. *The treasurie of the French tong teaching the waye to varie all sortes of verbes: enriched so plentifully with wordes and phrases (for the benefit of the studious in that language) as the like hath before bin published. Gathered and set forth by Cl. Hollyband. For the better vnderstanding of the order of this dictionarie, peruse the preface to the reader.* London: Henrie Bynneman, 1680.

Hollyband, Claudius and Peter Erondell. *The Elizabethan Home, Discovered in Two Dialogues by Claudius Hollyband and Peter Erondell* (rev. ed.). Edited by M. St. Clare Byrne. London: Methuen, 1949.

Honan, Park. *Shakespeare: A Life.* Oxford: Oxford University Press, 1998.

Honigmann, E. A. J. *Shakespeare: The 'Lost Years.'* Totowa, NJ: Barnes & Noble Books, 1985.

Hope, Jonathan. *The Authorship of Shakespeare's Plays: A Socio-Linguistic Study.* Cambridge: Cambridge University Press, 1994.

———. *Shakespeare and Language: Reason, Eloquence and Artifice in the Renaissance.* The Arden Shakespeare Library. London: Methuen Drama, 2010.

Hotson, Leslie. *Shakespeare versus Shallow.* London: Nonesuch Press, 1931.

Jackson, Macd. P. "Vocabulary and Chronology in Shakespeare's Sonnets." *Review of English Studies* n.s. 52:205 (February 2001), 59–75.

Jaggard, William. *Shakespeare, Once a Printer and Bookman, Lecture One of the 12th Series of Printing Trade Lectures*. Stratford-on-Avon: Shakespeare Press, 1933.

Jamieson, John. *Supplement to the Etymological dictionary of the Scottish Language*. Edinburgh: Printed at the University Press, 1825. Available online at http://books.google.com/books?id=9w8oAAAAYAAJ&source=gbs_book_other_versions.

Kastan, David Scott. *Shakespeare After Theory*. New York: Routledge, 1999.

————. *Shakespeare and the Book*. Cambridge: Cambridge University Press, 2001.

Keats, John. *Letters of John Keats 1814–1821*. 2 vols. Edited by Hyder Edward Rollins. Cambridge, MA: Harvard University Press, 1958.

Kellner, Leon. *Restoring Shakespeare: A Critical Analysis of the Misreadings in Shakespeare's Works*. New York: Alfred A. Knopf, 1925.

Kipling, Rudyard. *The Sussex Edition of the Complete Works in Prose and Verse of Rudyard Kipling*. 35 vols. London: Macmillan, 1937–39.

Kirschbaum, Leo. "Shakespeare's Hypothetical Marginal Additions." *Modern Language Notes* 61:1 (January 1946), 44–49.

Knowles, Ronald, ed. *Shakespeare and Carnival: After Bakhtin*. London: Macmillan, 1998.

Kozuka, Takashi and J. R. Mulryne, eds. *Shakespeare, Marlowe, Jonson: New Directions in Biography*. Aldershot: Ashgate, 2006.

Lancashire, Ian. "An Early Modern English Dictionaries Corpus 1499–1659." *CCH Working Papers* 4, 1994. Available online at http://projects.chass.utoronto.ca/chwp/lancash2/.

————. *Forgetful Muses: Reading the Author in the Text*. Toronto: University of Toronto Press, 2010.

Lee, Sidney. *The French Renaissance in England: An Account of the Literary Relations of England and France in the Sixteenth Century*. London: Oxford at the Clarendon Press, 1910.

Levins, Peter. *Manipulus Vocabulorum: A Rhyming Dictionary of the English Language (1570)*. Edited, with an alphabetical index, by Henry B. Wheatley. London: N. Trübner & Co., for the Early English Text Society, 1867. Reprint, New York: Greenwood, 1969.

Lewis, Charlton T. and Charles Short. *A Latin Dictionary. Founded on Andrews' edition of Freund's Latin dictionary*. Revised, enlarged, and in great part rewritten. Oxford: Clarendon Press, 1879.

Liddell, Mark Harvey, ed. *The Elizabethan Shakspere: A New Edition of Shakspere's Works with Critical Text in Elizabethan English and Brief Notes Illustrative of Elizabethan Life, Thought, and Idiom.* New York: Doubleday, Page, 1903.

Logan, William. *The Undiscovered Country: Poetry in the Age of Tin.* New York: Columbia University Press, 2005.

MacKay, Charles. *New Light on Some Obscure Words and Phrases in the Works of Shakespeare and His Contemporaries.* London: Reeves & Turner, 1884.

Madden, D. H. *The Diary of Master William Silence: A Study of Shakespeare and of Elizabethan Sport.* London: Longmans, Green, 1907.

Madden, Sir F. *Shakespeare's Autograph; Observations on It; As Also on the Orthography of His Name.* London: Royal Society of Antiquaries, 1837.

[Maggs Bros.] *Books and Readers in Early Modern Britain V: A Selection of Books, Manuscripts and Bindings.* Catalogue 1471. London: Maggs Bros., 2013.

Mahood, M. M. *Shakespeare's Wordplay.* London: Methuen, 1957.

Manly, John M. and Edith Rickert, eds. *The Text of the Canterbury Tales.* 8 vols. Chicago: University of Chicago Press, 1940.

Martindale, Michelle and Charles Martindale. *Shakespeare and the Uses of Antiquity: An Introductory Essay.* London: Routledge, 1990.

McLoughlin, Cathleen T. *Shakespeare, Rabelais, and the Comical-Historical.* New York: Peter Lang, 2000.

Melchiori, Giorgio. *Shakespeare's Garter Plays: "Edward III" to "Merry Wives of Windsor."* Newark: University of Delaware Press, 1994.

Meres, Francis. *Palladis Tamia. Wits Treasury. Being the Second Part of Wits Commonwealth.* Ann Arbor: University of Michigan, Scholars' Facsimiles and Reprints, 1938. First published 1598.

Metz, G. Harold, ed. *Sources for Four Plays Ascribed to Shakespeare: The Reign of King Edward III, Sir Thomas More, The History of Cardenio, The Two Noble Kinsmen.* Columbia: University of Missouri Press, 1989.

Milward, Peter. *Shakespeare's Religious Background.* Chicago: Loyola University Press, 1973.

Murphy, Andrew. *Shakespeare in Print: A History and Chronology of Shakespeare Publishing.* Cambridge: Cambridge University Press, 2003.

Myers, Robin, Michael Harris, and Giles Mandelbrote, eds. *Owners, Annotators and the Signs of Reading.* New Castle, DE: Oak Knoll Press and the British Library, 2005.

Nares, Robert, J. O. Halliwell-Phillipps, and Thomas Wright. *A Glossary or the Collection of Words, Phrases, Names, and Allusions to Customs, Proverbs, Etc., Which Have Been Thought to Require Illustration, in the Works of English Authors, Particularly Shakespeare and His Contemporaries.* 2 vols. London: Reeves and Turner, 1888.

Nicholl, Charles. *The Lodger Shakespeare: His Life on Silver Street.* New York: Viking, 2008.

Nicoll, Allardyce, ed. *Shakespeare Survey 6.* Cambridge: At the University Press, 1953.

Norton, David. *The King James Bible: A Short History from Tyndale to Today.* Cambridge: Cambridge University Press, 2011.

Nuttall, A. D. *Shakespeare the Thinker.* New Haven, CT: Yale University Press, 2001.

Onions, C. T. and Robert D. Eagleson. *Shakespeare Glossary* (rev. ed.). Oxford: Clarendon Press, 1986.

Orgel, Stephen. *The Authentic Shakespeare and Other Problems of the Early Modern Stage.* New York: Routledge, 2002.

Palmer, Rev. A. Smythe. *Folk-Etymology, a Dictionary of Verbal Corruptions or Words Perverted in Form or Meaning, by False Derivation or Mistaken Analogy.* New York: Greenwood, 1969. First published 1883 by Henry Holt.

Parker, Patricia. *Shakespeare from the Margins: Language, Culture, Context.* Chicago: University of Chicago Press, 1996.

Pearson, Lu Emily. *Elizabethans at Home.* Stanford, CA: Stanford University Press, 1957.

Pepper, Robert D., ed. *Four Tudor Books on Education.* Francis Clement, *The Petie Schole with an English Orthographie* (1587); Thomas Elyot, *The Education or Bringing Up of Children* (1533); Dudley Fenner, *The Artes of Logike and Rethorike* (1584); William Kempe, *The Education of Children in Learning* (1588). Gainesville, FL: Scholars' Facsimiles & Reprints, 1966.

Phillips, O. Hood. *Shakespeare and the Lawyers.* London: Methuen, 1972.

Phin, John. *The Shakespeare cyclopaedia and new glossary . . . with the most important variorum readings, intended as a supplement to all the ordinary editions of Shakespeare's works, with an introduction by Edward Dowden.* London: K. Paul, 1902.

[Phillip, William]. *A booke of secrets shewing diuers waies to make and prepare all sorts of inke, and colours: as blacke, white, blew, greene, red, yellow, and* other colours. *Also to write with gold and siluer, or any kind of mettall out of the pen: with many other profitable secrets, as to colour quils and parchment of any colour: and to graue with strong water in steele and iron. . . . Translated out of Dutch into English, by W.P.* EEBO facsimile reprint edition, 2013. First published 1596.

Phipson, Emma. *The Animal-Lore of Shakespeare's Time.* London: Kegan Paul, Trench, 1883.

Plutarch. *The Lives of the noble Grecians and Romanes compared together by that grave and learned philosopher and historiographer, Plutarke of Chær-nea; translated out of Greeke into French by Iames Amiot, abbot of Bellozane, Bishop of Auxerre, one of the Kings priuie counsell, and great Amner of France, and out of French into English, by Thomas North.* Imprinted at London: By Richard Field for Bonham Norton, 1595.

Pollard, Alfred W. *Shakespeare's Fight with the Pirates and the Problems of the Transmission of His Text.* London: Cambridge University Press, 1967. First published 1923.

————, W. W. Greg, E. Maunde Thompson, J. Dover Wilson, and R. W. Chambers. *Shakespeare's Hand in the Plays of Sir Thomas More, with the text of the Ill May Day Scenes.* London: Cambridge University Press, 1967. First published 1923.

Porter, Stephen. *Shakespeare's London: Everyday Life in London, 1580–1616.* Stroud: Amberley, 2009.

Prescott, Anne Lake. *Imagining Rabelais in Renaissance England.* New Haven, CT: Yale University Press, 1998.

Preston, Jean F., and Laetitia Yeandle. *English Handwriting, 1400–1650.* Asheville, NC: Pegasus Press, 1999.

Prickett, Stephen. "Psalm 46," *TLS,* January 13, 2012.

Robertson, John M. *Montaigne and Shakespeare, and Other Essays on Cognate Questions.* London: Adam and Charles Black, 1909.

Rolfe, William J. *Shakespeare the Boy, with Sketches of the Home and School Life, the Games and Sports, the Manners, Customs and Folk-Lore of the Time.* New York: Harper & Brothers, 1896.

Rouse, W. H. D. *Shakespeare's Ovid, being Arthur Golding's Translation of the Metamorphoses.* London: At the De La More Press, 1904.

Rowe, Nicholas and Charles Nicholl. *Life of Shakespeare.* London: Pallas Athene Arts, 2009. First published 1709.

Schaar, Claes. *Elizabethan Sonnet Themes and the Dating of Shakespeare's Sonnets.* Lund: C. W. K. Gleerup, 1962.

Schoenbaum, Samuel. *William Shakespeare: A Compact Documentary Life.* Oxford: Clarendon Press, 1975.

――――. *William Shakespeare: A Documentary Life.* New York: Oxford University Press, in association with the Scolar Press, 1975.

――――. *William Shakespeare: Records and Images.* New York: Oxford University Press, 1981.

Seager, H. W. *Natural History in Shakespeare's Time; Being Extracts Illustrative of the Subject as He Knew It. Also Pictures Thereunto Belonging.* London: Elliot Stock, 1896.

Shakespeare, William. *Oeuvres complètes de Shakespeare.* Traduites de l'Anglais par Letourneur. D'une notice bibliographique et Littéraire de Shakespeare par F. Guizot. Paris: Chez Ladvocat. Tome Dixième, 1820.

――――. *The Works of William Shakespeare.* London: Edward Moxon, 1857.

Shapiro, James. *Contested Will: Who Wrote Shakespeare?* London: Faber and Faber, 2010.

――――. *A Year in the Life of William Shakespeare: 1599.* New York: Harper Collins, 2005.

Sherbo, Arthur, ed. *Notes to Shakespeare* by Samuel Johnson. Augustinian Reprint Society Publication Los Angeles: William Andrews Clark Memorial Library, University of California, 1956–58.

Sherman, William H. *Used Books: Marking Readers in Renaissance England.* Philadelphia: University of Pennsylvania Press, 2008.

Shorter, Alfred M. *Paper Mills and Paper Makers in England, 1495–1800.* Hilversum, Holland: Paper Publications Society, 1957.

Singer, Samuel Weller, and Charles Symmons. *The Dramatic Works of Shakespeare, with Notes Original and Selected… and A Life of the Poet.* Chiswick: Charles Wittingham, 1826.

Skottowe, Augustine. *An Appendix to Shakspeare's Dramatic Works. Contents: The Life of the Author by Aug. Skottowe; His Miscellaneous Poems; A Critical Glossary, Compiled After Nares, Drake, Ayscough, Hazlitt, Douce and others.* Leipsig: Ernst Fleischer, 1826.

Sledd, James. "A Note on the Use of Renaissance Dictionaries." *Modern Philology* 49:1 (August 1951), 10–15.

[Sotheby's.] *A Catalogue of the Greater Portion of the Library of the Late Edmond Malone; Which Will Be Sold by Auction, by Mr. Sotheby on Thursday, Nov. 26, 1818, and Seven Following Days (Sunday Excepted).*

Spurgeon, Caroline F. E. *Shakespeare's Imagery and What It Tells Us.* Cambridge: At the University Press, 1966.

Stapfer, Paul. *Shakespeare and Classical Antiquity: Greek and Latin Antiquity as Presented in Shakespeare's Plays.* Translated by Emily J. Carey. London: C. Kegan Paul, 1880.

Starnes, DeWitt T. "John Baret's *Alvearie* (1573)." Chap. 14 in *Renaissance Dictionaries: English-Latin and Latin-English.* Austin: University of Texas Press, 1954.

Steevens, George, Isaac Reed, and Samuel Johnson, eds. *The Plays of William Shakspeare: With the Corrections and...* London: J. Johnson, 1803.

Stewart, Alan. *Shakespeare's Letters.* Oxford: Oxford University Press, 2008.

Stewart, Alan and Heather Wolfe. *Letterwriting in Renaissance England.* Washington, D.C.: Folger Shakespeare Library, 2004.

Stopes, C. C. *Shakespeare's Warwickshire Contemporaries.* Stratford-upon-Avon: Shakespeare Head Press, 1907.

Straznicky, Marta, ed. *Shakespeare's Stationers: Studies in Cultural Bibliography.* Philadelphia: University of Pennsylvania Press, 2013.

Tannenbaum, Samuel A. *The Handwriting of the Renaissance, Being the Development and Characteristics of the Script of Shakespeare's Time.* Introduction by Ashley H. Thorndike. New York: Columbia University Press, 1930.

————. *Problems in Shakspere's Penmanship, Including a Study of the Poet's Will.* New York: Kraus, 1966. First published 1927 by the Modern Language Association of America.

Taylor, George Coffin. *Shakspere's Debt to Montaigne.* Cambridge, MA: Harvard University Press, 1925.

Thompson, Sir Edward Maunde. "Handwriting." In Sidney Lee and C. T. Onions (eds.), *Shakespeare's England: An Account of the Life and Manners of His Age.* Oxford: Clarendon Press, 1932. First published 1916.

Thompson, Sir Edward Maunde. *Shakespeare's Handwriting.* Oxford: At the Clarendon Press, 1916.

Tilley, Morris Palmer. *A Dictionary of the Proverbs in England in the Sixteenth and Seventeenth Centuries. A Collection of the Proverbs Found in English Literature and the Dictionaries of the Period.* Ann Arbor: University of Michigan Press, 1950.

Upton, John. *Critical Observations on Shakespeare.* Dublin: Printed for George and Alexander Ewing, 1747.

Velz, John W. "Shakespeare and the Geneva Bible: The Circumstances." In Takashi Kozuka and J. R. Mulryne (eds.), *Shakespeare, Marlowe, Jonson: New Directions in Biography*, 113–18. Burlington, VT: Ashgate, 2006.

Vendler, Helen. *The Art of Shakespeare's Sonnets*. Cambridge, MA: Harvard University Press, 1997.

Vickers, Brian. *Shakespeare, 'A Lover's Complaint', and John Davies of Hereford*. Cambridge: Cambridge University Press, 2007.

Weis, René. *Shakespeare Unbound: Decoding a Hidden Life*. New York: Henry Holt, 2007.

Wells, Stanley. *Shakespeare for All Time*. London: Macmillan, 2003.

———, ed. *Shakespeare Survey 50: Shakespeare and Language*. Cambridge: Cambridge University Press, 1997.

Wells, Stanley, and Gary Taylor, gen. eds. *The Oxford Shakespeare: The Complete Works* (2nd ed.). Oxford: Clarendon Press, 2005.

Wells, Stanley, and Gary Taylor. *William Shakespeare: A Textual Companion*. Oxford: Clarendon, 1986.

West, Gilian. *A Dictionary of Shakespeare's Semantic Wordplay*. Studies in Renaissance Literature 17. Lewiston, NY: Edwin Mellen Press, 1998.

Wilson, Richard. *Secret Shakespeare: Studies in Theatre, Religion, and Resistance*. Manchester, UK: Manchester University Press, 2004.

Wolpe, Berthold. "John de Beauchesne and the First English Writing Books." In A. S. Osley (ed.), *Scribes and Sources: Handbook of the Chancery Hand in the Sixteenth Century. Texts from the Writing-Masters*, 228–40. Boston: David R. Godine, 1980.

Wooten, David. "The Vibes of Marx." *TLS*, January 4, 2008.

Wright, William Aldis. *The Bible Word-Book: A Glossary of Archaic Words and Phrases in the Authorised Version of the Bible and Book of Common Prayer*. London: Macmillan, 1884.

———. *The Bible Word-Book: A Glossary of Old English Bible-Words*. London: Macmillan, 1866.

———, ed. *Shakespeare: Select Plays. Julius Caesar*. Oxford: At the Clarendon Press, 1879.

Wright, William Burnet. "Hamlet." *The Atlantic Monthly* (May 1902), 686–95.

Yates, Frances A. *John Florio: The Life of an Italian in Shakespeare's England*. Cambridge: Cambridge University Press, 1934.

Notes

PROLOGUE (pages 3–4)

1 John Baret. AN ALVEARIE OR QUADRUPLE DICTIONA-
RIE, CONTAINING FOURE SUNDRIE TONGUES: NAME-
LIE, ENGLISH, LATINE, GREEKE, AND FRENCH. Newlie
enriched with varietie of Wordes, Phrases, Proverbs, and divers
lightsome observations of Grammar. By the Tables you may contrariwise finde out the most necessarie words placed after the
Alphabet, whatsoever are to be found in anie other Dictionarie:
Which Tables also serving for Lexicons, to lead the learner unto
the English of such hard words as are often read in Authors, being faithfullie examined, are truly numbered. Verie profitable for
such as are desirous of anie of those languages. Londini: excudebat
Henricus Denhamus typographus, Gulielmi Seresij vnicus assigna-
tus, anno salutis humanæ 1580. [852] p.; 2⁰. Dedication signed: Io.
Baretus Cantabrigiensis. An expanded edition of: AN ALVEARIE
OR TRIPLE DICTIONARIE (1573). Edited by Abraham Fleming,
whose name appears on 4A1v. First three words of title are xylo-
graphic. At foot of title: Cum priuilegio Regiæ Maiestatis. Imprint
from colophon. Signatures: A⁸ B-Y⁶ 2A-2Y⁶ 3A-3N⁶ 3O⁴ 4A-4S⁴
4T⁶. The first leaf is blank except for signature-mark "A.j."; the last
leaf is blank. Our copy lacks two leaves of the preliminary matter.
The dictionary text is complete and includes the indexes.

A FEW THOUGHTS ON OLD BOOKS (pages 5–10)

2 Georgiana Fullerton (1812–85), English novelist. For a biographical study see A. Craven, *Life of Lady Georgiana Fullerton* (London:
R. Bentley & Son), 1888.

3 T. W. Baldwin, *William Shakspere's Small Latine & Lesse Greeke* (Urbana: University of Illinois Press, 1944).

4 Beyond the better-known sourcebooks, one should consider the
extensive work in eight volumes edited by Geoffrey Bullough,
Narrative and Dramatic Sources of Shakespeare (London: Routledge
& Kegan Paul, 1966). Being that Bullough has focused on narra-

tive and dramatic sources, there is no mention of dictionaries (i.e., Cooper, or Baret's *Alvearie*).

EARLY MODERN DICTIONARIES (pages 11–16)

5 Ian Lancashire, "An Early Modern English Dictionaries Corpus 1499–1659" (*CCH Working Papers* 4, 1994), http://projects.chass. utoronto.ca/chwp/lancash2/: "A shortlist of seminal works in England up to 1660 might include (a) bilingual dictionaries such as *Medulla Grammatice, Promptorium Parvulorum* (1499), John Palsgrave's for English-French (1530), Thomas Elyot's for Latin-English (1538), Thomas Cooper's for Latin-English (1565), John Baret's for (Greek)-French-Latin-English, (1573-1580) . . . ." For more on Renaissance dictionaries including discussions of Baret, see James Sledd, "A Note on the Use of Renaissance Dictionaries" (*Modern Philology* 49:1, August 1951), 10–15; DeWitt T. Starnes, "John Baret's *Alvearie* (1573)," chap. 14 in *Renaissance Dictionaries: English-Latin and Latin-English* (Austin: University of Texas Press, 1954).

6 Baldwin, *Shakspere's Small Latine*, 1:715.

7 Many books emphasize the rigorous schooling that Shakespeare must have experienced in Stratford. See, for example, Stephen Greenblatt, *Will in the World: How Shakespeare Became Shakespeare* (New York: W. W. Norton, 2004); Jonathan Bate, *Soul of the Age: A Biography of the Mind of William Shakespeare* (New York: Random House, 2009).

8 See [Sotheby's]. *A Catalogue of the Greater Portion of the Library of the Late Edmond Malone; Which Will Be Sold by Auction, by Mr. Sotheby on Thursday, Nov. 26, 1818, and Seven Following Days (Sunday Excepted).*

9 Patricia Parker, *Shakespeare from the Margins: Language, Culture, Context* (Chicago: University of Chicago Press, 1996), 17.

10 [Bernard Quaritch.] *English Books*, Catalogue 1352 (London: Bernard Quaritch, 2007), Item 4.

11 The closest Baret came to being reprinted seems to have been in 1866, when the Early English Tract Society was planning to reproduce both Huloet and Baret, but it was determined that it would be too costly. The information regarding the planned reprint appears in the Early English Tract Society's published transcription of *Catholicon Anglicum,* an English-Latin wordbook manuscript dated 1483. A plethora of notes provided on each page reference

a number of early printed dictionaries in England, Baret included. Sidney J. H. Herrtage, *Catholicon Anglicum, an English-Latin Word-book, Dated 1483. Edited from the Ms. No. 168 in the Library of Lord Monson, Collated with the Additional Ms. 15,562, British Museum, with Introduction and Notes . . .* (London: Published for the Early English Text Society by N. Trübner & Company, 1881).

SHAKESPEARE GOES TO LONDON (pages 17–23)

12 Robert Greene, *Groats-Worth of Witte, Bought with a Million of Repentance. The Repentance of Robert Greene 1592* (London: John Lane, 1923).

13 As Chute, among others, has pointed out, acting was a competitive profession, and Shakespeare must have established himself over some course of time. Marchette Chute, *Shakespeare of London* (New York: E. P. Dutton, 1949). Guesses as to what Shakespeare was doing abound, so much so that practically any guess has been made.

14 For the "lost years," see E. A. J. Honigmann, *Shakespeare: The 'Lost Years'* (Totowa, NJ: Barnes & Noble Books, 1985).

15 See, e.g., Charles Nicholl, *The Lodger Shakespeare: His Life on Silver Street* (New York: Viking, 2008), 175–78.

16 David Scott Kastan's *Shakespeare After Theory* (New York: Routledge, 1999) is one of many books wherein the position, long in the main, is taken that Shakespeare cared little about seeing his plays in print. But two very recent studies have taken an alternative stance. See Lukas Erne, *Shakespeare and the Book Trade* (Cambridge: Cambridge University Press, 2013) and Marta Straznicky, ed., *Shakespeare's Stationers: Studies in Cultural Bibliography* (Philadelphia: University of Pennsylvania Press, 2013).

17 Katherine Duncan-Jones, *Ungentle Shakespeare: Scenes from His Life* (London: Arden Shakespeare, 2001), 5.

18 René Weis, *Shakespeare Unbound: Decoding a Hidden Life* (New York: Henry Holt, 2007), 22.

19 Bate, *Soul of the Age*, 145.

20 Weis, *Shakespeare Unbound*, 280.

21 Ibid., 183.

22 Ibid., 280.

23 Baldwin, *Shakspere's Small Latine*, 1:718.

24 Stanley Wells, *Shakespeare for All Time* (London: Macmillan, 2003), 147.

25 Andrew Murphy, *Shakespeare in Print: A History and Chronology of Shakespeare Publishing* (Cambridge: Cambridge University Press, 2003), 15.

26 William Jaggard, *Shakespeare: Once a Printer and Bookman, Lecture One of the 12th Series of Printing Trade Lectures* (Stratford-on-Avon: Shakespeare Press, 1933), 2–4.

27 William Blades, *Shakspere and Typography: Being an Attempt to Show Shakspeare's Personal Connection with and Technical Knowledge of the Art of Printing* (New York: Burt Franklin, 1969; first published 1872), 25–36.

28 Shakespeare Birthplace Trust website, http://www.shakespeare.org.uk.

29 E. K. Chambers, *William Shakespeare: A Study of Facts and Problems* (Oxford: At the Clarendon Press, 1930), 1:24.

A HEAVILY ANNOTATED COPY (pages 24–28)

30 To L is written in the lower margin and clearly represents an interrupted annotation. The mouse-foot indicates that the word would have fallen between lap and laps. There is one place name in the concordance that falls between lap and laps, and it could have concluded the annotation had the annotator not been interrupted. It appears in *Comedy of Errors*, one of the earliest plays, and near the denouement, when Antipholus of Syracuse comes to Ephesus and is mistaken for his identical twin, Antipholus of Ephesus (whom he did not know of because the twins were separated at birth), and is inexplicably catered to by all the inhabitants. Lapland was noted in folklore for its inhabitants who were giants, witches, and sorcerers. The OED gives its first appearance in English as by Marlowe in 1590, where he mentions the gyante of Lapland. It is fun to imagine what distracted the annotator from completing his annotation – even more fun for those swayed by our arguments as to who has authored the annotations. To L could also have been the start of a verb phrase involving to lap or to lapse, both used by Shakespeare and fitting alphabetically, but we still like Lapland. Marlowe in *Doctor Faustus*, Shakespeare in *Comedy of Errors*, and Milton in *Paradise Lost* all use Lapland as the realm of giants, sorcerers, or magicians.

31 A recent catalogue from Maggs Bros. Ltd., a colleague in London,

includes an interesting annotated copy of *Coryats Crudities*, published in 1611. Two early owners provide the provenance, the earlier belonging to the poet and writing-master John Davies of Hereford (1564/5–1618), who adds verse to the book. An image is provided for what we have termed a "mouse-foot," described in their catalogue as "squiggles surmounted by triple dots." It is curious that while this device is not rare (other sixteenth- and early seventeenth-century English books in our inventories contain them), there does not seem to be a standard name for it. Another image illustrates a series of frequent dots in pencil appearing in the margin that are described as running throughout. Also described are underlined words, marginal florets, and manicules; but the book is almost entirely free of spoken annotations, per se. It is noted that there is also not a single annotation marking any of the Latin contained in the book. For the underlined words in pencil, the cataloguers have demonstrated linguistic parallels to the work of John Davies and have determined him to be the more likely candidate to have made the annotations, and not the later owner Pierre de Cardonnel (1614–67). But what is most significant to us is the acknowledgment in the description that William Sherman had not before seen this blend of an annotation method: the profusion of little pencil dots, the underlining, and manicules. Although the annotation method is, overall, clearly different from the one our annotator employs, enough similarities are there to suggest that our annotator's method is equally unusual. As the Maggs cataloguer asserts is the case for their copy of *Coryats Crudities*, we have never before, in our history of examining books, seen anything like the annotation method in our copy of Baret's *Alvearie*. [Maggs Bros.], *Books and Readers in Early Modern Britain V, A Selection of Books, Manuscripts and Bindings*, Catalogue 1471 (London: Maggs Bros., 2013).

32 See B. Efron and R. Thisted, "Estimating the Number of Unknown Species: How Many Words Did Shakespeare Know?" *Biometrika* 63:3 (1975), 435–37, for one study that has calculated that Shakespeare wrote 31,534 different words, of which 14,376 appear only once. The exact numbers, impossible to know, of course, are of less concern than the extraordinary number of single usages relative to the whole.

33 John W. Velz, "Shakespeare and the Geneva Bible: The Circumstances." In *Shakespeare, Marlowe, Jonson: New Directions in Biography*, ed. Takashi Kozuka and J. R. Mulryne (Burlington, VT: Ashgate, 2006).

34 Bate, *Soul of the Age*, 138.

35 Peter Milward, *Shakespeare's Religious Background* (Chicago: Loyola University Press, 1973), 86.

36 *The Strand* magazine, April 1934. "Proofs of Holy Writ" was completed too late to be included in Kipling's last collection, *Limits and Renewals*, published in April 1932. It later appeared in *The Sussex Edition of the Complete Works in Prose and Verse of Rudyard Kipling* (35 vols.) (London: Macmillan, 1937–39).

37 Stephen Prickett, "Psalm 46," *TLS*, January 13, 2012. The series of comments began in the *TLS* issues of December 23 and 30, 2011, in Prickett's review of Harold Bloom's 2011 publication *The Shadow of a Great Rock: A Literary Appreciation of the King James Bible*.

38 David Norton, *The King James Bible: A Short History from Tyndale to Today* (Cambridge: Cambridge University Press, 2011). This is an example of the scholarship that is currently being devoted to the making of the KJB. The unlikeliness of the notion that the KJB translators who were selected from the leading members of the Anglican and Puritan clergy would have been receptive to including the work of poets who wrote for the theater can be seen in the list of publications of John Rainolds who, in 1599, published *Th' overthrow of Stage-Playes, . . . wherein all the reasons that can be made for them are notably refuted . . . as that the iudgement of any man, that is not froward and perverse, may easelie be satisfied. Wherein is manifestly proved, that it is not onely vnlawfull to bee an actor, but a beholder of those vanities.* John Rainolds or Reynolds (1549–1607), president of Corpus Christi College, was the leader of the Puritan delegation to the Hampton Court conference (1604) that set the procedures in place for the new translation.

Another aspect of recent scholarship is the inspection of the extant and identifiable books from the translators' libraries. Much can be revealed, of course, by marginal addenda, but also, in at least one case, by the overall contents of the library itself. Greek scholar William Branthwaite left an enormous library of 1,405 books that is almost intact at Gonville and Caius College; in it one finds, surprisingly, an almost complete lack of English literature. This would seem to open the door, if only slightly, to the possibility that informal contact with leading poets might have been advisable as the translation was drawing to an end.

39 Henry N. Ellacombe, *The Plant-Lore and Garden-Craft of Shakespeare* (London: Edward Moxon, 1896), 125.

40 The most comprehensive survey of the Lancastrian Shakespeare discoveries can be found in Richard Wilson's *Secret Shakespeare: Studies in Theatre, Religion, and Resistance* (Manchester, UK: Manchester University Press, 2004).

PALEOGRAPHY (pages 40–54)

41 For a general introduction to the handwriting of the period, see Giles E. Dawson and Laetitia Kennedy-Skipton, *Elizabethan Handwriting, 1500–1650: A Guide to the Reading of Documents and Manuscripts* (Sussex: Phillimore, 1981; first published 1968 by Faber and Faber).

42 Leon Kellner, *Restoring Shakespeare: A Critical Analysis of the Misreadings in Shakespeare's Works* (New York: Alfred A. Knopf, 1925), 20.

43 For a discussion on historical figures and their signatures, see Charles Hamilton, *In Search of Shakespeare: A Reconnaissance into the Poet's Life and Handwriting* (San Diego, CA: Harcourt Brace Jovanovich, 1985), 45.

44 For an excellent introduction to Hand D, including arguments relating to those that have come out against it or in its favor, see G. Harold Metz, ed., *Sources for Four Plays Ascribed to Shakespeare: The Reign of King Edward III, Sir Thomas More, The History of Cardenio, The Two Noble Kinsmen* (Columbia: University of Missouri Press, 1989), 135–206.

45 Metz, *Sources for Four Plays*, 170–2. Hand D is now said to likely date between 1600 and 1605, after the speculated dating of our annotations. Metz's discussion on the reasoning behind various estimates on the dating of the ascribed Shakespeare contribution highlights the difficulty in assigning an exact date. But the feeling seems to be that the contribution is later than first thought, probably around 1603.

46 See Stanley Wells and Gary Taylor, *William Shakespeare: A Textual Companion* (Oxford: Clarendon, 1986), General Introduction, 9–10.

47 Sir Edward Maunde Thompson, "Handwriting," in Sidney Lee and C. T. Onions (eds.), *Shakespeare's England: An Account of the Life and Manners of His Age* (Oxford: Clarendon Press, 1932; first published 1916), 1:307.

48 Ibid., 300.

49 Ibid.

50 Ibid., 303.

51 Ibid., 302.

52 We should note that in a few instances, a majuscule letter "B" bears some resemblance to the capital "B" as printed in Baret. But these "B" examples are spread out and not contained within the letter, as is the case with the "W" and the "S" imitations. Also, the majuscule "B" letters as printed in Baret are closer – unlike the attempted copies of the "W" and the "S" – to genuine representations of the majuscule "B" as seen in period handwriting. Consider the majuscule "B" in "By Me" on Shakespeare's will.

53 See interview with Stanley Wells and Carol Rutter of the University of Warwick. Wells describes the existence of signatures in a couple of books as "disputed, but not impossible to believe." Warwick/SBT [Shakespeare Birthplace Trust] Shakespeare Collection, *Anonymous – A Shakespeare Authorship Discussion with Prof Stanley Wells and Prof Carol Rutter*. November 1, 2011. Available at http://www2.warwick.ac.uk/newsandevents/podcasts/culture/100-warwick-sbt-shakespeare.

54 D. H. Madden, *The Diary of Master William Silence: A Study of Shakespeare and of Elizabethan Sport* (London: Longmans, Green, 1907), 362.

55 Ibid.

56 Sir F. Madden, *Shakespeare's Autograph; Observations on It; As Also on the Orthography of His Name* (London: Royal Society of Antiquaries, 1837), 116.

57 D. H. Madden, *The Diary of Master William Silence: A Study of Shakespeare and of Elizabethan Sport* (London: Longmans, Green, 1907), 361.

58 Thompson, "Handwriting," 1:308.

59 Robert Ellrodt, "Self-Consciousness in Montaigne and Shakespeare," *Shakespeare Survey* 28 (1975), 38.

60 Frances A. Yates, *John Florio: The Life of an Italian in Shakespeare's*

England (Cambridge: Cambridge University Press, 1934), 245.

61 In an obscure book from 1901, *Shakespeare Not Bacon: Some Arguments from Shakespeare's Copy of Florio's Montaigne in the British Museum* (London: At the Unicorn, 1901), Francis P. Gervais argues not only that the signature is genuine, but that the marginal notes in the British Museum's copy come from the same hand. The title of his book aggressively takes aim at the "Baconites," and even reproduces a page in Bacon's hand, showing it having neither the feel nor the characteristics of the marginal hand in the Montaigne. Gervais's book also reproduces each of these manuscript additions over a series of plates, and Gervais goes on to explicate each of the annotations and the Shakespearean parallels that are found. The annotations are of a relatively very small quantity, and nowhere near as impressive as what is contained in our book, but along the paleographic front, the overall gestalt when comparing the Montaigne with our Baret is within range. We can report a nearly identical majuscule "H" in the Montaigne (an abbreviated reference to Hippocrates, "Hipp,") to the one we see in our Baret annotation hurlyeburlye. The minuscule "d" of "dos" in the continuation of "purgan-dos" is likewise a close approximation to examples we see from our annotator. So are several others. We even see, in the British Museum book, a nearly identical "+" symbol beside a penned reference to Seneca, which is also found leading in to one of our most important annotations in the Baret: as fat as Browne. In that instance, the + symbol is repeated at another point on the page to indicate the alphabetical placement.

SHAKESPEARE ON HANDWRITING (pages 55–62)

62 In 1600, *A New Year's Gift for England: The Art of New Brachygraphie* was printed by Richard Field.

63 Isaac Disraeli, *Curiosities of Literature* (London: Edward Moxon, 1849).

64 Ibid., 3:175.

65 Berthold Wolpe, "John de Beauchesne and the First English Writing Books." In *Scribes and Sources: Handbook of the Chancery Hand in the Sixteenth Century. Texts from the Writing-Masters*, ed. A. S. Osley (Boston: David R. Godine, 1980), 232.

66 Ibid.

67 Jonathan Goldberg, *Writing Matter: From the Hands of the English*

Renaissance (Stanford, CA: Stanford University Press,2003), 129.

68 Ibid., 124.

69 Inks were handmade at the time and this, in part, accounts for the difficulty in being able to do more than assess that it is of the general period. For a typical recipe, see [William Phillip], *A booke of secrets shewing diuers waies to make and prepare all sorts of inke, and colours: as blacke, white, blew, greene, red, yellow, and other colours. Also to write with gold and siluer, or any kind of mettall out of the pen: with many other profitable secrets, as to colour quils and parchment of any colour: and to graue with strong water in steele and iron. . . . Translated out of Dutch into English, by W.P.* EEBO facsimile reprint edition, 2013. First published 1596.

SHAKESPEARE AS READER (pages 63–68)

70 Stanley Wells and Gary Taylor, gen. eds., *The Oxford Shakespeare: The Complete Works*, 2nd ed. (Oxford: Clarendon Press, 2005), "Additional Passages," section M. For *Hamlet*, as well as for other plays, where earlier quartos contained somewhat different versions of entire scenes, individual lines, or, most commonly, individual words, the editors had to choose which variants to include in the actual text, and which to relegate to notes in an "Additional Passages" addendum if they seemed important enough to retain. This example is the first we encounter in our quotations from Shakespeare's works. In each instance, instead of the line number, we provide the page number of the "Additional Passages" section from the *Oxford Shakespeare* and the line number given therein at which the passage would have been included had it been selected.

71 James Black, *Edified by the Margent: Shakespeare and the Bible* (Calgary: University of Calgary, Faculty of Humanities, 1979), 8.

72 Parker, *Shakespeare from the Margins*, 182.

73 Ibid.

74 Goldberg, *Writing Matter*, 194.

BECOMING A BELIEVER (pages 69–76)

75 Greenblatt, *Will in the World*, 173.

76 For a look at alternative candidates, see James Shapiro, *Contested Will: Who Wrote Shakespeare?* (London: Faber and Faber, 2010). Shapiro's book is a rarity among volumes produced by Shake-

speare scholars, in that its principal subject is the authorship question. In the blogosphere, where – contrary to mainstream academia – anti-Stratfordian views are widespread, the exchanges between participants are especially contentious. The mean-spirited banter is unlikely to subside anytime soon, and may even be elevated once our website is made public, particularly if we are correct in imagining the desire of many of those who deny Shakespeare authorship to eagerly assign the annotations in our copy of Baret to the Earl of Oxford.

HAMLET (pages 79–100)

77 John Keats, *Letters of John Keats 1814–1821*, ed. Hyder Edward Rollins (Cambridge, MA: Harvard University Press, 1958), 2:67.

78 Ibid., 2:73.

79 Nicholas Rowe was the first to suggest that Shakespeare probably played the role. See a reprint of Rowe's famous 1709 introduction, Nicholas Rowe and Charles Nicholl, *Life of Shakespeare* (London: Pallas Athene Arts), 2009.

80 Alfred Hart, "The Growth of Shakespeare's Vocabulary," *Review of English Studies* 19:75 (July 1943), 242–54. Hart used the term "peculiar words" to denote words that were used only once in the entire corpus, thus "peculiar" to a particular play. He came up with a total of over 17,000 such instances.

81 Wells and Taylor, *Oxford Shakespeare*, "Additional Passages," section M.

82 Caldecott, Thomas, ed. *Hamlet, and As You Like It. A Specimen of a New Edition of Shakespeare* (London: John Murray, 1819).

83 For a discussion on rare words (appearing between two and seven times), consider A. Kent Hieatt, Charles W. Hieatt, and Anne Lake Prescott, "When Did Shakespeare Write 'Sonnets 1609?'" *Studies in Philology* 88:1 (Winter 1991): 69–109.

84 Wells and Taylor, *Oxford Shakespeare*, "Additional Passages," section A.

85 See Nicholl's lively and vivid account, *The Lodger Shakespeare*. Many of the ingredients of Elizabethan life that Nicholl imagines as integral to Shakespeare and his experience, both in and out of his lodging room, are represented in manuscript in the margins of our Baret.

86 Wells, *Shakespeare for All Time*, 15.

87 See Caroline F. E. Spurgeon, *Shakespeare's Imagery and What It Tells Us* (Cambridge: At the University Press), 1966.

88 Lancashire, "Early Modern English Dictionaries Corpus," 148.

89 Ibid.

90 *Middle English Dictionary*, s.v. "viage." Available online at http://quod.lib.umich.edu/m/med/.

91 John M. Manly and Edith Rickert, eds. *The Text of the Canterbury Tales*, 8 vols. (Chicago: University of Chicago Press, 1940).

92 William Burnet Wright, "Hamlet," *The Atlantic Monthly* (May 1902), 686–95.

THE NARRATIVE POEMS (pages 101–119)

93 Many books discuss the natural history allusions in Shakespeare as being out of character relative to the writers of his day. See H. W. Seager, *Natural History in Shakespeare's Time; Being Extracts Illustrative of the Subject as He Knew It. Also Pictures There unto Belonging* (London: Elliot Stock, 1896).

94 Weis, *Shakespeare Unbound*, 17.

95 Bate, *Soul of the Age*, 294.

96 Weis, *Shakespeare Unbound*, 81.

97 Robert Nares, J. O. Halliwell-Phillipps, and Thomas Wright, *A Glossary or the Collection of Words, Phrases, Names, and Allusions to Customs, Proverbs, Etc., Which Have Been Thought to Require Illustration, in the Works of English Authors, Particularly Shakespeare and His Contemporaries* (London: Reeves and Turner, 1888), 1:342.

98 Cited by Dalya Alberge, "Shakespeare's Fingerprints Found on Three Elizabethan Plays," *The Guardian* (October 12, 2013).

THE SONNETS (pages 120–146)

99 Frances Meres, *Palladis Tamia. Wits Treasury. Being the Second Part of Wits Commonwealth* (Ann Arbor: University of Michigan, Scholar's Facsimiles and Reprints, 1938; first published 1598).

100 Views from both sides are abundant in the critical literature. From the perspective of the sonnets being authorized, see *Shakespeare's Sonnets*, ed. Katherine Duncan-Jones (The Arden Shakespeare. London: Thomas Nelson, 1997), 151–171.

101 Duncan-Jones 1977, 13.

102 [Thomas Heywood], *An apology for actors Containing three briefe treatises. 1 Their antiquity. 2 Their ancient dignity. 3 The true vse of their quality. Written by Thomas Heywood*. EEBO facsimile reprint edition, 2010. First published 1612.

103 Duncan-Jones 1977, 6.

104 Ibid., 46.

105 Ibid., 72.

106 Ibid., 74.

107 Helen Vendler, *The Art of Shakespeare's Sonnets* (Cambridge, MA: Harvard University Press, 1997), 72.

108 Parker, *Shakespeare from the Margins*, 182.

109 Stephen Booth, ed., *Shakespeare's Sonnets* (New Haven, CT: Yale University Press, 1977), 322.

110 Ibid., 390.

THE EARLY COMEDIES (pages 147–169)

111 Wells, *Shakespeare for All Time*, 147–48.

112 Samuel Weller Singer and Charles Symmons, *The Dramatic Works of Shakespeare, with Notes Original and Selected…and a Life of the Poet* (Chiswick: Charles Wittingham, 1826).

113 Greenblatt, *Will in the World*, 130.

114 Michelle Martindale and Charles Martindale, *Shakespeare and the Uses of Antiquity: An Introductory Essay* (London: Routledge, 1990), 69.

115 John Phin, *The Shakespeare cyclopaedia and new glossary . . . with the most important variorum readings, intended as a supplement to all the ordinary editions of Shakespeare's works, with an introduction by Edward Dowden* (London: K. Paul, 1902), 264.

116 H. H. Furness, ed. *A New Variorum Edition of Shakespeare: A Midsummer Night's Dreame* (Philadelphia: Lippincott, 1895), 178.

117 Ibid.

118 Park Honan, *Shakespeare: A Life* (Oxford: Oxford University Press, 1988), 58.

119 C. T. Onions and Robert D. Eagleson, *Shakespeare Glossary*, rev. ed. (Oxford: Clarendon Press, 1986), 145.

THE EARLY HISTORIES (pages 170–199)

120 Nares et al., *A Glossary*, 957. The change to *while* by "modern" editors no longer holds, as today's editors all seem to have restored it.

121 As is pointed out in Wells and Taylor, *Shakespeare: A Textual Companion* (219), there would likewise be in that instance no Shakespearean parallel.

122 A. D. Nuttall, *Shakespeare the Thinker* (New Haven, CT: Yale University Press, 2001), 30.

123 Wells, *Shakespeare for All Time*, 147.

124 R. W. Dent, *Shakespeare's Proverbial Language: An Index* (Berkeley: University of California Press, 1981), 144.

125 Efron and Thisted, "How Many Words Did Shakespeare Know?"

FALSTAFF (pages 200–218)

126 Greenblatt, *Will in the World*, 69.

127 Ibid.

128 Plutarch, *The Lives of the noble Grecians and Romanes compared together by that grave and learned philosopher and historiographer, Plutarke of Chærnea; translated out of Greeke into French by Iames Amiot, abbot of Bellozane, Bishop of Auxerre, one of the Kings priuie counsell, and great Amner of France, and out of French into English, by Thomas North* (Imprinted at London: Richard Field for Bonham Norton, 1595).

129 See Starnes, "John Baret's *Alvearie*"; Sledd, "A Note on the Use of Renaissance Dictionaries."

130 Alexander Dyce, *The Works of William Shakespeare*, Vol. 1 (London: Edward Moxon, 1857), 426.

131 James Orchard Halliwell, *An account of the only known manuscript of Shakespeare's plays, comprising some important variations and corrections in the Merry wives of Windsor, obtained from a playhouse copy of that play recently discovered* (London: John Russell Smith, 1843), 13.

132 Quotation available online at http://books.google.com/books?id=avkFi5GuvNoC&lpg=PT854&ots=IxWAKGqdNi&dq=%22so%20we%20now%20say%2C%20in%20low%20language%2C%20a%20thwacking%20or%20swinging%20thing%22&pg=PT854#v=snippet&q=thwacking&f=false. Arthur Sherbo, ed., *Notes to Shakespeare* by Samuel Johnson. Augustinian Reprint Society Publication Los Angeles: William Andrews Clark Memorial Library, University of California, 1956–58.

133 Barron Field, "Conjectures on some Obscure and Corrupt Passages of Shakspeare," *Shakspeare Society's Papers*, 2 (1845), 47.

134 Dent, *Shakespeare's Proverbial Language*, 70.

135 Singer and Symmons, *The Dramatic Works of Shakespeare*.

136 Phin, *The Shakespeare cyclopaedia*, 421.

137 Nares et al., *A Glossary*, 156.

138 W. G. Clark and W. A. Wright, eds. *Richard II*. (Oxford: Oxford University Press, 1884).

139 When considering the whole of our annotations combined with the Baret text, Hamlet would run second to Falstaff among all Shakespearean characters as far as our observations indicate. This may or may not over time be viewed as convenient, considering our conclusion as to the authorship of the annotations. Harold Bloom has remarked on the characters, Hamlet and Falstaff, that they represent "the fullest representations of human possibility in Shakespeare." Bloom, *Shakespeare: The Invention of the Human* (New York: Riverhead Books), 1998, p. 745.

THE TRAILING BLANK (pages 219–253)

140 See Alfred M. Shorter. *Paper Mills and Paper Makers in England, 1495–1800* (Hilversum, Holland: Paper Publications Society, 1957), an important series of books on European paper making. There was almost no paper making in England before 1700, as hard as that is to believe. Shorter gives several reasons: England was well behind mainland Europe in establishing printing presses, and sheep were so plentiful that it was more economical to print on parchment or vellum than paper. Paper making was hindered by the need for capital and the lack of skilled labor. But most important of all was "the ability of those foreign countries which held a good lead in paper making, especially Italy and France, to export and sell cheaply, coupled with their determination to maintain their position in the English market" (28). Shorter has found very few identifiable English watermarks before 1700, but quite a few by the early eighteenth and then a good number of examples toward the end of the eighteenth century. He has pictures of many of these, but none where a hunter's horn is by itself. And without exception, all of the watermarks included the paper maker's initials or other identifying elements. So the blank page most likely came from Italy, France, or Germany (as did the text paper as well). With such a generic figure as the one found on the trailing

blank, and the source possibly from any one of a number of different countries, any dating is by extension even more difficult.

141 Two lines in Latin at the bottom of the page are somewhat isolated from the word salad in English and French. These two lines are challenging on several levels. The variation in letter formation that one sees here does not so clearly belong to the rest (the "rest" implying not only the trailing blank, but the whole of the book), although our hunch is that is in in the same hand. If we are correct and it is the same hand, it reinforces how incredibly variable the hand of the annotator was, beyond even the radical variation on display throughout the English and French word salad on this single leaf that is replicated throughout the book. There are cancellations in the two Latin lines below the word salad, and the words are not easy to make out. They consist of the following: deus producat vitam (^ dominus), conseruat honorem / regat et regnum (^ viribus). We were able to locate all of these words in proximity, including the pairing conseruat honorem (protecting honor), in John Gower's *Vox Clamantis*, a Latin poem on the English peasant revolt, written circa 1380. This may or may not be relevant, but is intriguing given the "Gower" associations in the *Henry IV* plays and *Henry V* and later in *Pericles*.

142 Kellner, *Restoring Shakespeare*, 20.

143 William Shakespeare, *Oeuvres complètes de Shakespeare*. Traduites de l'Anglais par Letourneur. D'une notice bibliographique et Littéraire de Shakespeare par F. Guizot. Paris: Chez Ladvocat. Tome Dixième, 1820, 531.

144 For the most comprehensive recent take on the Lucy problem, see Weis, *Shakespeare Unbound*.

145 Alexander Dyce and Harold Littledale, *A Glossary to the Works of William Shakespeare* (London: S. Sonnenschein, 1902).

146 Edward Berry, *Shakespeare and the Hunt: A Cultural and Social Study* (Cambridge: Cambridge University Press, 2001), 154.

147 Dyce, *Works of William Shakespeare*, 273.

148 Georgio Melchiori, *Shakespeare's Garter Plays: "Edward III" to "Merry Wives of Windsor"* (Newark: University of Delaware Press, 1994).

149 *Edward III* first appeared as an anonymous quarto in 1596 (Shakespeare's quartos did not use his name until 1598).

150 Melchiori, *Shakespeare's Garter Plays*. Interesting that one of the

words visible in the difficult-to-decipher two lines in Latin at the bottom of the page is honorem or honor.

151 Ash, *A New and Complete Dictionary of the English Language* (London: Edward & Charles Dilly, 1775), 1:195.

152 Ibid.

153 Berry, *Shakespeare and the Hunt*, 147.

154 Ross W. Duffin, *Shakespeare's Songbook* (New York: W. W. Norton, 2004), 263–65. As previously discussed, more than one scholar has suggested that Shakespeare may have learned French through his connection to Richard Field and his French wife, formally the wife of Vautrollier. When Field assumed control over Vautrollier's press, he gathered, by extension, his books. The English version containing *Monsieur Mingo* may safely be assumed to have been one of them, and the annotator's reference to the ballad along with the variety of French words played with on the trailing blank is in complete keeping with what others have already imagined when considering both Shakespeare's library and his skill with the French language.

155 Anne Lake Prescott, *Imagining Rabelais in Renaissance England* (New Haven, CT: Yale University Press, 2004), 228.

156 Thorton Shirley Graves, "Notes on Elizabethan Theatres," *Studies in Philology* 13:2 (April 1916), 112.

157 Observe that the "doting chronicles" relate to Edward III, grandsire of King Henry IV (Bolingbroke) and the great-grandfather of Prince Thomas, Duke of Clarence. Melchiori (*Shakespeare's Garter Plays*) lists *Edward III* as one of the six Shakespeare Garter Plays, and the editors of the *Oxford Shakespeare* (Wells and Taylor) have included it with at least partial authorship taking up several scenes.

BARET AS SHAKESPEARE'S BEEHIVE (pages 255–274)

158 John Jamieson, *Supplement to the Etymological dictionary of the Scottish Language* (Edinburgh: Printed at the University Press, 1825), 411. Available online at http://books.google.com/books?id=9w8oAA AAYAAJ&source=gbs_book_other_versions.

159 Nuttall, *Shakespeare the Thinker*, 117.

160 Charlton T. Lewis and Charles Short, *A Latin Dictionary. Founded on Andrews' edition of Freund's Latin dictionary*, revised, enlarged, and in great part rewritten (Oxford: Clarendon Press, 1879).

161 David Wootton, "The vibes of Marx," *TLS*, January 4, 2008.

162 Chambers, *Shakespeare: A Study of Facts*, 1:547-48.

163 T. W. Craik, ed. *King Henry V*. The Arden Shakespeare, 3rd series (London: Thomson Learning, 1995).

164 William Aldis Wright, ed. *Shakespeare: Select Plays. Julius Caesar* (Oxford: At the Clarendon Press, 1879), 122.

165 Norman Blake, *Shakespeare's Non-Standard English: A Dictionary of His Informal Language* (London: Continuum, 2004).

WHAT'S IN A NAME? (pages 275–283)

166 Onions and Eagleson, *Shakespeare Glossary*, 309.

167 R. H. Case, ed., *The Tragedy of Antony & Cleopatra*. The Arden Shakespeare (London: Methuen, 1906).

"MY DARLING" (pages 284–298)

168 Greenblatt, *Will in the World*.

169 Honan, *Shakespeare: A Life*.

170 Blake, *Shakespeare's Non-Standard English*.

171 William Chomsky, *Hebrew: The Eternal Language* (Philadelphia: Jewish Publication Society of America, 1957). The linguistic pathway from the earliest texts of the Hebrew bible to the Hebrew word that was translated as "my dearling" is at once straightforward but also largely unknown. The word itself comes down to us intact because of careful scribal copies made over the centuries, but its original semantic meaning is not easy to reconstruct, for a number of reasons. As Chomsky sums up, "The center of interest in Hebrew grammar and lexicography . . . shifted from Jewish to Christian scholars. The father of Hebrew grammar among the Christians was the famous humanist Johann Reuchlin (1455–1522). His book, *De Rudimentis Hebraicis*, ushered in the Hebrew philological movement among Christians" (p. 133).

172 Chambers, *A Study of Facts*, 1:479. It is also worth noting Chambers's comment on the following page where he dismisses the suggestion of as late a date of 1612 for *Coriolanus* despite the fact that the 1612 edition of North's Plutarch has *vnfortunate* in Volumnia's lines that we quote (which would have matched her *vnfortunate* that we find in Shakespeare's text) instead of *vnfortu-*

nately as we see in Richard Field's 1595 edition which is the one that Shakespeare would have used.

173 Nuttall, *Shakespeare the Thinker.*

174 Ibid.

175 Philip Brockbank, ed. *Coriolanus.* The Arden Shakespeare (New York: Routledge, 1988; first published 1976), 293.

A Note on the Authors

George Koppelman and Daniel Wechsler have independently both spent more than two decades working with rare books. Each is a member of several respected rare books organizations, including the Antiquarian Booksellers' Association of America, The International League of Antiquarian Booksellers, and the Grolier Club. Since first meeting at Mr. Wechsler's Upper West Side shop, Book Ark, in 1995, they have shared a common bond over a love for, and a devotion to, the labyrinthine world encompassed by books. Mr. Koppelman, in operating Cultured Oyster Books (1993–), and Mr. Wechsler, in operating Sanctuary Books (2001–), have each gone through the process of cataloguing thousands of books, spanning all fields and time periods. They have also handled countless additional books and manuscripts apart from those that they have owned personally or as part of their respective businesses. Occasionally the two firms have combined forces on cataloguing projects, but none as significant, or as spectacularly time-consuming, as the present one: the annotated copy of John Baret's *Alvearie; or Quadruple Dictionarie*, 1580, that is the subject of *Shakespeare's Beehive: An Annotated Elizabethan Dictionary Comes to Light*, and that is represented in complete digital facsimile on shakespearesbeehive.com, along with additional content and information. Because of the delicate nature of the project, and the possibility of particularly sensitive reactions that have for some time been anticipated, an independent company, Axletree Press LLC, was formed subsequent to the joint acquisition of the Baret, to more carefully manage the acquisition and to oversee all by-products of research related to the book.

Two thousand copies printed,
of which 26 lettered copies are bound
in quarter leather & signed by the authors,
and 100 are signed by the authors & numbered.
Set in Van Dijck and Caslon types
with Fell ornaments. Printed on
Mohawk paper. Design
and typography by
Jerry Kelly.